W9-AEK-066

26-24

THE CHRISTIAN FUTURE

harper torchbooks

A reference-list of Harper Torchbooks, classified by subjects, is printed at the end of this volume.

"The time span of the length of the Church goes from the beginning of the world to its end since the Church originated in her faithful from the start and shall endure until the end.

"For, we basically hold that from the beginning of the world to the end of times, no period exists in which there cannot be found those who trust Christ."

Hugo de Sancto Victore, † 1141

Patrologia Latina 176, 685

EUGEN ROSENSTOCK-HUESSY

THE CHRISTIAN FUTURE

Or The Modern Mind Outrun

Introduction

by

HAROLD STAHMER

HARPER TORCHBOOKS The Cloister Library

Harper & Row, Publishers

TO

Karl Muth
Courageous Roman Catholic layman in Germany

J. C. Oldham
Ecumenic Missionary in Great Britain

Ambrose Vernon
Onward Translator of Our Faith in the U.S.

EX EXPERIENTIA SPIRITUS

THE CHRISTIAN FUTURE

Printed in the United States of America.

This book was originally published in 1946 by Charles Scribner's Sons, New York, and is here reprinted by arrangement with the author.

First HARPER TORCHBOOK edition published 1966 by
Harper & Row, Publishers, Incorporated
49 East 33rd Street
New York, N.Y. 10016.

CONTENTS

PART THREE: THE BODY OF OUR ERA: BACKWARD, FORWARD, NOW

INTRODUCTION TO THE TORCHBOOK EDITION

by HAROLD STAHMER

I

There exists today among sensitive theologians, Biblical scholars, clergy and laymen a significant interest, on the one hand, in *hermeneutics*—the problem of *interpretation*—and on the other, in all those writings which might appropriately be associated with *religionless Christianity* or *Post-Christian thinking.* The names Bultmann, Fuchs, Ebeling and Wilder are associated with interest in the first, e.g. *hermeneutics;* while Bonhoeffer, Bishop Robinson, Tillich, and Harvey Cox are with the second, e.g. with *radical religion.* Actually, both are interrelated since language and communication are central to each. To those familiar with both of these current topics, I suggest that Eugen Rosenstock-Huessy not only anticipated these interests, but has proposed answers to those questions which our age may wish to listen to.

In 1946, before either of these topics had achieved the publicity which each now enjoys, Eugen Rosenstock-Huessy had published his *The Christian Future or The Modern Mind Outrun.* It is a work which, unfortunately, was ahead of its time in terms of interest in these themes and consequently received little public attention. In the scholarly world his correspondence with Franz Rosenzweig (1886–1929) on *Judaism and Christianity* had already occasioned serious recognition in the *Journal of Religion* by Professors Alexander Altmann and Dorothy Emmett.[1] Elsewhere, he has been compared on numerous oc-

[1] Alexander Altmann, "Franz Rosenzweig and Eugen Rosenstock-Huessy: An Introduction to their Letters on Judaism and Christianity," *The Journal of Religion,* XXIV, 4 (October, 1944); Dorothy Emmett, "The Letters of

casions with Martin Buber and Martin Heidegger because of his insights into language and his use of dialogical motifs.[2] From a different quarter his *Out of Revolution: The Autobiography of Western Man* (1938) has long been hailed as a major work by none other than W. H. Auden. In 1947 he was described by J. H. Oldham as "one of the remarkable figures of our time." In a *Foreword* to the English edition of *The Christian Future* Oldham acknowledged certain difficulties with Rosenstock-Huessy's lively style, but added that "His mind is too quick and fertile for most of us. . . . Those who refuse to be deterred by these occasional difficulties will find themselves amply rewarded by contact with an extraordinarily rich and vivacious mind, constantly emitting flashes of penetrating insight, and with an intensely vital and stimulating personality who lives all that he thinks and whose thinking grows out of his wrestling with life."[3]

Since 1946 more than eight published volumes of his writings and numerous essays and articles have appeared in German. In addition many of his projects such as the idea behind the Peace Corps have become a reality (his guiding insights have been acknowledged publicly by Sargent Shriver, the Peace Corps director[4]). It is hoped that this new edition of *The Christian Future* together with the planned publication of an American

---

Franz Rosenzweig and Eugen Rosenstock-Huessy," *The Journal of Religion,* XXV, 4 (October, 1945). Cf. also Rivka G. Horwitz, "Franz Rosenzweig on Language," *Judaism,* vol. 13, no. 4 (Fall Issue, 1964).

[2] In English, cf. Maurice S. Friedman, *Martin Buber: The Life of Dialogue* (New York: Harper and Brothers, 1960), pp. 162 and 268; cf. also Walter L. Ong, S.J., "Philosophical Sociology," *The Modern Schoolman,* XXXVIII (January, 1960), Harold Stahmer, "Vocal Communication and Technological Society," *Social Order* (June, 1963).

[3] Eugen Rosenstock-Huessy, *The Christian Future or The Modern Mind Outrun* (London: SCM Press, 1947), "Foreword" by J. H. Oldham, p. xii.

[4] Article by Sargent Shriver on "The Peace Corps" in *The American Peoples Encyclopedia Yearbook for 1962.* His major works since 1946 include *Der Atem des Geistes* (Frankfurt: Frankfurter Hefte, 1951); *Die Europaischen Revolutionen und der Charakter der Nationen* (Stuttgart: W. Kohlhammer, 1951); *Heilkraft und Wahrheit* (Stuttgart: Evangelisches Verlagswerk, 1952); *Der Unbezahlbare Mensch* (Berlin: Kathe Vogt, 1955), a German edition of *The Christian Future* (München: C. Kaiser,

edition of his monumental two-volume *Soziologie* and speech-book, *Die Sprache des Menschengeschlechts,* will give the English-speaking world an opportunity to give his writings the respect and attention now being accorded them in Europe.

II

On the occasion of receiving an honorary doctorate in theology from the University of Münster in 1959 Eugen Rosenstock-Huessy was hailed as the new *Magician of the North,* the J. G. Hamann of the twentieth century. Eugen Rosenstock-Huessy was born Eugen Rosenstock to a respected German Jewish banker and his wife in Berlin in 1888, one hundred years after Hamann's death. At sixteen, he became a practicing Christian. Like Hamann, he has gnawed continually upon the bone of language and is appropriately hailed in Europe as *Der Sprachdenker—The Speech-thinker.*[5] Although addressing two radically different social and intellectual climates, the similarities in their writings with respect to their reverence for the sacramental power of speech is indeed striking.

Compare, for instance, the following statement of Rosenstock-Huessy's with two passages from Hamann.

> And this temporal character of my thinking is in fact the Alpha and Omega from which I grasp everything afresh. Speech reflects this mode of procedure, even for someone who has been influenced by philosophy. For that reason I prefer to talk about speech rather than about reason.

And now Hamann's statements:

1955); *Soziologie* I and II (Stuttgart: W. Kohlhammer, 1956 and 1958); and most recently, *Die Sprache des Menschengeschlechts,* I and II (Heidelberg: Lambert Schneider, 1963 and 1964).

[5] Georg Müller, "Der Sprachdenker Eugen Rosenstock-Huessy," *Evangelisches Theologie* (July-August, 1954), pp. 314–334. Dr. Müller has written numerous penetrating articles on various aspects of Rosenstock-Huessy's writings.

> I too know of no eternal truths save these which are unceasingly temporal.
>
> I speak neither of physics nor of theology: with me language is the mother of reason and revelation, its Alpha and Omega.
>
> With me the question is not so much: What is reason? but rather: What is Language?

For each, speech (or as Hamann put it, *verbalism*) constituted a *via media* between the Scylla and Charybdis of philosophical and theological discourse.[6] Each regards speech as sacred and each sees in language the answer to their age's obsession with artificial and abstract languages and systems reminiscent of Enlightenment and nineteenth century philosophers and their modern heirs. Kantian transcendental idealism which Hamann attacked for its devaluation of sensuous speech and its rejection of the testimonies of everyday experience had, together with the contributions of Fichte and Hegel, determined the acceptable religious, ethical, political and philosophical categories in the nineteenth and early decades of the twentieth centuries. What Hamann attacked at its inception had permeated in Rosenstock-Huessy's time every quarter of twentieth century European intellectual life. In attacking the Enlightenment Hamann had relied primarily upon sensuous poetic speech modeled upon the time-conditioned and time-oriented view of reality inherent in the Bible. For Hamann, sacred natural speech and poetry were practically synonymous. Both Hamann's deeply personal, if not individualistic, piety, as well as his earthiness, were shaped by his view of language and his preoccupation with esthetic and literary themes. In the normal use of the term he was not a social thinker. The social significance of the events preceding the French Revolution which for Rosenstock-Huessy and Franz Rosenzweig anticipated the beginning of the Johan-

[6] Eugen Rosenstock to Frank Rosenzweig (10/28/1916); J. G. Hamann, *Golgotha und Scheblimini* (1784); Hamann to F. H. Jacobi (1785, 1784 and 1787).

nine Age had little, if any, influence upon Hamann who by then was an old man. The attempts of certain Enlightenment thinkers to put Reason to use in freeing men not only from religious superstitions but also from political and economic subjugation went largely unnoticed by Hamann. Anything done in the name of Reason, despite its intent, was from Hamann's standpoint hopelessly *unnatural* and religiously *profane.* As is true of so many religious existentialists, their obsession with personal existence often makes them incapable of going beyond the solitary soul in conflict to those larger social conditions affecting the *human condition.* Preoccupation with the *rights of man*—with the alleviation of harsh working conditions associated with an industrial, technological society, for instance, was beyond Hamann's ken. Although anticipated in Hamann's time, the organization of the social sciences did not take place until the nineteenth century, and then only with the aid of the advocates of positivism and behaviorism. Most of all, current obsessions with the *soul* viewed from the perspectives of applied social and analytical psychology and psychiatry as well as other behavioral approaches was a phenomenon which aroused the general public only after the *assembly line* had entered the business of creating new kinds of creatures. Nor had the effects of historicism been felt then as they would be in Rosenstock-Huessy's student days. Equally unknown in Hamann's time were the modern-day problems generated by a mobile society, the atomic age, automation, shorter working hours and increased leisure time and, above all, by major advances in the field of communication: radio, television and electronics. The latter have appealed not only to man's visual, but especially to his oral and aural powers in a way totally unknown to earlier periods. Still to come was modern urban life with its division of life into urban work, suburban play and car pool limbo. Also absent was the recent questioning of the adequacy of traditional forms of institutional religion to speak to man's many-sidedness or, in Rosenstock-Huessy's words, to the *multiformity of man.* The *modern mind* with all its neuroses, assumptions, needs, value systems and sense of *estrangement* and *alienation*—its *prob-*

lematic elements—was as yet unborn in Hamann's lifetime. Were he alive today it would be interesting to discover the degree of concurrence which might obtain between these two *Magicians of the North* who see in speech the antidote for the needs of their respective societies. Because of Rosenstock-Huessy's preoccupation with speech, time, work, play and leisure, *The Christian Future* was certainly relevant twenty years ago, but its importance is only now becoming recognized.

III

Of the many possible intellectual precursors to Rosenstock-Huessy's thinking certainly the names Saint John, Saint-Simon, Paracelsus, Hamann, Jakob Grimm, Wilhelm von Humboldt, Friedrich von Schlegel, Otto Gierke, B. G. Niebuhr, and William James deserve mention. In his first lecture on the *Philosophy of Life* Schlegel began by paraphrasing Hamlet, "There are more things in heaven and earth than are dreamt of in our philosophy." Half way between heaven and earth ". . . lies the true road; and the proper region of philosophy is even that inner spiritual life between heaven and earth." For Schlegel the thinking soul was the center of consciousness and speech was the language of the soul. Many of the themes dealt with by twentieth century *speech thinkers* are contained within the leaves of Schlegel's *Philosophy of Life, Philosophy of Language,* and his *Lectures on History.* For example, the Gospel of John is referred to by Schlegel as the Evangel of Life, and later on he extols language as the highest creation of artistic genius. "It is only . . . in poetry or some other form of language . . . that we meet with the perfect harmony of a complete and united consciousness, in which all its faculties work together in combined and living action."[7] In anticipation of Rosenstock-Huessy's *cross of reality* and *grammatical thinking,* Schlegel's observations about the fourfold nature of man's consciousness, his multiform character and the equation of this fourfold structure with gram-

[7] Friedrich von Schlegel, *The Philosophy of Life* (London: Henry G. Bohn, 1847), pp. 1–2, 207–208, 387.

mar, are most remarkable. Schlegel's understanding of the hierarchy and complexity of those forces which operate upon the solitary creature, his convictions about the inability of reason and its categories to know life *absolutely,* and his insistence that life can only be *lived,* certainly provide a link in the chain between Hamann and Rosenstock-Huessy. When asked in 1949 to mention a precursor whose works would be helpful in understanding his thought, Rosenstock-Huessy immediately mentioned Schlegel, and especially his *Lectures on History.*

Though regarded by Rosenstock-Huessy as one of the devil's many advocates, certainly Hegel's preoccupation with time and history and his insights into the successive ages of the Spirit were familiar to Rosenstock-Huessy as were the millenarian themes in Schelling's writings. Ludwig Feuerbach's name is also worth mentioning, not so much because of any acknowledged influence upon Rosenstock-Huessy, but because of the task he envisioned for future philosophers. In an early preface to his *Principles of Any Future Philosophy* (1843) Feuerbach discussed this in a way that helps us appreciate the general setting for Rosenstock-Huessy's own intellectual pilgrimage.

> The Philosophy of the Future has the task to lead philosophy from the realm of *departed souls,* back into the realm of embodied and living souls; to pull philosophy down from the divine, self-sufficient bliss in the realm of ideas into human misery. To think, speak and act in a pure and truly human fashion will, however, be granted only to future generations. At present the task is not to present man as such, but to pull him out of the mud in which he was embedded. These principles are the fruit of this unsavory work of cleansing.

In the opening sentence of this same work he discussed the future shape of Christianity in a way closely resembling Johannine millenarian thinking and suggestive of the quality it was to take in Rosenstock-Huessy's thinking as outlined in his *Out of Revolution* and *The Christian Future.* Feuerbach proposed that, "Protestantism is no longer concerned . . . about what God is in Himself, but rather only about what He is for man."[8] This theme is developed at length in the Johannine focus in Rosenstock-Huessy's thought and is best summed up in *Out of Revolution* where he discusses a proposed sequel to Michelangelo's painting of God creating Adam in the Sistine Chapel in Rome. God, in the upper right hand corner, is shown creating Adam, reclining naked and helpless, in the lower left hand corner. He suggests that *in the beginning* all of God's angels were on God's side, contained within the folds of His robe. "We might conceive," he suggests, "of a pendant to this picture; the end of creation, in which all the spirits that had accompanied the Creator should have left him and descended to man, keeping, strengthening, enlarging his being into the divine. In this picture God would be alone, while Adam would have all the Elohim around him as his companions."[9]

This is but one expression of the Johannine millenarian quality which permeates all his writings and which places him in the company of all those who shared John's vision on Patmos of the future ages of the Spirit—Tertullian, Joachim of Fiore, and more recently, Hegel, Schelling, Feuerbach, Franz Rosenzweig, and Dietrich Bonhoeffer. For Rosenstock-Huessy, we are approaching the conclusion of the second age—the unification of space, both geographical and technological, and are on the threshold of the third, the Johannine age—the *Age of the Spirit* which is dedicated to the task of the *creation and preservation of a truly human society.* It will be a time thirsted after by Jew and Christian but also one wherein men will feel incomplete simply as Jew or Christian. It will be a time wherein men will feel the need to live in the Spirit and by and through the Word now become fully clothed in its creaturely attire. Johannine, for Rosenstock-Huessy, combines the respect of John's sense of the future epochs of the Spirit which he described on Patmos together with the Incarnational effect of the

[8] Ludwig Feuerbach, *Grundsätze der Philosophie der Zukunft* (Zurich: Verlag des litarischen Comptoirs, 1843), pp. iii–iv, 1.

[9] Rosenstock-Huessy, *Out of Revolution* (New York: William Morrow, 1938. Latest edition: New York: Four Wells, 1964), pp. 727–728.

Word in the Prologue to John's Gospel. If the vision at the end of Revelation meant anything for John it served as a mark of "the New Jerusalem as a healing of the nations without any visible Church at its center." Early in *The Christian Future* he elaborates upon John's vision by stating:

> All things were made by the Word. In the beginning there was neither mind nor matter. In the beginning was the Word. St. John was properly the first Christian theologian because he was overwhelmed by the spokenness of all meaningful happening.

Thus, the Word and *speech,* Spirit and *history,* Eternity and *timing* are woven together with that same secret quality which has characterized the confidence of Jew and Christian in the future determination of the Creation. However, as even theologians are now suggesting, the Age of the Spirit may turn out to be a totally *areligious* and *atheological* one. "I believe that in the future, Church and Creed can be given a new lease on life only by services that are nameless and incognito." In another place he states, "In the third epoch, beginning today, Christians must immigrate *into* our workaday world, there to incarnate the spirit in unpredictable forms." Further on he sums up the reasoning behind this when he states that "... *each generation has to act differently precisely in order to represent the same thing.* Only so can each become a full partner in the process of Making Man." The inadequacy of the Church in its present institutional attire is a constant theme especially in *The Christian Future.* This does not imply the *death* or *eclipse of God;* rather, it suggests that new forms of spirituality must be discovered in order for the present *eclipse* to pass. In this connection, one of his favorite quotations is that of William James, who in 1903 anticipated our present religious dilemma. "The average church-going civilizee realizes, one may say, absolutely nothing of the deeper currents of human nature."[10]

[10] *The Christian Future,* pp. [159–160]; [129], [127], [130], [2].

For Rosenstock-Huessy, Incarnational speech, the *grammatical approach* (which should not be confused with Incarnational *theology*), provides the clue to the secret of the coming age. In *The Christian Future* this process is defined as *anthropurgy:* the act of winning "the true stuff of Man out of his coarse physical substance." This represents the final realization of the statement in Genesis, "Let us make man in our own image." The Holy Spirit from henceforth, "makes man a partner in his own creation" just as the early Church Fathers "interpreted human history as a process of making Man like God," e.g., *anthropurgy.*[11] Compare this presentation of man's divine role with Buber's rendition of Hasidic man as a "partner of God responsible for God's fate in the world."[12] The task of men living in the Johannine Age is captured in an oft-cited passage in *Out of Revolution:*

> The *Cogito ergo sum,* for its rivalry with theology, was one-sided. We post-war thinkers are less concerned with the revealed character of the true God or the true character of nature than with the survival of a truly human society. In asking for a truly human society we put the question of truth once more, but our specific endeavor is the living realization of truth in mankind. Truth is divine and has been divinely revealed—*credo ut intelligam.* Truth is pure and can be scientifically stated—*cogito ergo sum.* Truth is vital and must be socially represented—*Respondeo etsi mutabor.*[13]

While preoccupation with the creation of a truly human society is *the* religious concern of many liberals and unorthodox thinkers today, many *orthodox* religious thinkers have resisted this emphasis for fear of identifying the *sacred* with the *profane,* and thereby diluting the power of the Word. At the same time many religious *liberals* frequently view history and tradition as

[11] *Op. cit.,* p. [108].
[12] Martin Buber, *Mamre* (Melbourne: Melbourne University Press, 1946), p. 70.
[13] *Out of Revolution,* pp. 740–741.

a barricade which must be broken down in order for the Spirit to speak freely to men. Rosenstock-Huessy, because of his Johannine orientation, because of his emphasis upon the necessary stages of life through which individuals and societies must pass, and above all, because of his view of the way in which the Word may become the *fruit of our lips,* has managed to avoid the pitfalls inherent in traditional approaches. More recently, Harvey Cox in *The Secular City* has captured this fine distinction in his discussion of the creative spiritual-temporal process of *secularization* in contrast to *secularism.* He defines *secularism* as "any new closed world-view which functions very much like a new religion."

> While secularization finds its roots in the biblical faith itself and is to some extent an authentic outcome of the impact of biblical faith on Western history, this is not the case with secularism. Like any other ism, it menaces the openness and freedom secularization has produced; . . . . Secularization arises in large measure from the formative influence of biblical faith on the world, an influence mediated first by the Christian Church and later by movements deriving partly from it.[14]

The path traveled by Rosenstock-Huessy to arrive at these insights was, as with Hamann, an unconventional one. Each regarded himself as an *impure thinker* and *distemporary* in terms of traditional ways of thinking.[15] The subtitle of a published autobiographical statement by Rosenstock-Huessy, *The Nine Lives of a Cat,* captures this quality and stresses his insistence that true progress and growth is one involving perpetual death and rebirth, viewed as a continuous defiance and desecration of what many regard as normal or *natural* existence. His motto, "*I respond although I will be changed*" ("*Respondeo etsi mutabor*"), is an allusion to the fact not only that the social

[14] Harvey Cox, *The Secular City* (New York: Macmillan, 1965), p. 21.
[15] Rosenstock-Huessy, "Ich bin ein unreiner Denker," *Neues Abendland,* 8 Jg. (1953).

representation of truth involves costly commitment for each individual, but more significantly, that one's corporate community of *named* individuals is more sacred and deserving of concern and obligation than are the antinomies and anxieties surrounding the dark nights and moments of individual souls alienated and estranged from their fellowmen. *Society,* rather than the *individual,* is his main concern. And yet, because of his high regard for speech, individual needs are not overlooked. They are, however, met in terms of one's named *social* existence, rather than in any individualistic or *asocial* context. William James more than anyone symbolized for Rosenstock-Huessy the infinite possibilities for the soul's constant rebirth and renewal in behalf of "bringing about a growing universe of free people." In many ways, the substance of both William James' own credo as well as Rosenstock-Huessy's are captured in a letter of Henry James to William, his son. Rosenstock-Huessy has described it as containing James' "own practical attitude to finite things, to the right *name* for God, and to the unity of mankind." It certainly captures many of Rosenstock-Huessy's own sentiments. The words *underlined* are Rosenstock-Huessy's emphasis. Referring to Jesus, the elder James wrote:

> What a mere obscenity every *great name* in history confesses itself beside this spotless Judean youth, who in the thickest night of time—unhelped by priest or ruler, by friend or neighbor, . . . in fact, if we may so consider it, only by the dim *expectant sympathy* of that hungry rabble of harlots and outcasts who furnished his inglorious retinue, and still further drew upon him the ferocious scorn of all that was devout and honourable and powerful in his nation—yet let in eternal daylight upon the *soul,* by steadfastly *expanding* in his *private spirit to the dimensions of universal humanity,* so bringing for the first time in history, the *finite* human bosom into perfect *experimental* accord with the *infinite divine love.*

Later on in the letter the father confessed to the son that he found "the conception of any Divinity superior to this radiant human form inexpressibly treasonable to his own *manhood.*" He went on to add that:

> I shall always cherish the most hearty and cheerful *atheism* towards every *orthodox and popular* conception of Deity but him who has illustrated my own nature with such resplendent power as to make me feel that *Man* henceforth is *the only name of honor.*
>
> . . . Infinite wisdom compassed at length a direct and adequate access to the *most finite of intelligences* . . . in Jesus' sublime and steadfast *soul,* the divine and the human was at last perfectly consummated. Thenceforth the *infinite* expansion of our nature became the most strictly *inevitable.* Ever since, husband and father, lover and friend, patriot and citizen, priest and king, have been gradually assuming more human dimensions, have been gradually *putting on glorified lineaments. The universal heart* of man has been learning to despise and to disown all *absolute* sanctities. . . .[16]

IV

As with most visionaries, significant intellectual contributions and the events in one's life are almost synonymous. This is especially true in the case of Rosenstock-Huessy who, when asked to write an autobiographical introduction to his lengthy bibliography, entitled his response *biblionomics,* and began by stating that his "too lengthy bibliography" must be read from the standpoint of inward *necessity,* that is, "the necessity of remaining sane, or, to be more exact, of recovering sanity. . . . Any author lives in some kind of biblionomical field of force."[17] His early youth was spent mostly in devouring books, immersing himself in history, learning languages, translating the classics,

[16] Cited by Eugen Rosenstock-Huessy in a privately printed address entitled "The Soul of William James" delivered at Dartmouth College in 1942.

[17] Rosenstock-Huessy, *Bibliography/Biography* (New York: Four Wells, 1959), pp. 13 and 16.

making indexes and writing poetry. Even when playing with his collection of tin soldiers he would re-enact famous military battles, assuming the title of *Emperor Eugen I of Bergenau* and chronicling daily the course of each battle. His doctoral dissertation of 1909 is apt testimony to the incredible learning and disciplining of faculties which had taken place in his youth. Professor Bader, the editor of the *Savigny Zeitschrift* described his effort as "a good example of nineteenth century erudition." It was understandable, therefore, that he eventually became a *Privatdozent;* but, indeed, amazing that his life is one continuous record of an almost Kierkegaardian iconoclastic attack upon the dryness and irrelevance of those kinds of erudition which many associate with the term. Nevertheless, by 1919, then twenty-six years of age, he had already published three books and five articles, among them his first major contribution in the field of law, *Königshaus und Stämme in Deutschland Zwischen 911 und 1250.* Even at this early stage in his development he declared to his readers that law and history are intimately bound up with speech. In a lengthy privately published autobiographical statement (to my mind, one of his most enjoyable and informative essays) he draws the reader's attention to the two mottos for that work; the first taken from Socrates, the second from Goethe:

> Law and right and justice, these are words which sound and echo within me so loudly that I cannot hear anything else over their sound.

> The word was so important there, because it was a spoken word.

Of these two statements he writes: "The two mottos which preface a book on jurisprudence will, better than my assertion, prove to the reader that *language,* listening and speaking, have been my A and Ω."[18]

During this period he devoted himself to studying the works

[18] From a lengthy privately circulated autobiographical essay, p. 180.

and unprinted papers of the historian B. G. Niebuhr and came under the influence of the great jurisprudent, Otto Gierke. His *Von Industrierecht* (1926) was an attempt to do precisely for the field of law what he had contributed in the field of history.

In 1912 he was appointed lecturer in law at Leipzig and during this period continued his conversations with Franz Rosenzweig, then a secular Jewish scholar immersed in the study of Hegel, whom he had first met in 1910 at a convention of young scholars in Baden Baden. Their now famous encounter on the evening of July 7, 1913, its effect upon Rosenzweig's own development, and their subsequent exchange of letters in 1916 on *Judaism and Christianity* has been discussed at length by Professors Altmann and Emmet. As far as Rosenstock-Huessy was concerned, the encounter was a public declaration to the academic world that a man could be a competent scholar and nevertheless a deeply religious and committed Christian. It was precisely this combination of deep piety and erudition which had attracted Rosenzweig to this unusual and brilliant teacher of law.

Already in Baden Baden in 1910 those present were acutely aware of an impending world catastrophe of the first order. It was equally apparent to them that the intellectuals in the European universities were so involved in departmental and professional squabbling that they had completely divorced themselves from the deeper issues facing their culture. The outbreak of war convinced Rosenstock-Huessy that this *guild system* of professional compartmentalization and squabblings was detrimental to the very task for which universities and intellectuals ostensibly existed; ". . . the whole world of the educated was embodying a spiritual lag." When he wrote his *Biblionomics* in 1958 he compared the situation in 1914 to our own current one: "When, later, I came to America, I here found the term *Cultural Lag* in frequent use—unfortunately in the opposite sense. In the United States today, as in Europe in 1914, the alleged custodians of culture are lagging behind the allegedly uneducated masses. Greenwich Village seemed to me to belong to the Stone Age as much as the German Universities during

World War I."[19] Unfortunately, as he noted, this "breakdown of the old standards was communicable to a few friends only." When war broke out and the breakdown in communication was complete, he was commissioned a second lieutenant in the army, spending most of the war-years as transportations officer at Verdun. During a leave he married a warm, great and wonderful woman, Margrit Huessy and, according to Swiss custom, added his wife's name to his own. They had one child, Hans R. Huessy, now a professor of psychiatry in this country. Everyone who knew Margrit Huessy loved her as a tremendously patient and loving individual who experienced deeply the many joys, vicissitudes and adventures which they as a family were to encounter. Her death in 1959 affected deeply all those who knew her.

V

Rosenstock-Huessy's profound preoccupation with speech and communication grew out of the kinds of cultural crises viewed as *speech impasses* which he experienced in the years just prior to the outbreak of World War One. Increasingly, he realized that the few with whom he could converse *must* talk to one another to survive as persons. More significantly, they began to realize that small groups like theirs must assume the responsibility for speaking out and inspiring the dead branches of society about them. Through *speech,* they hoped to heal the social divisions and overcome the professional rifts which mark social decay and any impending cultural crisis. This kind of *remedial speech* is sacred for Rosenstock-Huessy because it is the means whereby men are capable of either destroying one another or giving birth to a new and truly human society. Though philosophers like Heidegger have devoted their lives to existential systems of language and have often been compared to Rosenstock-Huessy (and *vice-versa*), they differ dramatically and precisely because of the asocial origin of Heideg-

[19] *Bibliography/Biography,* p. 17.

ger's thought as opposed to the sacred character of speech which men discover together in periods of social crisis. Similarly, each has wound up where he started; Heidegger is read and discussed by existential intellectuals as an intellectual with little social application, whereas the thrust of Rosenstock-Huessy's influence has been felt most acutely outside the salon and the learned journals. His greatest impact has been in the classroom, in work camps, and in those social situations which cut across class and disciplinary lines and include members from every section of society.

As a matter of record, Rosenstock-Huessy's purely academic interest in language is undoubtedly comparable to Heidegger's. In the lengthy autobiographical statement referred to earlier, he notes that in the four decades, "from 1902 to 1942, *speech* made me the footstool of its new articulation." Subsequently he wrote, "Since 1902 I have lived consciously under the banner of *speech.*" In retrospect, that particular aspect of language which he investigated was conditioned by the particular *front* or linguistic crisis which he himself was facing at the time. According to his *cross of reality,* individuals, societies and nations, are understandable in terms of four *fronts* or *vectors:* past, future, inner and outer. Thus his autobiographical statement constitutes, in effect, his "love affair with the German language as mother tongue, as bridal tongue, as the tongue of marriage and work." For students interested not only in this subject but in biography and the history of ideas his lengthy account of his own involvements with language is a fascinating one.

> Since 1902 I have lived consciously under the banner of speech. I was in my fifteenth year, and asked for Kluge's *Etymological Dictionary of the German Language* as a gift. I myself bought Jakob Grimm's *German Grammar* of 1819 and his *Legal Antiquities,* in which the Word plays such an important part. At that time, Hamann's observation caught hold of me! "language is the bone upon which I shall gnaw forever." In addition to the usual languages of the *Gymnasium* I added Egyptian and became excited about the highly

talented Heinrich Brugsch. Reading of Carlyle's *Sartor Resartus,* this Song of Songs of speaking, of Bengel and Chesterton, supported the excessive interest in pure linguistics and philology (for I also at the time wrote dictionaries and made translations from all languages); but of course, the child knew nothing else but that only the philologists deal with language. Thus a tension arose between that which I longed for and that which seemed to be the only universally recognized expression of this longing: I wanted to decipher the organisation of humanity on the basis of language, and strangely, I studied everything philological with a zealous fanaticism and awe, as if this sort of linguistics would lead into the sanctuary. Deepest respect for the German university was beyond question for me. Thus I read every scrap of every acknowledged philologist from Scaliger to Ludwig Traube with devotion. But, fortunately, I fell in love for the first time in that same year and started to write poetry. For many years I always carried the little paperback containing the works of Hoelderlin around with me. And Nietzsche, Goethe, Homer, Schiller, Lessing, Pindar, and towards the end of the century, Chesterton, built a more genuine empire of language alongside the philological one of the Boeckh, Niebuhr, Grimm, Bopp, Erman, Brugmann.

The study of classical philology under its masters Otto Schroeder, Eduard Meyer, Wilamowitz-Moellendorf, Johannes Vahlen, Hermann Diels, and the study of law which I had undergone "against the longing of my heart" sought after a compromise. I had dreams for a while, of becoming another Ludwig Traube and of co-founding a new western philology for the Middle Ages. My main contribution to this I dedicated in 1912 with great pathos to the "Prince of Philology," Johannes Vahlen. I just was able to go to his funeral when the book was finished.

Two comments have to be made in retrospect about this decade, looking from 1912 back towards 1902. I had learned to mix all the essences and tinctures of philology. I had published papers about lower and higher criticism, had done investigations of diplomatic documents, copied and edited manuscripts, dealt with stylistic and archival investigations. I had planned dictionaries and grammars, published investigations of liturgical calendars, and I had placed the credibility of B. G. Niebuhr's chronicles in a new light. I had investigated buildings and monuments iconographically; and through it all, I felt that the entire body of classical philology plus Indo-germanic linguistics and Egyptian were walking by my side as a bride. Since then I have followed the developments and ups and downs of these branches of knowledge consistently and constantly; without having any official relationship to them, they remained my home. I kept track of humanism and classicism in their study of antiquity from 1450 until nowadays, with all their splendid achievements. Never have I forgotten August Boeckh's wonderful word about philology. "Knowledge of the known" he called his doings. We have added to this only the knowledge that it is not proper to recognize without acknowledging and disallowing.

His early passion, if not veneration of formal philological studies, soon gave way to a disenchantment brought about by his recognition that "Language is wiser than the one who speaks it."[20] It marked the beginning of his *public* as against *private* involvement with language; *speech* rather than *language* in the sense of mere philology became as for Hamann, the bone upon which he gnawed. With this insight, his future had direction; "the cat had been let out of the bag," and he now began to experience each of the cat's *nine lives* abridged into the decades beginning with 1902 right up to the publication of his two volume *Sprachbuch* in 1963 and 1964.

At the heart of his own speech *conversion* lay not only his awareness that speech is greater and more profound than any speaking individual, but with von Humboldt, that the key to

[20] The preceding citations are all from his privately circulated autobiographical essay, pp. 172–176.

an individual's speech lies in the language of a people. Thus in 1912 he wrote:

> ... the living language of people always overpowers the thinking of individual man who assumes that he could master it; it is wiser than the thinker who assumes that he thinks, whereas he only *speaks,* and in so doing faithfully trusts the material of language; it guides his concepts unconsciously towards an unknown future.[21]

Suddenly, the significance of names, historical and ecclesiastical holidays and calendars, and especially those grammatical forms of speech which call people to new powers and actions as *imperatives* are capable of, took on new significance. At the same time, the crisis of his own era, and his reliance upon the stimulation and life which his conversations with his friends produced, made him aware that the fate of his own thinking was intimately tied to those questions which he and his *co-respondents* recognized. He and his friends knew that the times beget that particular question which each must respond to in terms of his particular social role. In the words of a Presbyterian ordination hymn, "Each age its solemn task may claim but once." They were convinced that somehow men are driven together, and at the same time driven out of their particular niche in society precisely in order to survive and respond to those questions which have seized them. Recognition of the historical and temporal factors which condition all real speech and subsequent serious thinking was an insight which distinguished this circle, known as the Patmos group, from those scientists and intellectuals either ignorant of this fact or unwilling or unable to accept its consequences. *This* serious speech about *their* times meant for them that as scholars *their* thinking and research must address itself to those questions which had been raised in *their* time. This insight, incidentally, has been appreciated increasingly in Europe

21 *Ostfalens Rechsliterature unter Friedrich II* (Weimar: H. Bohlaus Nf., 1912), p. 144.

today in sharp contrast to the obsession by most academicians in our own country, particularly in the social sciences, with *value neutrality* and *scientific objectivity.*[22]

VI

The name *Patmos* is particularly appropriate for our interests in *speech-thinking* since for the members of the *Patmos* group it combined the significance attached to the Incarnate Word by John in the prologue to the Fourth Gospel with the sense of loneliness and vision of another age felt by the other, or same John, when he wrote *Revelation* on the island of *Patmos.* For Rosenstock-Huessy and those associated with the Patmos circle, the problem of their age was, as it had been for St. John in his time, a *speech* problem. This was their conclusion after having appraised the effects of nineteenth century idealism, historicism, and positivism upon their generation's culture. In many ways their reaction was similar to that of Hamann and his friends during the *Sturm* and *Drang* protest against the presuppositions behind the Enlightenment. The problem as the Patmos group viewed it was characterized by an absence of real personal encounter together with a lack of a common language able to bridge the cultural and academic compartmentalization which prevailed not only in academic circles, but at every level of European, and especially German culture. According to Kurt Ballerstedt's comments on the situation: "How can a human being teach credibly of history, society or language in monologues? Only a human being who has lived and experienced the *thou* and the *we* in their fullness can reveal the *secret* of the university."[23] The Patmos circle was founded in response to

[22] Cf. for example, the recent exchange at the Weber Centenary Congress in Heidelberg (April, 1964) between Professors Herbert Marcuse and Benjamin Nelson. Herbert Marcuse, "Industrialization and Capitalization," *The New Left,* London: Issue No. 31 (May-June, 1965); Benjamin Nelson, "Diskussion uber Industrialisierung und Kapitalismus," *Max Weber und die Soziologie heute, Verhandlung des 15. deutschen Soziologentages* (Tubingen: J.C.B. Mohr, 1965).

[23] *Bibliography/Biography,* p. 36.

this dilemma; the name served as a symbol of their need for a common speech as well as a sense of the past and a vision of their responsibility to shape a common future. Rosenstock-Huessy has, rather vividly, spoken of the significance of Patmos upon his own life on a number of occasions and in several books and articles. Most recently he stated:

> From 1915 to 1923 this group of friends felt as though living on Patmos. And Patmos we called the publishing house founded in 1919 for the purpose of giving us a first opening into the official world of books. In the main, we remained *extra-mundane,* so to speak. But all the seed of my later work, and if I may say so, of my peculiar contribution, stems from this period of total renewal and overhauling. If any period may be called one of emigration, this was it. When I immigrated into the United States with my wife in 1933, it was nothing like our inner immigration upon Patmos achieved after 1915. After that year, we lived totally unconcerned with the prevalent departments or divisions of existing social order and thought. The niceties of the antitheses faith and science, capital and labor, object and subject, Protestant and Catholic, lost their vitality. We entered a much more open situation. I suppose that any crisis brings this experience. We, however, were dedicated now to never going back behind it and to devoting the rest of our lives, instead, to a return to normalcy, to the new norm of this extraordinary experience.[24]

Between 1910 when several from this group met in Baden Baden to discuss these problems and 1930 when the final issue of their periodical, *The Creature,* appeared, a number of important works bearing upon speech, encounter, and communication were published. While not all the authors were identified with the Patmos group they certainly shared the group's concerns. Rosenstock-Huessy's comments about the purpose of the editors of *The Creature* captures the spirit which animated their various responses.

[24] *Op. cit.,* pp. 17–18.

The Creature represented the sum of the struggles of Kierkegaard, Feuerbach, Dostoevsky, Nietzsche and William James. They had all discovered, that no one has really anything to say, if they all say the same thing. The creature does not speak as God does. A husband does not speak as his wife, nor does a Christian as a Jew, nor a child as a professor. For that very reason and solely for that reason are they able to speak to, and must they speak to, one another. . . . What the editors of *The Creature* discovered, were the spiritually nourishing processes experienced by genuinely speaking and existentially thinking persons.[25]

In addition to Rosenstock-Huessy, those directly connected with the Patmos group included the publishers of *The Creature,* Joseph Wittig, Martin Buber, Victor von Weizsacker and also contributors like Frank Rosenzweig, Hans Ehrenberg, Karl Barth, Leo Weismantel, Werner Picht and Rudolf Ehrenberg. The works which these men produced during this period were actually responses to the fundamentally human and social issues which they experienced. Hence, Rosenzweig's remark, "The dialogue which these monologues make between one another I consider the whole truth." Similarly Rosenstock-Huessy stated in the introduction to his first major speech book, *Angewandte Seelenkunde* (Applied Psychology) (1924) that, "The occasion for this work is rooted in the association of the author with a small circle of speakers and listeners."[26] Their individual contributions had, therefore, a responsive and dependent quality about them. For example, Rosenzweig was not only indebted to Rosenstock-Huessy's insights into speech which he had gleaned from a rough draft of *Angewandte Seelenkunde* in 1916, but he actually intended that his *Star of Redemption* (1921) complement it. Other related works produced during this period include, Buber's *I and Thou* (1923), Ferdinand Ebner's *The*

[25] Rosenstock-Huessy, "Rückblick auf die *Kreatur*," *Deutsche Beiträge* (Chicago: University of Chicago Press, 1947), pp. 209–10.
[26] Eugen Rosenstock, *Angewandte Seelenkunde* (Darmstadt: Roether-Verlag, 1924), p. 8.

Word and the Spiritual Realities (1921), and Karl Löwith's *The Individual as Person* (1928).

VII

Of all those cited, Rosenstock-Huessy and Franz Rosenzweig were undoubtedly most attuned to one another's insights, both personally and intellectually. For example, their verbal encounter in 1913 and subsequent exchange of letters on Judaism and Christianity in 1916 were cited by the late Fritz Kaufmann as a model of *existential* dialogue in connection with his excellent analysis of Jaspers' philosophy of communication. "True co-Existenz," Kaufmann wrote, "in the consummation of face-to-face relationships is no less intensive and forceful for being unobtrusive, a model of non-violence." Such was the quality "alive in the highly charged controversy between Eugen Rosenstock and Franz Rosenzweig in 1913 and '16."[27] In retrospect, Rosenstock-Huessy made the following comment: "Much to their own surprise the two partners found themselves reluctantly put under the compulsion to face up to one another in a struggle with no quarter to be given or asked for . . . For only in this last extremity, of a soul in self-defense is there hope to realize the truth in the questions of life."[28] Their respective works are, in fact, established upon the significance of speech of this quality, rather than upon any kind of *philosophy of language* of the kind which one finds in the writings of Martin Heidegger or Karl Jaspers. While for both Rosenzweig and Rosenstock-Huessy speech is *the* way of entering into meaningful existence, in the latter's writings one finds a much more explicit attempt to make speech as *grammar* the methodological basis for curing *social* ills and effecting social unity. He is quite emphatic when he stresses methodological and social concerns

[27] Fritz Kaufmann, "Karl Jaspers and a Philosophy of Communication," *The Philosophy of Karl Jaspers* (Ed. by P.A. Schilpp) (New York: Tudor, 1957), p. 214.

[28] *Ibid.* Cited from Eugen Rosenstock's "Introduction" to his correspondence with Franz Rosenzweig in the latter's *Briefe* (Berlin: Schocken, 1935), p. 638.

as against those of the individual creature. In a recent essay on our social grammar he says quite explicitly that his "analysis of the dangers and ills of society will omit all the individual evils of the single and lonely human being."[29] Although his writings abound with insights into our individual linguistic powers, they are always related to methodological and social problems, rather than being an outgrowth of an essentially personalist orientation of the kind developed by Buber in his *I-Thou* or *dialogical* philosophy.

Of all the works cited, Buber's *I and Thou* is undoubtedly the best known. While his name and the term *dialogue* are practically synonymous, the American Buber scholar, Maurice Friedman has noted that, "Those who have arrived at a dialogical or I-Thou philosophy independently of Buber and without influencing him include Ferdinand Ebner, Eberhard Grisebach, Karl Jaspers, Gabriel Marcel, Eugen Rosenstock-Huessy, Franz Rosenzweig and Max Scheler."[30] It is unfair, however, to identify Rosenstock-Huessy's speech writings with most of the above in view of his open criticism of a number of them—especially Buber's *I-Thou* approach. Although they shared the *Patmos* experience, Buber tended to emphasize the more personal dimensions of encounter while Rosenstock-Huessy emphasized the methodological implications of speech insofar as it spans at least two generations or two social groups.

> Our historical mutability . . . is effective as a mental relation between two people, two generations, two times. . . . In so far as we act or speak, we can act or speak meaningfully only

[29] "In Defense of the Grammatical Method" (1955) (privately printed), p. 2. In the same essay he writes, "The circulation of articulated speech is the life blood of society. *Through speech, society sustains its time and space axes.* . . . When speech is recognized as curing society from the ills of disharmony and discontinuity in time and space, grammar is the most obvious organon for the teachings on society. . . . A science is sought by which we may diagnose the power, vitality, unanimity and prosperity of the life blood of society, of speech, language, literature. . . . Our method represents remedial linguistics. . . ." p. 5.

[30] Maurice Friedman, *Martin Buber: The Life of Dialogue,* p. 162.

> between the two other generations preceding and succeeding us, because we always come too late to ourselves.[31]

In contrast to Buber, Rosenstock-Huessy insists that we can only create and preserve a truly human society if we take seriously *names, history, time, calendars* and *tradition.* This means that we must apppreciate *formal* as well as *informal* speech and the *impersonal* as well as *personal* qualities in Western Man's autobiography. Significant or sacramental speech embraces therefore for Rosenstock-Huessy third person *I-It* speech as well as the more direct *I-Thou* forms of address and encounter. But above all, as will be indicated, the major difference between Buber and Rosenstock-Huessy's stress upon language lies in the latter's insistence that nouns precede pronouns, that formal impersonal address are more crucial than the mostly informal and personalist qualities stressed by Martin Buber.

When the war ended, three attractive positions were offered Rosenstock-Huessy; Breitscheid, Minister of the Interior, invited him to become his under-secretary and to draft a new constitution for the Republic; and Karl Muth, the editor of the Roman Catholic magazine *Hochland,* invited him to become its co-editor. The third offer was from the Law Faculty of Leipzig to continue his university lecturing with a promotion in status. He rejected all three offers, and in so doing their implications as well. The first demanded that he become a Marxist, the second that he become a Roman Catholic, and the third that he "fall in line with the agnosticism prevailing in academic circles." He was determined that any commitment he should make would not result in departmentalization—in an isolation of his energies in any single area, whether politics, religion or scholarship. The time was behind him when he could view life categorically in terms of recognized divisions and compartments. In the trenches he had experienced the breakdown of the civilization which included these three intellectual pillars. To him "the professors seemed as wanting as the princes, the ministers of the Word as secluded as their laity, the makers of political

[31] *The Christian Future,* p. [222].

constitutions and of party platforms as unaware of the judgment of God upon our world as the blind masses."[32]

His renunciation of the three offers was countered by the passionate affirmation that labor and labor camps were the means by which he might see unity restored in the post-war era. He first accepted a post with Daimler-Benz as editor of a weekly journal and while there developed in detail his views on labor. After this he helped found, and was leader of, the *Academy of Labor* at Frankfurt for two years. In 1923 he accepted an appointment at Breslau as Professor of the History of Law and Sociology because, as he described it, "no legal basis of existence was open except this academic position" (B & B p. 18). Fortunately, he was able in his spare time to devote his energies to the founding of voluntary work camps, such as the one founded in Lowenberg in Silesia in 1926. It was projected as a *universitas* in the wilderness where farmers, industrial workers and students attempted through their common labors and conversations to bind together people in that region in a common creative social enterprise. From these projects, various forms of work service spread throughout Germany. However, by 1932 the State had taken control, and the initiative of the student element had been changed from one of freedom to one of regimentation.

He has described his literary production between 1923 and 1933 as *three-stranded. Industrierecht* was a straggler from his *pre-war campaigns* while *Applied Psychology* (1923), "formulated for Franz Rosenzweig in a manuscript of 1916," was a product of his *Patmos* experience. Although less known than *Applied Psychology,* he regards his three-volume *The Age of the Church* (1928), written in conjunction with the Roman Catholic priest, Joseph Wittig, as "the most ambitious and certainly the most unplanned" work during this period.

> In Breslau, the comradeship with Wittig gave me the sense of still having a foothold on Patmos. As the inspiration

[32] J.H. Oldham in his "Foreword" to the 1947 English edition of *The Christian Future,* p. viii.

> of 1914 had allowed me to penetrate into the eternal origin of States, our *Alter der Kirche* paid tribute to the role of the Church through the ages.[33]

Their work amounted to a justification and presentation of the Johannine view of the Church which bound them together in their Patmos activities. Having been excommunicated for his views, Wittig was restored to membership in the Church some twenty years later after Pius XII, upon reading the *Age of the Church,* telegrammed Wittig saying that he had never read anything more beautiful. Like his earlier dialogue with Rosenzweig, this exchange was an example of their reliance upon the power of the Spirit revealed in speech through the creature to his fellow creature. Each lived off the other's words and letters; the result of their conversations was a work whose insights neither alone could have fathomed or discovered. In his *Biblionomics* the power of a true co-respondent is eloquently portrayed.

> Sound calls forth sound, song calls forth song; and innumerable books given to friends bear witness, by their often lengthy, poetical inscriptions to this infectious character of confabulation. I mention this so the reader may see . . . that the printed word was not radically different to me from the words spoken or written between friends. Fittingly, letters have played an immense role in my life. The letters printed in Franz Rosenzweig's volume of letters are a good example of their role in my own existence. Many books got started as letters.[34]

Again, the Patmos reliance upon the miracle of speech was a living reality which each discovered in the midst of personal crisis. The principle which evolved and is stated in countless works was a *product* of their common existential crises rather

[33] *Bibliography/Biography,* p. 19.
[34] *Op. cit.,* p. 23.

than something which evolved subsequent to detached speculation.

He remained at Breslau until February 1, 1933 when, opposed to Nazism and having been offered a post at Harvard University, he decided to come to the United States. The period from 1931 to 1938 was devoted to the social problems of revolutions, *Out of Revolution* (1938) being the product of several revisions beginning with the first German edition which appeared in 1931. (The latest revised edition appeared in German in 1951.) His *calendar thinking* which influenced Rosenzweig's own *Star of Redemption* so significantly is fully developed in this lengthy tome, as are significant insights into his Johannine orientation and speech-thinking, which have preoccupied his later years. Like his earlier efforts, his plan for the work on revolutions was conceived amid crisis and social involvement—in this instance, on the battlefield of Verdun in 1917. The fuller significance of his *calender thinking* will be discussed in connection with his *speech-thinking* and cross of reality since these three themes must be viewed in their interrelatedness in order to do justice to any one of them.

In 1935 he was appointed Professor of Social Philosophy at Dartmouth College and in 1940 President Roosevelt invited him to train leaders for the Civilian Conservation Corps. The training center, Camp William James, in Tunbridge, Vermont was created in response to this need. Unfortunately, with the advent of the Second World War and the draft, most of the active workers were enlisted for military service and the CCC movement came to an abrupt end.

VIII

Although it received little or no recognition in this country when it appeared in 1946, *The Christian Future or the Modern Mind Outrun* is a *bridge book* since it spans the sum of his previous contributions and links them with his summary insights into the mysterious interpenetration of Johannine and speech themes with his *cross of reality.* At the same time, the work integrates his experience as a German European in the pre-Hitler period with his American experience during and after World War II. It was his first truly post-war proclamation and it has taken twenty years for it to be accorded the recognition it now begins to receive. For only recently have problems dealing with *hermeneutics,* and *radical religion* or *post-Christian thinking* been receiving not only serious attention by all those connected with contemporary religious life, but for the first time, these themes are seen as interrelated, since the problem of language and communication is central to each. With this recognition, commentators on the contemporary religious scene like Martin Marty and Harvey Cox have singled out *The Christian Future* as a truly pioneering work. Actually, the stage arrived at, on the one hand in the field of *hermeneutics* or *interpretation* by men like Bultmann, Fuchs, Ebeling and Wilder, and on the other, in the area of *religionless Christianity* or *radical religion* by Bonhoeffer, Bishop J. A. T. Robinson, Paul Tillich and Harvey Cox, is precisely the stage where *The Christian Future* begins. *Speech-thinking* in a Johannine Age looking desperately for *religionless forms* of sacred expression geared to the creation and preservation of a truly human and sacred society is *the* concern not only of theologians, but of men in every field of human endeavor today. The *ninth life* of this remarkable *cat* has provided us with an abundant storehouse of insights central to these contemporary concerns. *The Multiformity of Man* (1949), *Der Atem des Geistes* (1951), *Heilkraft und Wahrheit* (1952), his two volume revised *Sociology* (1956 and 1958), and most recently, his two-volume *Sprachbuch* (1964 and 1965), represent the *fruit of his lips* and help us appreciate the marvelous way in which the themes last in print indeed were the driving power throughout his earlier stages or eight *lives* as he refers to them. It was not until he read Shakespeare in English after coming to this country that the meaning of Mercutio's taunting of Tybault in *Romeo and Juliet* was revealed to him as the secret of his own crises, rebirths and transformations. "Good king of cats, nothing but one of your nine lives; that I mean to make bold withal, and, as you shall use me hereafter, dry-heat the rest of the eight." He reflected on this passage at the conclusion of his *Biblionomics:* "I . . . before I came to the States, had not heard of the nine lives of the cat. Now it seems to me, that though ignorant of their very existence, I had begun to live them quite a while ago."[35] An awareness that each individual goes through definite stages or lives is essential to an understanding of his insights into speech. The power of words is intimately connected with one's own personal history; words, therefore, betray our times and spaces as much as they enable us to overcome previous or unnecessary stages. Hence this statement:

> Man is reverberating the Word. How can he do this if he runs away from the first periods of life, in which he should acquire forever the resounding qualities of obedience, of listening, of singing and of playing? These first periods have made me. From them, the power has sprung of giving the slip to any one outdated later period of style or articulation, and to grow up to one more comprehensive. . . . The best pages of my *Sociology* may be those in which I have vindicated these four chapters of the life of the spirit as creating our true time, our full membership in history.[36]

Herbert Marcuse in his recent work, *One Dimensional Man,* discussed one of the tragic obsessions of the modern mind which makes it difficult to grip the subtlety of Rosenstock-Heussy's understanding of man: first, the common assumption that we creatures speak a single language and play a single role; and secondly, that a single linguistic methodology—the language of a single social science—can adequately treat our multi-formed, multi-roled, hierarchical existence. Rosenstock-Huessy's son, Dr. Hans R. Huessy, has discussed this difficulty in a recent unpublished paper devoted to applications of his father's thought in the field of psychiatry. In discussing the effect of the revolution

[35] *Op. cit.,* p. 25.
[36] *Op. cit.,* pp. 23–24.

in the exact sciences he notes that "it became evident that insights at higher levels along the pyramid were not always derived from the building stones below, but that the new insights at the higher levels required a re-explanation of the lower building stones."[37] He adds that:

> The five levels of human functioning described by my father allow an application of this philosophical revolution to the study of man. If we . . . think of a pyramid as five levels, the bottom level of functioning would be physiological and autonomic; the second . . . would deal with eating, sleeping, and playing, the third . . . with work; the fourth . . . with love, the re-creation of values; and the fifth . . . with heroism and self-sacrifice.

To treat man adequately requires an understanding of his particular operational level of existence. At the highest level it may be, for example, that some form of *inspiration* or confrontation is required "which allows him to rise above his past, and, at times, to overcome his past."

> The hallmark of a large percentage of psychiatric patients is their inability to live at all on levels four and five. For these patients (at these levels), the psychological determinism of psychoanalysis would be quite invalid. . . . Events on the upper two levels are almost totally dependent on things having their origin outside the individual and, therefore, will always be unpredictable from a study of mankind.

This hierarchical factor accounts for another difference between Martin Buber and Rosenstock-Huessy with respect to the former's *I-Thou* formulation, which Rosenstock-Huessy insists must begin with *Thou,* rather than *I*—with forces which

[37] These remarks are contained in a paper delivered by Dr. Hans R. Huessy at a symposium on Rosenstock-Huessy's thought held at the Miramar Conference Center at Woods Hole, Mass. during July, 1965. It was entitled, "Some Applications to Psychiatry of the Work of Eugen Rosenstock-Huessy." The citations which follow are also from Dr. Huessy's paper.

originate outside the *I.*[38] Hence, the priority of the *grammatical* second person over the first in Rosenstock-Huessy's grammatical approach. His son has appropriated this in terms of its application to the upper two levels of existence where events

> have their origin outside the individual. . . . Our formulation states that there must be a Thou before there can be an I. Support for this formulation is found in the observation that children learn the pronoun *I* last. This demands a 180° shift in our thinking about man. If Thou *precedes* I, then something outside of man is essential. The first human being had to be addressed as a Thou before he could become an I. This immediately leads to some kind of formulation of God.

In *Liturgical Thinking, Dich und Mich,* and other essays, Rosenstock-Heussy dwelt upon this theme at considerable length. Our first liturgical and grammatical figure is *Thou* which is the "health principle of the soul." "The soul must be called *Thou* before she can ever reply *I*, before she can ever speak of *us* and finally *it.* Through the four figures, *Thou, I, We, It,* the Word walks through us. The Word must call our name first. We must have listened and obeyed before we can think or command."[39]

For those capable of living at times on all five levels speech, *encounter, inspiration,* and *social confrontation* may possibly change the configurations of lower levels during those periods when we are operating at the highest level of existence. Furthermore, the *way* we speak our roles and *what* we say at any single level, for example, as son, husband, father, teacher, is dependent not only upon that particular level, but also upon

[38] "Liturgical Thinking" (II) *Orate Fratres* (Collegeville, Minn., January, 1950), pp. 12–13. Cf. also a related essay which deals with his differences with Martin Buber, "Dich und Mich, Lehre oder Mode.", *Neues Abendland,* 9 Jg. (1954, November). An account of his subsequent exchange with Buber is contained in *Philosophical Interrogations* (Ed. by Sydney and Beatrice Rome) (New York: Holt, Rinehart and Winston, 1964), pp. 31–35.

[39] "Liturgical Thinking" (II), p. 12.

the outside community which calls forth each role we play. All of these permutations are possible within a relatively short period of time. Compound this with our various roles during an entire lifetime and one gets some idea of the wide variety of roles, the diverse kinds and qualities of speech, and therefore the mystery, problematic and speech-dependent character of human existence. During every moment of our lives it is possible for us to live in a wide variety of times and spaces, and simultaneously to create and undergo an untold number of new time and space configurations and transformations. Rosenstock-Huessy's own pilgrimage in language since 1902 is an excellent illustration of this insight as it affects an individual's life. In each decade *what* he pursued formally in the area of language was determined by the particular *front* on which he was fighting.

In all his writings Rosenstock-Huessy repeatedly insists that the creaturely existence of a named person is *unnatural* in contrast to that of those creatures living exclusively on the natural or animal level. For *natural man,* names which span several generations, history, time and social groups are meaningless as are memory, inspiration and the possibility open to all persons of overcoming one's past and participating in the creation of a new speech-conditioned future. He deplores the assumption that we develop our natural reason and true powers between fourteen and twenty-five, that this is the normative stage for determining values and meaning in life. Actually, it is but a *transient phase* about which he says: "It is the Reason of the classroom student. Greek philosophy, eighteenth century enlightenment, American common sense or pragmatism, are gigantic superstructures of these uprooted minds and unloved bodies in their in-between age, when one set of names has faded and the new call of love is slow to resound."

The liturgy, the call to be a named responsible person, the *soul*'s being confronted and its resulting inner dialogue, all contribute to both the uniting of our passions and thoughts and their receiving direction, as well as enabling us to declare to ourselves and to society that certain experiences and questions are more significant than others, that a part of us is now past and a new future and new community await us! Hence his statement, "From the liturgy I have learned to think rightly!" The missionary charge, "Go ye into all the world," demands from the missionary himself a change of his own mind, a price!

> True partnership puts my mind at the service of my partner, and his mind at my service. *Our minds work much better for our partners than for ourselves.* The Spirit was not given to man for himself. Self-reliance is an abuse of the greatest gift of the Spirit, or our reason.[40]

The alternative to self-reliance, the missionary *submission* to the Word—to those crucial words which call us into responsible action—highlights the risk, possible sacrifice, and above all, the *unnaturalness* of this kind of response. Dwell on the significance of the *etsi,* the 'although' in his motto, "I respond *although* I will be changed!" To be a *person* in this setting means more than simply the fact that we utter many sounds, and enact a wide variety of roles; it involves the willingness to take on those forms of responsibility which run counter to our *natural* inclinations.

As developed in his *Applied Psychology* and later works, our *grammatical life* is one involving named persons whose involvement in the *modes, tenses* and *intonations* enable us to experience the rebirth and transformations which the Word makes possible. In *Liturgical Thinking* he notes that before 1500 to be called a *person* in canon law meant that:

> A person was always responsible for a functioning part of the whole community, he held an office of some kind. The smallest 'office holders' were the fathers and mothers who presided over households. We forget too readily that not everybody or anybody was free to marry, but that to establish a home was itself a privilege.[41]

40 "Pentecost and Mission" *The Hartford Seminary Foundation Bulletin* (Winter, 1954), p. 21.
41 "Liturgical Thinking" (I) *Orate Fratres* (Collegeville, Minn., Nov. 1949), p. 2.

More recently at the University of California he re-emphasized that our *names* link us to universes of discourse which go beyond an individual's existence. At the very least names signify the unity provided by the home, as well as national and historical ties. "House from Moses to Edwards meant that spiritual unity, which forges two or three generations and an inner sanctum and some space into a cross of reality whose center is not to be formed in any one person."[42]

In the light of numerous variations upon the theme of modern assembly line existence which so many in our society lead, is it not a strange assumption as is so often asserted that we are *persons by nature!* With Kierkegaard, Rosenstock-Huessy would insist, that humanity is a *task* and not a *fact!* Up until the late Middle Ages before a monk received his monastic name signifying his responsible entry into a new community, he underwent a previous ceremony during which he formally renounced the name given at birth. He renounced his worldly person by renouncing his worldly name just as in the ancient world you could destroy a man by writing his name on an earthenware jar and dashing it to the ground in pieces. Each decision, each new act is a unique and irreversible one which announces to those affected that one part of us has died, and another reborn. It is belittling to the nobility of *named* persons, as presented by Rosenstock-Huessy, to categorize a richly lived life as merely a form of *natural* existence. *Persons* are precisely those who often through costly decisions, have defied the natural laws of determinism.

IX

Names are important not only as the focus and standard bearer of sacred speech, but they are essential for an understanding of the named individual's involvement in history, in the *autobiography of Western man.* Names are our link with history. This is the theme of *Out of Revolution* and this work helps us realize the significance of his *calendar thinking* referred to earlier, especially as it relates to his *speech-thinking* and the

[42] A report in a letter to the author dated 12/26/65.

cross of reality. Hence, his concluding statement in *Out of Revolution:* "Regeneration of Language would be no faulty name for the due process of Revolution. This process was the means of survival during the sixth day of creation."[43] In *Out of Revolution* the calendars of world history and personal biography are wedded as an attempt to "read world history as our own autobiography. The *calendar form* of thinking accords to time, history and names their proper place in the development of our own autobiographies."[44] Calendar thinking, alone, does justice also to the historical millenarian emphasis so evident throughout Rosenstock-Huessy's writings. Thus, there can be no speech, no time, no history of any consequence unless all these elements are involved. As Rosenzweig and Rosenstock-Huessy developed it, *God, man* and *world, creation, revelation* and *redemption,* and *speech, time, names* and *history,* are connected in such a way that to omit the influence of any single element lessens our collective human potential. *Out of Revolution* is probably the first attempt to understand European history through a blending of these themes. *Calendrical thinking* presents this heritage in terms of our *festivals, holidays, holy days* and *national revolutions.* These calendars represent Western man's corporate memory, his determination of what it is that is worth preserving, observing and remembering.

> The holidays which you and I respect are composed of the memories of all the vicissitudes of man. So much then must be said in emphatic defense of the calendar: . . . I . . . have written the history of the last thousand years around the holidays and the calendars instituted during this epoch; and I am sure that this new method places the historian in the center of human history.[45]

The degree to which his entire orientation in every field has been influenced by his respect for and veneration of calendars is

[43] *Out of Revolution,* p. 739.
[44] *Op. cit.,* p. 8.
[45] *The Christian Future,* p. [209].

captured in a passage from his *Biblionomics.* Referring to *the bricks* of his *house of history* he writes:

> Ever since my lines on Notker and Clodius, and my first printed essay on the Medieval Calendars, research in the calendars of all religions and countries, and in the lives of workers, scientists, saints, revolutionaries, businessmen, etc. has been perpetual. Therefore, if I may say so, *lifetimes* and *holidays* are my bricks of time, although the bibliography does not list more than half a dozen titles in either field.[46]

The central theme of *Out of Revolution* is stated in the *Prologue:*

> Mankind has always, with the utmost tenacity, cultivated its calendar. One of the innovations of this book in point of method consists in taking the political and ecclesiastical calendar seriously. A day introduced into the calendar or a day stricken out of the calendar, means a real change in the education and tradition of a nation. Mankind writes its own history long before the historians visit its battlefields; days, festivals, holidays, the order of meals, rest, and vacation, together with religiously observed ritual and symbols, are sources of political history, though rarely used by the average political or economic historians. . . . A holiday is always a political creation and a political instrument.[47]

Earlier, he distinguished between the *reasoning mind* for whom time is a matter of months, days and years, and the time sense of the man of faith whose calendar is "independent from nature's mechanism." For the Christian, "from Christmas to Easter, a whole lifetime of thirty years is remembered, and from Pentecost to Advent, the whole experience of mankind through the Old Testament and our whole era is remembered."[48] Any sense of a presence fraught with meaning depends for its content upon the intersection of four of these calendars,

[46] *Bibliography/Biography,* p. 22.
[47] *Out of Revolution,* p. 8.
[48] *The Christian Future,* p. [209].

each of which should be regarded as essentially a *speech event* where formal named address, rather than informal pronominal speech, was uttered to give direction to Western man's destiny.

The use of *four* for Rosenstock-Huessy is central to his *cross of reality* and forms an essential part of his methodological interests. In this instance its application reveals the ingredients of the presentness of a people consisting of the intersection of four speech calendars representing *nature, secular* history, *sacred* or Church history and our own private uniquely personal calendar. Being confronted and torn in this manner leaves the *present,* as Homer described it, "as inconvenient to sit on as the blade of a razor." As individuals, we live similarly at the crossroads, at the juncture of four *fronts:* "*backward* toward the past, *forward* into the future, *inward* among ourselves, our feelings, wishes and dreams, and *outward* against what we must fight or exploit or come to terms with or ignore."[49] In the discussion which follows the cross of reality and speech will be presented as the basis for determining those speech forms which determine social health as well as indicate the possibility of social decay.

X

The significance of the cross of reality and speech can be highlighted by examining Rosenstock-Huessy's methodological insights into speech as contained in *Applied Psychology* (1924) and subsequent works and essays. *Applied Psychology* is a reworking of a *Sprachbrief* (speech letter) addressed to Franz Rosenzweig in 1916; it was offered as a defense against the then prevailing interest in scientific linguistics. It first appeared in print in 1924, and was presented as "an attempt, in the most compact style, to offer for the first time an appropriate '*discours de la methode,*' a *Sic et Non;* for our day."[50] This task, to which the man has devoted his total energies, was outlined in the three-page Foreword almost fifty years ago. On the occasion of his seventieth birthday, and more recently in his lectures

[49] *Op. cit.,* pp. [167–68].
[50] *Angewandte Seelenkunde,* p. 8.

at Columbia, this devotion was reaffirmed. The appearance of his two-volume *Sprachbuch* in 1964 represents truly the "fruit of his lips" since it contains his own selection of his numerous insights into the sacramental character of speech. In the following pages an attempt will be made to state briefly and then indicate applications of the *grammatical method;* first, to the life of the individual as it is discussed in the fifth chapter of *Applied Psychology;* secondly, to society as described in chapter nine; and lastly, as it relates to the intimate connection which exists between these insights and his application of the *Cross of Reality* to social unity as discussed in his essay *In Defense of the Grammatical Method,* which first appeared in English in 1955. Though necessarily brief and sketchy, it may be possible to both outline the focus of his remarks and also give the reader a sense of his style.

One of the clearest statements about the aim and purpose of his grammatical method appears at the beginning of his essay *In Defense of the Grammatical Method* (1955). A comparison of this with the earlier Foreword to *Applied Psychology* will testify to Rosenstock-Huessy's faithfulness to his earlier manifesto on this subject. The essay begins, "Grammar . . . is the future organon of social research."

> In this way, following the astounding developments of dialectics and mathematics, from ancient analytics and arithmetics, to their modern standards, grammar, too, will ascend beyond the grammar school, and become from a dry-as-dust textbook-obsession, the open sesame to the hidden treasures of society.[51]

The complete breakdown of the German language between 1933 and 1939 was, for Rosenstock, "one of the speediest and most radical events of all times in the field of mind and speech." Reflecting on this breakdown he remains more convinced than ever that ". . . the science of this lifeblood of society (i.e. language) should . . . be exalted to the rank of social research."

51 "In Defense of the Grammatical Method," p. 1.

> The originality of social research hinges on the existence of a method that is neither stolen from theology nor from natural science. We intend to prove, in the terms of grammar, of theology and of natural philosophy, that such a particular method exists, and that by using it Roman Catholics and Protestants and Free Thinkers, are united in a common enterprise. Without such a unity, the revolt of the masses must find the various intellectual groups in a helpless division, as helpless as in the new war, the single neutral country in Europe is found. . . . We must discover a common basis for social thinking.[52]

It is fascinating to follow Rosenstock-Huessy's development of this methodology in a work like *Applied Psychology,* not only because of the compactness of the argument, but because of the structure of its development, which proceeds from a discussion in the first four chapters about our having substituted the *soul* for real *named persons* to outlining in chapter nine a complex program for co-ordinating art, religion and law. The early chapters reflect his reasons for choosing the title, *Applied Psychology,* which he took over from a popular paperback tract on social psychology. Having lured a particular audience with that popular title, he hoped to reach those who, in his opinion, were most in need of hearing such words. The fascination of psychologists in his time for the *soul* was, from his standpoint, a "de-souling" of people since it meant that the soul was more important than one's *name;* hence, of more significance than the creature's link with time, history and his actual biography. Descartes' preoccupation with the cogitating mind and his admitted disdain for his own autobiography prior to his vision in a country hut is a good example of the split which such emphases could produce. Actually, Descartes' mind-matter dualism made it theoretically possible for either *mind* or *matter* to do justice to precisely those aspects of reality with which each was ostensibly concerned. In Descartes' case, he mistakenly viewed his *second mind* as the authoritative one. From such a

[52] *Op. cit.,* p. 2.

split the *subject-object, inner-outer* characterization of reality inevitably follows, with the thinking mind determining the truth and meaning of the concrete experimental world. At the heart of this dilemma lies the false assumption that the *soul* is an *object,* a *thing.*

The fifth chapter is devoted to the question of whether the soul has its own peculiar grammar. He begins with an attack upon those false grammars which reflect the dominance of the perceiving *I*—e.g., those which begin with the *I* rather than as experience tells us, with the *Thou.* Not *amo, amas, amat,* but rather *amas, amo, amat* is the correct order of our proper grammatical posture. This is confirmed by his responses to external forces and pressures which address him as they did primitive man, namely as a *thou.* It is through outside address that we gradually become persons, conscious of our identity—our names become meaningful. During this period we are most aware of the imperative forms of speech: "Go! Come! Listen! etc." Similarly, the child's response, "No! Yes!" represents an assertion by the child that gradually his identity is being established. In each instance, *personality* is rooted in the fact that we have a name within a community and are capable of being addressed and responding. This, for Rosenstock-Huessy, is basic to our grammatical life.

It is only after we have utilized the grammatical forms *I* and *Thou* that we begin to employ the grammatical third person *He, She,* or *It.* Our normal grammatical existence informs us that both the personal as well as the impersonal are integral parts of our vocabulary. The transition from childhood to adulthood is marked by this distinction. While the second person is our primary grammatical form, the complete grammar of the soul is revealed in the changes and transformations resulting from the basic grammatical laws. "Every change in the life of the soul appears as an inflection of its grammatical configurations."[53] The various grammatical *moods* become the medium through which our grammatical *persons* are expressed. They constitute, in effect, the particular garb of the soul in

[53] *Angewandte Seelenkunde,* p. 27.

each moment of its existence. As with the three grammatical persons, all grammatical moods and tenses manifest the "soul's possibilities." ". . . the soul can swing to the melody of becoming just as it may resound with existence's tune of the rhythm of transformation."[54] Thus love, being *in* love, is the supreme force capable of transforming the *I*—releasing it from its own thoughts and obsessions with individual freedom. Like Augustine, love surpasses all the pagan virtues since love alone can bend the *I.* We can be courageous, temperate, etc., but we cannot *be* love: we are always *in* love. To be *in* love is to admit the priority of the grammatical second person over the first.

Crucial for grammatical existence is the temporal factor of *timing.* While for many, to quote a popular saying, "Thoughts are free," just the opposite is true of speech which is the creature of time, bound to various time sequences, and yet capable of creating new times and ages. Timing, inspiration, transformation, and speech always go hand in hand with grammatical living. He concludes chapter five with the following summation about the *grammar of the soul.* "It is the theory of the transformation of shapes. Inflection, transformation, changes of time are its contents. Our school grammar speaks of umlauts and ablauts; the Urgrammar of the transformation of shapes."[55]

As indicated earlier, chapter nine is the appropriate complement to five because of its devotion to the social implications of the grammatical method; namely, its concern for the *we* rather than the *I,* with *community* rather than the *individual.* The *we,* for Rosenstock-Huessy, is more than merely the total sum of a number of individuals. As he puts it, "The Urgrammar blends God, Man and World in the resounding 'We'." In their grammatical attire the first person plural embraces the world of *art*—lyric song, drama, and prose, etc. These are the elements of the aesthetic world which unite us most intensively as a people (*Volk*). The second person plural embraces those *legal* norms which again define the nature of communal existence whether they be the laws of the secular or spiritual

[54] *Op. cit.,* p. 31.
[55] *Op. cit.,* p. 37.

realm. Finally, the language of the *scientific* world is subsumed under our grammatical third person plural. In each of the three realms he has singled out one example as embodying the *purest* form of that particular grammatical voice. Thus *lyric poetry* is the purest example of art, *jurisprudence* the purest and simplest expression of the social order, and lastly, *natural science* the purest, but also most elementary kind of science.[56] It is noteworthy that *religion* is discussed not only in connection with law-giving and law-making in the field of jurisprudence and ethics, but also as that vital force which is present when significant personal and collective transformations occur in any of the three realms. Here, as in other writings, Rosenstock-Huessy identifies religion and religious experience with that force which enables us to speak and respond during any period of our spiritual biographies. These two chapters contribute greatly to an appreciation of the transforming and sacramental powers inherent in speech as evidenced in his motto, "I respond *although* I will be changed." It also helps us to understand that "Speech is the body of the Spirit."

Finally, let us note his application of speech as the means whereby social unity is determined by examining his essay, *In Defense of the Grammatical Method,* referred to earlier. This essay is particularly relevant as it illustrates the interrelatedness of his *grammatical approach* and his *cross of reality.* The trinity of speech, both individual and collective, constituting the authentic spiritual biographies of all those involved, can be appreciated at any one moment only in terms of the intersection of at least four vectors which represent the meeting of the spatial and temporal axes within which all life unfolds. In his two-volume *Sociology,* in *Applied Psychology* and elsewhere, he has reiterated his conviction that dualisms like *subject* and *object* never do justice to the complexity of any situation. He has described himself as an *impure thinker* because of his unwillingness to settle for the normal polarization which typifies most thinking. His use of the four vectors of a cross enables him to give appropriate recognition to the traditional

[56] *Op. cit.,* pp. 51 and 53.

subject-object distinction representing the *spatial* axis as inner and outer. To this he adds the *temporal* axis represented by the two vectors which embrace *past* and *future, traject* and *preject.* The rationale behind this division he explains as follows:

> The terms preject and traject above we have chosen out of respect for the inveterate usage which divides the world in mind and body, in subjects and objects. It did not seem wise to by-pass these well-established terms of our tradition in logic. The battle had to be joined on the battlefield defined by the classical tradition; and we tried to make room for two more aspects of the real by introducing the time cup. Of any time cup the subject and the object were fragments because the future was anticipated by the prejective or imperative, the past ascertained by the report or narrative (trajective).[57]

Note his application of the *cross of reality* when analyzing first, those evils which destroy unity. It is *anarchy* that "prevents translocal units from cooperating"; *decadence* destroys our sense of future because it means that people "do not have the stamina of converting the next generation to their own aims and ends": in *revolutions* men do violence to the past and to the existing order, and it is *war* that forces a country to "incorporate external territory." Corresponding to his *Cross, anarchy* and *war* represent the inner and outer "space in society." Thus, he writes:

> We are compelled, by the two facts of anarchy and war, to distinguish between an inner and an outer space in society. The twofold character of space is that, in any society, a border-line . . . cuts the world of space into two parts, one inner, one outer.[58]

Similarly, *decadence* and *revolution* destroy the possibility of future and the necessity of past so essential to the growth of

[57] "The Individual's Right to Speak and Some Final Terms of Grammar" (privately printed) (1946), p. 25.
[58] "In Defense of the Grammatical Method," pp. 2–3.

any healthy society. Upon such discussions Rosenstock-Huessy bases his claim that this represents "an undebatable basis for the social system." "For the two axes of time and space, with their fronts backward, forward, inward, outward, are not merely verbal definitions of the social order; they are open to a unanimous experience and an identical consciousness of all human beings." These social truths are, he claims, "universally valid as any mathematical and logical truths." It is only when one realizes that we are threatened on any one of our "time or space fronts" that we are compelled to acknowledge the existence of social processes and the need for integration and preservation. The fight to restore social health is akin to that described by William James in his insistence upon the need for a *Moral Equivalent of War.* When one front is threatened, we become aware that the "four fronts of life perpetually must be balanced." Where these evils are allowed to continue unchecked, "no social research is meaningful or possible." Corresponding to the four "evils" enumerated above, are the tasks confronting social research to restore the perpetual balance vital to a healthy society.

> Social research is imprisoned in a reality, in a cross of reality between four simultaneous tasks to cultivate faith, power, unanimity, respect, all four. Social research is the search for the restoration of the perpetual balance.[59]

Perhaps the only advance made in this most recent presentation of the grammatical method is its relatively striking clarity of style and the concreteness of application. The more theoretical pronouncement of 1924 is enhanced by Rosenstock-Huessy's practical and concise exposition of 1955 and more recently in his *Speechbooks* of 1964. His discussion of social evils is an excellent illustration both of his method and of the relevance of speech to it. In short, the above four evils "hurt language" since it is "speech" which defends society against these ills. Thus the heading of his third section: "Society lives by Speech, dies without speech." We speak out of need and out of fear; our of fear that decay, anarchy, war and revolution will destroy

[59] *Op. cit.,* p. 3.

the time and space axes of society which "give direction and orientation to all members of society." In order to prevent social disintegration, men reason, pass laws, tell stories, and sing. In so doing, "The external world is reasoned out, the future is ruled, the past is told," and "the unanimity of the inner circle is expressed in song."

> Without articulated speech, men neither have direction nor orientation in time and space. Without the signposts of speech, the social beehive would disintegrate immediately. When speech is recognized as curing society from the ills of disharmony and discontinuity in time and space, grammar is the most obvious organon for the teachings of society.[60]

By means of this method, we become conscious of our "place in history (backward), world (outward), society (inward), and destiny (forward)." The grammatical method constitutes "an additional development of speech itself" which fulfills itself in our new powers of "direction and orientation." Thus, "Grammar is the self-consciousness of language, just as logic is the self-consciousness of thinking." Rosenstock-Huessy's constant use of language as the means of social unity and peace is never stated without reference to the space and time axes of society.

> Without common speech, men neither have one time nor mutual respect nor security among themselves. To speak has to do with time and space. Without speech, the phenomenon of time and space cannot be interpreted. Only when we speak to others (or, for that matter, to ourselves), do we delineate an inner space or circle in which we speak, from the outer world about which we speak. . . . And the same is true about the phenomenon of time. Only because we speak, are we able to establish a present moment between past and future.[61]

It is interesting to note his rejection of scientific notions of time and space. "Grammatical time and space precedes the

[60] *Op. cit.*, p. 5.
[61] *Op. cit.*, p. 8.

scientific notions of an outer space or of a directed time. For they presuppose an inner space between the scientists and some contemporaneity between them, too." The types or forms of speech which are our social watchdogs are, in words resembling Schelling's in his *Introduction* to his *Weltalter,* "speaking and listening, teaching and studying."

XI

The time spent pursuing the various themes in Rosenstock-Huessy's writings is a forceful and imaginative journey into the secrets and mysteries of human meaning. Each reader must appropriate this meaning depending upon his own particular style of traveling. For at least one student, such a journey means both direction and hope at a time when men everywhere are questioning traditional modes of approaching ultimate problems from every quarter of the social order. The universality of the questioning is a good sign for those who, in Rosenstock-Huessy's sense, have waited for our age to take seriously the universal sacramental power of speech. If the *cross of reality* has any meaning, it must by definition affect every quarter of human existence. No single style can bring life to all others; only a harmonious blending of numerous styles confident in their oral and aural powers can bring about the continued creation and preservation of a truly human society, namely, complete the envisioned sequel to Michelangelo's painting in the Sistine Chapel. In the concluding pages of *Out of Revolution* this is admirably stated:

> *Mankind does not try to speak one language.* He does not monotonously speak the same words. But this is because in every dialogue the two partners assume different parts, represent different points of view, use different arguments. Variety is the essence of real speech between men. . . . By the multitude of dialects we are reminded of the innumerable quarrels, dialogues, disputes between the men of the past. But interplay and mutual relation are at the bottom of the tower of Bable which linguists study today by the queer method of

approaching each language separately. Each human variety has its particular coagulated speech. Every speech is dissoluble; it is retranslatable into the universal language behind one separate tongue. Through translation, each variety of man remains in contact with all other varieties.[62]

Thus speech is indeed the means whereby men become conscious of their variety and at the same time, aware that speech provides the clue and means to healing the rifts between men and creating a viable, healthy society. In all of this there has been notably little mention of God or use of traditional theological categories. For those oriented in traditional forms of Petrine and Pauline Christianity this presentation will undoubtedly present serious difficulties. Such a reader may simply wish to reject these concerns as not related to religion as he sees it. For those willing to submit themselves to a Johannine approach, such a presentation may provide a means of overcoming the present rift between *sacred* and *secular* concerns. For such creatures the answer to the question about the *place* and *nature* of God within such a vocal setting, is a simple one. "The power who puts questions into our mouth and makes us answer them is our God."[63] Such was the condition for David and Jeremiah; it is equally ours today.

The living God thus revealed by Jesus must be forever distinguished from the merely conceptual God of philosophers. Most atheists deny God because they look for Him in the wrong way. He is not an object, but a person, and He has not a concept but a name. To approach Him as an object of theoretical discussion is to defeat the quest from the start. Nobody can look at God as an object. God looks at us and has looked at us before we open our eyes or our mouths. *He is the power which makes us speak. He puts words of life on our lips.*[64]

[62] *Out of Revolution,* p. 738.
[63] *Op. cit.,* p. 225.
[64] *The Christian Future,* p. [94].

PREFACE

OUR DATE WITH DESTINY

THE LINKING TOGETHER of the material which the waves of life threw upon my beach in more than thirty years is largely the work of George Morgan. The author of *What Nietzsche Means,* he challenged me repeatedly about my stubborn religious conservatism: Since you admit that Nietzsche's Antichrist and the two World Wars made an epoch, why do you play the mooncalf and remain a Christian?

I let him have all the utterances in which I tried to answer this very question long before he asked it. Before George Morgan entered the army, he worked over the manuscript for a year. Another four years, and thanks to the interest of Reinhold Niebuhr, Douglas Horton and George Thomas, here it is in print.

I had two classes of readers before me when I wrote: one the free fighters, men and women between twenty and thirty who struggle with the spirit in the form of the spirit of their own age and time. To them their generation is a secret society, and it has incommunicable tastes, enthusiasms and interests which are a mystery both to its predecessors and to posterity. The other class contains the men who have experienced the spirit as the great translator from age to age because they themselves have been drafted for this supreme service. The three men to whom this book is dedicated belong to this group.

The dedication of this book is part of its ambitious aim. And the reader will understand this better after I have said a word about the merits of these three friends.

Karl Muth has raised the quality of Roman Catholic literature infinitely by his *Hochland*. Founded in 1903, this monthly has reeducated the clergy and the laity of Germany in a new sense of quality in all matters of religious art and literature. From 1933 to its suppression by the Nazis in 1942, it never once, as far as I have found, mentioned the Nazis; it kept on the highway of the soul, yet dealt freely with social, political, and historical themes. In the midst of lunacy, it imparted the true spirit.

J. C. Oldham is so widely known in the Anglo-Saxon world that I only have to mention his work for the ecumenic movement and his *Christian News-Letter* which valiantly presses home the double sense of news: translating the gospel into everyday revelation.

Ambrose Vernon, in the United States, twice has founded a college department for biography—at Carleton and at Dartmouth. The life of Christ, he felt, would meet the students through the lives of other great souls in history, if the spiritual core of biography could be opened up to them as a lawful order.

All these men have retranslated the forms of the spirit, for their own Church and day. They have strengthened my faith. In them I have been able to recognize the life-giving power of the Church's spirit.

The book, however, which I am allowed to inscribe with their names, is a kind of apology for my different approach to the same eternal problem. For it tries to present the difficulties of a new era and of a new generation: of the generation who showed their faith by becoming soldiers of war. The crux of my life and of the life of the young has been the same: to break the impasse between the tradition of the Holy Ghost and the workings of the spirit of the times in the courage and faith of simple soldiers. The soldier in an army has faith in some spirit. How is this related to the faith in the Holy Spirit, of the Christian tradition?

Until we rediscover their relation, the gospel cannot be truthfully preached to the soldiers, nor can the soldiers make themselves understood to the Christian missionaries of the spirit through the ages, and wars will have their way.

The spirits must get together, the One Holy One, and the many of each time. The three friends have translated the One Holy One into new forms. O my friends, will you believe me when I introduce to you the simple faith of the next generation and request you to hear the spirit speak out of their acts of faith?

EUGEN ROSENSTOCK-HUESSY

Advent, 1945
Four Wells
Norwich, Vermont

PART ONE: THE GREAT INTERIM

"The average church-going civilizee realizes, one may say, absolutely nothing of the deeper currents of human nature."

William James, July 23, 1903.
(Perry II, 317)

I

MY DISQUALIFICATION

The Conflict of Functioning and Speaking—The Conflict of Words and Names

The Conflict of Functioning and Speaking

Some time ago an American returned from abroad with high dreams, for he was going to develop a real theater in this country. On his first evening in New York he went to a downtown restaurant for dinner. Next to him a young couple spent the evening and he could not help listening in. She bravely would try to say something with real eagerness. Then the fellow, looking bright and handsome enough, would respond with a short "To h—." This would go on for the whole evening. It must be admitted that the raucous "To h—" was not without some modulation; it actually covered in its repetition a number of keys. But it remained the young man's sole contribution as far as articulate speech went. The observer went home and buried all dreams of a new future for the stage. For, he would say, when a lover has nothing more to say, the stage, which is based on the plenitude of speech, and its public have grown too far apart.

In this story, the dilemma of our age is well stated. This dilemma has been the theme of my life ever since 1905.

We are entering upon a speechless future. In this new society the eloquence of neither Daniel Webster nor Phillips Brooks, of neither St. Paul nor Shakespeare is going to be heard by the masses; the wave length on which men listen or speak has changed to "infra-eloquence," to an offhand "I don't care" and "what-the-h—" style.

If this is the future, then Christianity has no future. For the flow of vital speech is the sign of living Christians. They represent Pentecost and its gift of tongues or they do not exist.

The future of our economic order and the future of Christians are in conflict. This conflict seems to be decided at the outset in favor of the economic order. For the great languages of Church as well as State, of the Bible as well as of the Constitution, are losing their power in a daily process of advertising, commercialization, mechanization. People become indifferent to the hullabaloo of all verbiage.

This indifference is more serious than any attack on Church or State. Persecution helps a Church, and an aggressor may save a nation. But this is a withering from within.

It has been the strangeness of my life that I should have believed with everything I did or wrote in the solubility of this conflict, ever since 1905. To me, the years 1905 to 1945, this last period of human history, are of great simplicity and grandeur. A powerful hand has lifted up the particles of the human race and now puts them down again under a new horizon of existence. We see this horizon as dimly as the eastern sky one hour before sunrise; yet it determines already the lives and livelihood of all of us despite our nation or denomination. Granted that twelve generations or so lived happily within "Church" and "State" (the very word "State" is not older than 1500) and got their orientation from these two sources of light; this no longer is true.

We are unemployed, impoverished, inflated, killed, moved around, in nations great and small, in Churches free and orthodox, because of a new "within." Against this new "within," the millions find little protection, either within their nation or within their Church. Global economic cooperation is the new "within." Neither the New Deal nor the GOP nor Hitler nor Stalin can guarantee prosperity because the globe is not governed by any one statesman. The Great Society, this speechless giant of the future, does not speak English (neither does it speak Russian). And it is this Great Society which claims all of us who have to make a living, as her material, her victims, her assets or liabilities in terms of capital and labor.

The two world wars were the form of world revolution in which this new future reached into everybody's life; the nationalist and communist ideologies with their dreams of revolution were checkmated and are mere foam around the real transformation. The real transformation was made by the wars and it made the Great Society final. She is the heiress of State and Church.

Now, as I said before, it has been the strangeness of my life that I always believed in this powerful hand which called the new Giant into being and placed us all within the new horizon. I always considered the wars more decisive than the party slogans, but I was not at all impressed by the Great Society as though it were the Good Society. I concentrated on the inevitable conflict between this daughter "Society" and the mother "Church," between toiling and speaking man, between daily bread and Pentecost. I accepted the general division of labor in the new universe. But I believed that it was void of any consecration in any of its particulars.

Most people distributed hope and fear differently. Some would stick to the good old society, others would think that the new Great Society would also be good. And in this party fashion, neither group admitted that events moved without any regard to their moral judgments in this matter. For forty years the revolutionary events have been listed by the press under the headlines of the hour or the day of the single sensational happening: sinking of the *Lusitania, Panay* incident, Bruening dismissed, Black Friday, etc., etc. Thousands of events were photographed upon our memory one upon the other.

Gradually, however, this Niagara of disconnected facts impressed itself on the human mind as a—Niagara. The time atoms flew around our ears so thick and fast that we had to coin a common name for the puzzle; the single events ceased to make sense when treated singly. Who was Man that he did unchain this flood of destruction and confusion?

The young man in the restaurant used the stereotyped label "to h—." Though pertinent, it did not suffice for people who already found themselves in this place. They now wished to get out of it.

The Conflict of Words and Names

But a hell which functions so well as the world wars do will not let us climb out unless we can find new words, new names of faith, unheard tones of hope by which to appeal to each other. The old names are shopworn. A Spirit of Pentecost has become our immediate political necessity since we must say more to each other than "war of survival." War of survival is a term which in its denudedness fails to give to the hundreds of millions who are engulfed any common direction. To survive is one thing for each individual, and quite another for all of us together. If we hope to survive *together,* obviously we must distinguish very clearly indeed the way by which this may be achieved from the panic in which we ourselves try to survive by cutting our neighbor's throat. For any distinction of this type, we must speak again with growing conviction. It becomes crucial to go beyond stereotype because the new shores of a common and more extensive survival can only be reached on the wings of new names and, in turn, these new names must be spoken in such a setting that their speakers strike us as trustworthy and free and not fettered by partisan interest. It will not suffice to find "another set of words," but we must address each other with such vigor that the term "set of words," appears wholly inadequate for this compelling new speech.

Yet from the leading educator of this country and the Western World, we receive this advice: "We have to find another set of words to formulate the moral ideal." [1]

Nobody seems to see the horrors of this phrase. And people will think that I am insane because I feel that the world comes to an end unless this sentence is pilloried. The sentence demands action from us and, by the way of saying it, it paralyzes the action. This vicious circle, that we are told in a way which impedes our chances of achieving, is our dilemma. In the sentence quoted, we are treated like school teachers who are asked to tell their children in one form or another what "the moral ideal" is. But in real life, there are no school teachers or children but people who pray that they might believe themselves despite disillusionment. I shall never trust a man's attempt to formulate our faith if I know that he considers his formula as a mere set of words. I shall not listen to sets of words. They are like sets of china or any other dead things. You cannot draft soldiers for "sets of words." Man will not act unless he is asked in the name of more than mere words. I shall act in the name of the One and Real or I shall despise myself and the talker and not act at all. With John Dewey's statement, we are in the center of our crisis. He is throwing a wet blanket while admitting that we had better get hot under the collar. This is the self-contradictory attitude of all the good people during this strange half-century in which we have seceded from our own tradition. All the Liberals have poked fun at all sacred names as mere verbalisms or mere generalizations. Now when the wars and the revolutions have come and destroyed the peace cemented in the name of God, these same good people begin to tremble and invite us to march for the Four Freedoms and to reinstate the songs, the prophecies, the names which can restore peace, hope, and patience. But the style of their invitation is hollow and impersonal and as abstract as their sciences. Modern

[1] John Dewey, *The Living Thoughts of Thomas Jefferson,* New York, 1940, p. 25.

man's relation to The Word is bankrupt. John Dewey speaks of his and our language as we may speak of a kitchen set or of any set which one buys in the Five-and-Ten store.[2] And the worst thing is that if somebody cringes under their way of icing all important names, they laugh at him. This is at the core of our chaos: John Dewey confuses the consumption of words and the creation of compelling names. He, with all the idealists, takes his notion of speech from the commercial aspects of social communication. It is true that in the world of give and take, words are like poker chips. In trading, society uses words *as they are*. And so they are consumed just as we eat our daily bread—in the form of descriptions, advertising, propaganda, bills. In this realm of speech-consumption, a manufacturer is clever if he hits on a Doolittle cigar or a Lincoln car. He makes use of an existing set of names and builds on their popularity his own market for his product.

But how did Doolittle and Lincoln acquire their reputations? How did they become household words? Certainly not by using language as a set, but by impressing the people with the unity of their words and actions. They made us feel that by word and deed they served in the same name. Names are so sacred because they constitute the unity or the conflict of words and deeds in human life. Hence names are priceless; words have their price. Words can be definite, *names must have an infinite appeal.* Names must make us act in ways which seemed unbelievable before they were done; words express the things which are to be had at a known price in figures.

At this point, we may anticipate the defense of the Liberal or the Pragmatist: but are we not right? Are not all sacred names as they love to call it, "arbitrary"? Every American college student

[2] Dewey is now becoming aware of "the startling diagnosis of linguistic disease" in his "A Search for Firm Names," *Journal of Philosophy,* 1945, p. 5, where he still confounds words and names totally. But words are used to speak of something, names to speak to somebody. The direction is the opposite by 180 degrees of the compass, and this Dewey and pragmatism ignore.

feels safe, as far as I can see, behind the barbed wire of this argument: words and names both are "arbitrary." They have confused "transient" and "arbitrary." It is true that all sacred names have a limited span of life. A man too is not immortal and yet, during his lifetime, he has certain inalienable rights. So it is with names. The names which excite our hearts are not of the same urgency at all times. All names rise and fall.[3]

But rise they must from the dead. And of this rise, the small talk of modern man is ignorant. We cannot go naked without any binding and inspiring names. And for this reason, we must wage war against the throwers of wet blankets, against the term, "set of words" for the power that makes the soldiers march, and against the term "arbitrary" for the most necessary expressions of our hearts' desires or our country's laws.

Perhaps it is here that the usefulness of my life may be found. I am disqualified for daily politics which decide the election or the new League of Nations.

A period of wars, of world wars, was prophesied before 1910 and I believed it then.[4] "The Moral Equivalent of War" was postulated by William James in 1910, and I began to act upon this assumption as early as 1911. And, therefore, I am afraid, I have believed too early and known too long. A statesman or any man of action will not have success unless he is a first-class last-minute man.

However, the conflict between mechanization and creation, between the Great Society and the Future of Christianity, is the theme of my life. And this dilemma of my life seems to become the dilemma of everybody today. Naturally, I would like to make life easier for myself by turning it into a signpost for everybody's dilemma.

[3] Cf. the extraordinary concession about the name of God, by a Jesuit Father, on p. 128.

[4] See William James' and my own' proposals as reprinted in "American Youth," edited by Winslow and Davidson, Cambridge, 1940.

The order of this book results from the task on hand. The setting of our daily life is examined in suburb and in factory; and here we shall find the millstones which grind all important names to pieces incessantly. Our environment as we have created it, and as it creates us every day, does not allow us to speak with the power by which new names must be invoked and new communities founded.

We shall find that this environment is perfect for production and education, and impotent for reproduction and creation.

Against this background (Chapter Two), we have to discuss the qualities necessary to creating future communities. This creation of Future is a highly costly and difficult process. It can be done but it does not happen by itself. The progress made so far always has been a progress by Christians; especially in the natural sciences, progress is the fruit of Christianity. For Christianity is the embodiment of one single truth through the ages: that death precedes birth, that birth is the fruit of death, and that the soul is precisely this power of transforming an end into a beginning by obeying a new name. Without the soul, the times remain out of joint.

Our discussion continues in Part Two. This belief in death and resurrection is the condition of progress in science. It patently is difficult for the modern mind to acquiesce in the Creed's former formulations. It is impossible to drop the belief itself (Chapters Three, Four, and Five). There are eternal conditions under which alone life can go forward among men.

The Third Part (Chapters Six to Eight) bases its assessment of our own time on these eternal conditions. The body of our own time embraces our past, future, and present. The deadwood of our past must be thrown out. So, Chapter Six shows the crucial experiences of the Church of which we must be aware as her weakness impedes us. Chapter Seven confronts us with the unsolved future; in bringing in the Far East, we actually become critical of the further possibilities of our faith.

Can the Cross penetrate and encompass the wide world? For, otherwise, the eternal truth would remain impractical.

The answer in both cases is that Church and Man are in a more crucial situation and that the Cross is more real than theology or philosophy cares to admit.

In the last chapter, we return home. By now, we know why life in the factory, suburb, around the campfires of the soldier, or on the academic campus, is incomplete. We have recast the Christian truth. And we know that the Future of Christianity will be decided by the courage with which we shall apply this recast truth.

II

INTERIM AMERICA: 1890 TO 1940

The Suburb—The Factory—The Soul on the Highway—The New Nature of Sin—Secession from Our Era—No Child Is Father to the Man—Our Invasion by China—John Dewey —Charles Darwin

The Suburb

Year by year the suburb spreads its tentacles and absorbs town after town that used to be a genuine all-round community. I have seen this happen to my own small town in Vermont. So typical of modern life has the suburb become that we are justified in taking it as representative of our non-working hours.

Suburban life is unreal because it shuns pain and conflict. A town or city includes all kinds of people; a suburb tends to contain only members of one income group, one race, one type of cultural background. They live elsewhere their most vital economic relations, the struggle for a livelihood. They may invite business friends for a weekend, but not the boss who has fired them, or the secretary they have snubbed. Suburban marriage is a kind of spiritual inbreeding: there is little room for adventure when boy and girl have known each other since high-school days. No Romeo or Juliet can come to life in a suburb because Montagues and Capulets do not wage their Homeric battles there, and no Miranda is courted on an island after a tempest; love's labor is lost. Children are not born in suburbs but in maternity wards—yet how can a man respond to emergencies of war or peace with the full depth of heroism if he has not quaked in the presence of shattering travail, when woman wages her corresponding fight against death? A woman's travail places her at the opposite pole from her bridal state. And from this tremendous revolution of the soul when in blood and agony the fruit of love enters the world, modern husbands are excluded by the science of medicine. But where else do we ever experience the law of creation? These husbands who, as the saying goes, marry for fun and in order to have fun together, may go with their wives on Church parade, on Sundays, with the Cogshells and Thickhides. But on the crucifixion mentioned from the pulpit as the universal sign which sums up the law of life, they must miss out as they are spared the corresponding agony of their wives.

Similarly, sick people are isolated, and death, as far as possible, is not allowed to happen visibly in a suburb. Even the word "death" is almost taboo; people find the whole subject embarrassing.[1] But how can you appreciate the miraculous unity of mind and body, spirit and incarnation, unless you have watched the last breath of a person you loved?

Suburban life accordingly is prudent, kind, and barren. There is a special word for its lukewarm atmosphere: it has a mentality. Mentality is what is left of the soul when you subtract the crucifying experiences that bear fruit in more energetic and vital human relationships. Mentality knows nothing of jubilant joy and black despair, of yelling and cursing, moaning and groaning, shouting and dancing and weeping and singing.

Small wonder, then, that teaching and preaching become verbiage in the suburb. Its mentality emasculates the Word. How can we speak deeply about God or King Lear in an environment

[1] The movie, *Peter the Great,* contains a death scene in which the Tsarina weeps passionately over the dying Tsar. The whole audience in our suburban theater laughed at this scene, and I later asked my students, who were present, for an explanation. After a day's reflection the most serious among them said, "We laughed because we felt perfectly sure that under no circumstances would we cry so desperately."

that has been artificially preserved and sterilized? The wife of a minister in a fashionable suburb once naively remarked that her husband was really quite a social reformer, but since he moved to his present wealthy parish he had had no occasion to mention his radical ideas.

At the same time there is a paradox about suburban man: he lives amid too much peace, but he knows little peace within. He is a veritable battleground for a hundred organizations and pressure groups. He is cleft and torn by the inevitable inner conflicts which suburbia cannot abolish but can only repress. The cross of reality is an indelible pattern of conflict engrained in the very structure of all life, and a society which makes it indecent to share the agonies of our souls puts a burden on the individual which he is far too weak to bear. Only together can we man the various fronts of life adequately, stand the strain of decision which they entail, and bear the risk of the inevitable wrong choices which occur. Neurosis and nervous breakdown flourish in the suburb for lack of a fellowship based on the deeper urgencies and passions.

The curse of modern man, in consequence, is to become more and more non-committal for fear of going too far in any direction. He plays safe, adopts a minimum attitude, never acts on any front without a sideglance in the other directions. The prudence of the suburb begets a corresponding philosophy which pervades most popular psychology and sociology today: the philosophy of adjustment, of golden mediocrity. This doctrine means no real excitement, no real devotion, no real fight, no real love. It invites us into a future in which all the energies which made possible our own existence have cooled down. The values and institutions on which we live were created by maximum effort. The philosophy of minimum life would never make possible one work of art, one song, one discovery, one free constitution. The future it advocates would see no children born, from sheer precaution; no sorrow felt, for fear of pain; no loyalty cherished, for fear of being old-fashioned. Man is in process of being completely secularized.

Are we condemned to extinguish the fires of life because they are too dangerous? Is prudence really the last human word? A real man puts his whole heart into the incarnation of his soul on earth. His problem is how to give maximum effort, an all-out movement of his heart, on every front, yet how to select the right deed, the divine, value-creating act at any given moment. And the only way to strengthen him for this task is to take from him the curse of loneliness. Conversely, the cure for loneliness cannot be created in small, piecemeal steps. The division between people has to be overcome by the same infinite effort by which we throw a rope across a stream before we can build a bridge foot by foot. The heart must yield itself with singleness of purpose to its trust in the fellowship of mankind, else it will remain split and alone. We obtain freedom only through infinite effort and devotion.

The cross fulfills its meaning when it is shared. The power of love surpasses and heals our riven selves. Christianity reveals to man that his being torn is a human privilege, because no society could develop among people who were self-contained. Man is divided so that he may cease to be an individual. If a man does not know that it is perfectly normal to be thus torn, and that a divine power exists which integrates persons by uniting them in communion, he will surrender to any man-made power that seems to promise unity, fixity, and security. Many Germans accepted the Nazis because, in their despair, they felt that mad decisions were better than none. Torn men are dangerous men. They will go to hell and worship the devil of power for power's sake, in the form of any wild desire, unless we reestablish the power of the Spirit in its original white heat. That is the challenge to Christianity today.

The Factory

As toil, sweat, and tears are hidden, in the suburb, so inspiration, which alone redeems man's toil from the curse of Adam, must not be mentioned in the business and industrial district. And this is increasingly so for all our lives as the industrial revolution sweeps in its wake the last of the pre-industrial crafts and professions. Rare is the office, studio, farm, pulpit or classroom which has not been invaded by factory atmosphere.

The essence of the industrial system, from a human point of view, is the utilization of men as labor forces in the same way that physical energies are put to work to secure maximum efficiency in production. This means that man in a factory is treated virtually like an inanimate object. He is no longer a person but a function, a replaceable cog in a machine—the way workers replace one another in shifts makes this particularly vivid. The labor molecule which the management has to employ, consists of the two, three or four shifts of workers which fill one twenty-four-hour day. No decent worker will break his cohesion with the man who precedes or follows him on his shift. The solidarity of the workers is not the loyalty of the football team, but it is the identity of the drops of water in the unending stream of work which is done day and night; the triumph of the machine is this creation of a *second* nature in which nothing but the laws of nature prevail. These natural laws are the laws of energy and matter, of raw materials and power, and the labor forces are among them. A factory is not a human habitation. For a human home houses man and wife, old and young, people who sleep and wake, are sick and healthy, age and grow, play and pray. A factory houses Nature. And Nature with a capital N, is concerned with man as a part of a force and as part of material. The watering of labor, of which any industrialist is well aware, means that nobody on factory shift-work is allowed or expected to go all out in his personal effort. He must stoop to the level which can be maintained in the incessant stream of twenty-four-hour processes of production. He is "laid on" or "laid off," as steam or light are turned on or turned off. I am a part of Nature, in the process of production, and as a part of Nature, I am just my "self." The style of Nature is to unite all Self in capital letters, for what it is worth. Homes do the opposite: they drown self: a boy is treated here as his father's son, a woman as her husband's wife, her children's mother, her brother's sister, etc. But in the factory it is the very "self" who counts. Homes appeal to me in my qualities which transcend my age or sex or class. The suburb is so sweet because we all are just human beings in the suburb, sympathizing with each other in a quite real unselfishness. For "self," and "human being," are not questions of ethics or good intentions. These positions or attitudes are imposed on us by our functions in a specific environment. In the suburb, we are received and looked upon as family men. In the factory we are elements of a labor force. Only the cold-blooded analysis of the difference between these two agglomerations will give us the key to the strange spectacle that a man in town and a man in his suburb are treated, one as "self," the other as a family man. In the shift work of the factory system, this deep rift reaches perfection. For, in the factory, the "self" is used to compose a compound; the labor molecule and the inner cohesion of this molecule demands from its elements the avoidance of all personal traits, especially of the traits of zeal and ambition. Now, we take our hat off to the miracles of modern production. I am not sentimentally deploring the facts of this situation. Nevertheless, I am bored by the people who won't see the profound change in the nature of Man which it entails. It is Man without his family who enters the factory. And, it is the family in which man first receives and on which he later bestows his name. Of this receiving and bestowing of our name, the act of ensouling consists. And this act, quite naturally, is missing in mass production. The demands of technical efficiency require that factory work become more and more automatically successful and perpetual. But there is no soul in work that is automatic because things must be *things to come* if they shall have a soul; there is "soul" in the life of an individual craftsman who experiences the joys and pains of uncertainty about the outcome of what he is doing. The factory reserves this privilege for a few scientists, engineers and managers. And the pressure for continuous production means that even these men and all of us tend to become slaves of a time schedule. Also the fluctuations of business conditions mean that neither a factory nor an individual's employment in it is likely to last long; the factory chops our lives up into short units of time, and infects them with a radical instability. It is not a house or a home, in which people eat and play as well as work together and where generations succeed each other, but an essentially partial and transient arrangement.

As a result, modern man's work is no longer something he can throw himself into for a lifetime, something through which his whole personality can ripen and take shape. The rapid shifting of his work makes him shiftless. I know a mechanic who had held more than fifty jobs by the time he was thirty-two, and the young men of my acquaintance assure me that this sort of thing is not unusual. In the days of the New Testament, binding and loosing were momentous processes that would occur only once or twice in a lifetime, and the awe with which they were regarded was symbolized by the power of the keys traditionally given to St. Peter—the power to dissolve and rebuild allegiances. Today radical changes of mind, body, soul and environment are so frequent that we have ceased to feel them deeply and to recognize them as events of birth and death. Tragedy has become diluted into a long series of endings and beginnings.

In such circumstances we are taught to take all human relations lightly and irresponsibly. Modern labor conditions drain the resources by which we grow into and out of human fellowships. Change is so rapid that we can hardly be expected to take the plunge of committing ourselves with complete dedication either in joining or leaving anything. We buy ease of change at the price of superficiality; frequency does away with intensity of feeling; we come without joy and leave without sorrow.

In consequence personality is dwarfed.[1] The normal processes

[1] Cf. Eugen Rosenstock, *Politische Reden,* Berlin, 1929, pp. 48 ff., and *Werkstattaussiedlung.* Unters-über d. Lebensraum d. Arbeiters, 1922; J. H. Oldham *The Christian News-Letter,* 1941, No. 88.

of maturing through joy and sorrow no longer reach the core of man. Nobody can become a person in a void, but only in relations with other people, and if he plays safe in these relations he remains childish and undeveloped. So in work as in leisure we shun not only superfluous pains, which is right, but growing pains, which is wrong. Jesus on the Cross rejected the drug which would have diminished his agony. Who even understands his rejection today?

The greatest temptation of our time is impatience, in its full original meaning: refusal to wait, undergo, suffer. We seem unwilling to pay the price of living with our fellows in creative and profound relationships. From marriage to teaching, from government to handicraft, man's relation to man has become segregated, impatient, non-committal in the machine age. To be non-committal means to keep all relations without important consequences, to rob them of their reproductive, fruit-bearing quality. We meet so many people on our journey through life that we do not take the risk of belonging to any of them. As we eat wheat bread without wheat and drink Sanka, so we love without children, have friends without inspiration, schools without discipleship, factories without skills, government without succession. "So what?" is the echo of every effort on the stony surface of our cities. Tremendous ado and not even a mouse born. Everything is over so quickly. We have no time.

The rootless, rhythmless quality imposed on our lives by the factory is reflected in the general hectic pace of modern life. Our existence is an uninterrupted interruption. At the office, train of thought is cut short by the telephone; at home, someone dials the radio. The news becomes a sort of drug habit, like cigarettes. We become a bundle of nerves responding to red and green lights, all stops and starts. We are obsessed with speed at all costs, and live perpetually as on a highway, with the world flashing past like a motion picture. A warm friend of mine drove several hundred miles to see me; he had looked forward to the visit, but when he finally arrived he tried to leave in ten minutes!

Modern man's temptation to impatience accordingly expresses itself in the craving for panaceas and short cuts. He wants to escape from his nervous pace by finding some sure-fire scheme that will offer a final solution of all his problems and make him a smooth-running machine, as regular as ants or bees. So men like Marx, or Hitler, or Huxley proclaim ideas—the classless society, four thousand years of the swastika, a "brave new world"—that would put an end to history, and Joyce's Ulysses cries, "History is the nightmare from which I must wake up."

As in previous millenniums of the Christian story men found and testified and fought for one God and one earth, so now we must find and testify and fight for God's one time against impatient men's private plans for history. Schemes to usher in the end of history overnight defy the Christian belief in a dispensation of time, whereby God is taking care of his world from beginning to end.

Of course machine industry is here to stay. It is undesirable and impossible to turn the clock back to the sixteenth century. The evils of modern life cannot be escaped in any such unrealistic fashion. They are rather a challenge to us to find constructive ways of overcoming the sterile divorce of labor and leisure, and of mastering the sequence of changes which industrial society makes inevitable in every individual life.

The Soul on the Highway

"They really try to run a nation
By factories and education."

A whole world has been built on this dichotomy of residential and business district. We have achieved a maximum of production as well as of education by this division of the mass producer and the family man. I think we should go on producing and educating in this manner. Both are about the best things of the modern world. It has given all its thinking to these two things and they, therefore, are next to perfect.

I would consider it insanity to abandon ways of life which have proved efficient. I am, however, interested in the price of this achievement. We can't get something for nothing. Being masters in production and education, in work and leisure, we have done harm to the two other aspects of life, to reproduction and creation, the processes which renew life and which found real communities. In the old days, the formula for these two acts read: to renew heaven and earth. But prosaically expressed, it means fecundity and communal roots; the latter was considered heavenly, the former earthly.

Our analysis of suburb and factory is in no way nostalgic of the good old past; neither do we assume that Willow Run and the Armour meat packers are not miracles of efficiency. Let them proceed.

But let us now take stock of the man who results from this dichotomy into a family man and a cog-in-the-wheel. In one peculiar trait, we may discover his special problem. It is in the fact that he is expected to speak two languages. In the business district words are tools. To write the right ad is a great art there. In the suburb, in club and church and home, you are expected to use the right set of words and suburban peace is shattered when somebody does not repeat the expected phrases. In the factory, besides, we are best off if we are nameless, "regardless of color, race, and creed." In the suburb we are mindful of all the sacred names and loyalties of the group.

This makes the new phenomenon clear: Here is a human being who is full of names half of the time, and void of names during the other half. The two worlds of the average employee are mutually impenetrable. Downtown the man belongs to organized labor, or to the group which impersonally represents his "interests." At home he really is interested personally. And so, the one man within myself leaves the other man pretty much behind when he commutes. Modern commuter's peace of mind is served best by a careful dividedness.

Who, then, is this man if he himself is the dual personality composed of the Man downtown and the Man uptown, if so to speak he is "Md. plus Mu."? How does he recognize himself as still one and the same man?

The real man who is trying to recognize his deepest identity, would have to focus his attention on the rudimentary situation in which he is neither suburban nor factorial, and yet knows of both situations as waiting for him. When we said that "Md. plus Mu." equalled the modern man, we omitted one essential element. It may be infinitesimally small in actual claims on our time and space; but it exists in all of us. There is an "x" which we have to add to "Md" and "Mu," Man down- and uptown, and this is the man in the hour or two when he commutes. Who are we while we commute between office and home? Is the full-sized man not to be found on the highway, driving his car as a commuter? Perhaps he is very tired. All the same, in one respect, this tired animal is highly central. On the highway, while commuting, the real man talks to himself alone.

Of this commuter, modern literature more and more takes cognizance. Our writers look for the person behind her or his appearance either downtown or in "Honeypots," his dream home, and they find him on the highway. In his novel, *When Winter Comes,* A. S. Hutchinson summed it up in one paragraph:[1] "The commuter, on his solitary ride on his bicycle [today it is his car], is mysteriously suspended and has magically escaped from vulgarity. Hence he returns to his home and enters his business world both, with feelings of condescension." His term "condescension" struck me forcibly: "my high grade personality," the commuter feels, "is alone on the highway. The two social forms between which I alternate, are petty in comparison."

The full-sized person, in other words, can only be met where he feels condescension for his smaller selves.

[1] Boston, 1921, p. 41 ff.

From this, we may conclude: we are not going to come to full life by going into the business district or into the suburb. Long enough we have been told that the apostles, if they came in our own days, would be newspapermen or would go to house-parties. I deny it.

Man has his fullest potentiality on the highway as a commuter.

Try to meet him there. Build an oxygen tent for the soul on the highway. If it can be done, he will be himself there while he would stoop and become small under all the roofs of the city and suburb.

While man seems to speak in the suburb and seems to act in his business, yet we must not condemn him to speak or to act there exclusively. His true soul cannot become articulate unless it is met on the highway.

This meeting place will have to fulfill two requirements: He must be recognized by others in those qualities which are neither suburban nor official. He must wash himself of these two qualities which make him small; he should be allowed to differ from these two environments.

To differ and to be recognized in this difference are two requirements by which the trend of our times, that man becomes more and more a product of his environment, can be halted.

When the world offers man an opportunity of meeting man, it gathers people either of the "same background," or of the same foreground activity (profession, party, age, etc.) This is the world. The world chokes our soul and plunges us into the original sin of society, the self-adoration of interests separated by the division of labor which the world requires. Even laymen when convened as laymen are too-professional laymen. And the Annual Conference of Hobos is the ultimate in professional grouping.

A specific act or articulation in which the soul on the highway screws up its courage so as to reject this identity with foreground or background, with suburb and factory, will have to be instituted.

The meeting of the souls on the highway has two intelligible contents: severe judgment on the background and profession which hold me in bondage, gladness to have escaped and to join a fellowship not conditioned by the original sins of society. Cursing, accusation, muckraking are in order in a group which thereby intends to deliver the inner man from the barbed hooks of his background- and foreground-interests of "mentality" and "matter."

The pious hatred of the Puritans against curses by now has made man impotent to bless. Nobody has the power to bless or to be blessed who has lost the vigor to curse. Our society is so polite that it cannot curse social evils and prefers to blaspheme God instead. He who will not curse the shortcomings of his profession as a lawyer, a teacher, a doctor, a priest,[2] always will have to defend it beyond the health of his soul. The doctor who defends medicine as it is today, against all outside criticism, and nowhere bands together unselfishly with these same critics, must do harm to his soul. For on the highway, his soul knows better how much is wrong with his profession. Now, anything which the solitary man knows, he, for the sake of his salvation, must come to profess in fellowship, too. Hence, the souls on the highway must recognize the hell of mere functioning. The new form of fellowship must include the curses over my own social function since it is in my becoming distinguishable from this function that I have my hope.

The Soul on the Highway is in search of groups where people in the work of the cosmos, i.e., physical functioning, in patient silence, i.e., without heretical pride, in warm expectation, i.e., without the guarantees of any "background," gather so that the chaos, the darkness, and the confusion may die down within them. The souls in fellowship who admit that chaos, confusion, benightedness, are frustrating them, put an end to them. And the dawn of

[2] In Europe, the nations putrefied from this same deficiency that more and more—instead of less and less—people spoke to each other as representing their nations en bloc. Even the Churches were treated as part of the nation. Pentecost truly was abolished. These collective insanities formed the natural background for the opposite exaggeration: communism.

a cosmic order can only follow this end. The cosmic process called Christianity puts the end first, and the beginning later.

Admit that chaos, darkness, confusion, are our common heritage, and that the sins of this our heritage can be forgiven. The social chaos cannot become cosmos unless man takes this chaos upon his own mind as his own mental chaos, unless he drops his mask of academic observer and his pride of mental self-sufficiency, usually called objectivity.

A once great nation stands before us as a strange lesson for this cosmic law. La Grande Nation of the French will be glorious forever because here the single individual was hailed as the New Adam, and as the genius. Even the Church, who at first was rejected by the Revolution, became acceptable only after a writer in 1800 had given her status as genius. *Le Génie du christianisme,* by Chateaubriand, had one of the most astounding successes in the history of books. It draped the Church of the martyrs and monks as "genius" and, by linking it to the humanistic principle of genius, the ideas of 1789 became reconcilable with the Christian tradition. The Church got the French franchise when she, like everybody else, submitted her credentials for genius.[3]

But a young American diplomat described the impotency of these same individual geniuses to take the step into communal and group suffering, graphically in these terms:[4] "The poor French, they are suffering for everybody's sins as well as their own, for all the indifference and neglect of a hundred years. They are like the small dogs one finds in alleys who have been so often beaten that they snarl when you try to stroke them. Perhaps it is better in America. The French distress me. They are so completely disintegrated, every man alone with his own fears. They are like grains of sand, all alike, individual, sterile, grating against each other, instead of being a warm, thick, clinging soil as a nation should be.

[3] For the mania of the French for genius see the example on p. 77.

[4] From a letter written in 1942.

"Patience is the highest virtue nowadays. I had always thought that wars required a sort of devil-may-care courage, but actually war requires a sort of courageous patience. In these wintry times, if we are patient and calm and still, we can hear the first dark stirring of the roots underground where we dug and planted last year. I comfort myself by saying that even in a desert, you can dig a well or bring water, and if one is patient, the desert will blossom like a rose.

"Harry Hopkins, after his first visit to England, brought back one particularly vivid discovery, that the strength of a nation depended on the extent of its organization in depth. I think one of the great problems which it must be the task of our century to solve is the social disintegration brought about by the new techniques of industrial and political organization.

"The family, the guild, the church, and even the community (as in New England) have all disappeared. Work camps are one form of reintegration, but in other fields others are possible.

"The French offer a terrible example. Each one is isolated in his own hopes and fears. They have no means, nor forms of communication with each other. Every man is alone.

"Suppose that we should be conquered by the Germans. To organize our eventual liberation, we could not turn as we turned in 1775 and 1776 to our families and churches and town meetings. You and I could turn for one thing to the friends we made in Camp William James whom we know we can trust because we worked with them previously. But the French have no one to turn to at all. It is a horrifying sight.

"The principle of organization in depth is as valid for the needs of peace as for war. It can be used not only on our external but on our interior frontiers, to conquer the devils of waste and indifference as well as the Germans. . . ."

Christianity is essentially war in peace: it distributes the bloody sacrifices of the battlefront by an even but perpetual spread of sacrifices through the whole fabric of life. World wars can be replaced by daily wars. The Christian soldier of the future must wage war against the indifference and indolence, the coldness and barrenness, of human relations in the machine age. Why did my friend write this letter on the French to us? We, at one time, had done something together and he compared his experience in France with the great time we had had in our all-out effort. Since examples explain things best, I will now say a word about this war against indolence undertaken by Camp William James between 1939 and 1942.

Camp William James was founded a few years ago when forty-five young men from colleges and farms, with the blessing of the President of the United States, decided to move up to a Vermont town and represent in that community the age group that was conspicuous by its absence because the educational system makes young people dissatisfied with remaining on the farm and also drains all small communities of their youth by concentrating them on college campuses.

A petition subscribed to by 325 people from the nine neighboring towns was sent to Washington in favor of the undertaking. And as well may be imagined, it had taken some preparation to achieve such commotion. Also, the members committed themselves for a whole year of service.

The result was a vital process which remade the community and the members, boys as well as girls, themselves. The older people felt rejuvenated with a new vision of their town's future. Where before the Selectmen had dropped all pretense of expecting any future for the town, new life suddenly seemed possible. The town had a future! And the young men grew up to a stature observed by every one who met them. A friend remarked, "These boys are men now, and will never be childish or emasculate." They had put down roots, and now they belonged firmly in the chain of generations, not just as physical individuals but as proper representatives of the Spirit, contributing their own spirit to the other age groups as a tonic and an essential ingredient in the complete life of man.

The camp sent out its members to work on any farm in the township that needed labor, and in the evening the men from surrounding farms came back to the camp with the boys they hired, for talk and song and moral refreshment. The camp was not a workers' church nor a church factory; *it was a home of young volunteers to which their bosses went to get new faith and hope,* and it was, at the same time a cooperative of employees who went out to old-time farms to get century-old traditions in barn and field and church and town meeting. The words of the boys' mouths and the acts of their hands originated in one and the same orbit of life. Work and worship were united once more.[5]

What these boys achieved has encouraged me to publish this book. They proved that *spiritual immigration into this world* is not a dream. The hope of Camp William James was that by throwing into a declining community a unit of unbound, free youth, regardless of background and profession, even the most stagnating vested interests and backgrounds could be "desquamated," sloughed off by the older people who would live with them. Since our educational crusades have combed our cities and towns of their enthusiastic elements and concentrated the latter in boarding schools, kindergartens, or colleges, the community is tranquillized artificially. Camp William James repaid the small town for its loss of its native youth to the scholastic system by delegating youth from all schools for the purpose of enthusiastic comradeship in the older peoples' economic worries.

The "old" man or woman are all those who are responsible for some particle of the world—a loom, a piece of garden, a task. From this, they have to return into the middle of the Cross. And by meeting the "young," this holiday feeling was achieved.

The Interim America of 1890 to 1942 saw the Church recede

[5] The best description of Camp William James was given by Stuart Chase in *Survey Graphic,* May, 1942.

into suburbs. The ministry, thereupon, disintegrated into humanitarians, social workers, pacifists. The individual cannot be blamed. Social conditions made the Churches unreal. They no longer stood in the center of the cross of a man's life, but stood on the side of private leisure. We shall not enter into polemics with the suburban church mentality. Our whole desire in writing this chapter was to move the Church back to the middle of the Cross, from its place of a leisure activity.

However, one comparison may make clear the danger in which the factory and the suburb have plunged us. Once upon a time, the people were told that there could be no salvation outside the Church. *Extra ecclesiam nulla salus*. Then, Calvin burned Servetus, and the Lutherans burned witches, and the Inquisition burned Muslim and Jews and Giordano Bruno. Whereupon we dropped that harsh sentence which was so obviously abused. The modern ministers of the gospel have gone to the opposite extreme. They are threatened by the opposite adage. Having moved away from all claims, they must now remember that *Extra crucem nulla ecclesia*: Outside the Cross, there is no Church.

The New Nature of Sin

"But why should there be put such a superfluous extra burden on life as the Cross? Did you not admit that man became only too tame in suburb and factory? The way you have described this modern man is either a caricature or, if it is true, the conclusion is obvious: he cannot sin any more. Domesticated at home and 'taylorized' by scientific management in his shop, the poor fellow is so anemic, so regular, so predictable that one only could wish him to sin a little *more*. By his vices, he would make us feel his vitality. So why preach the Cross in a world without sin?"

This is a valid sermon. Yes, it is true that the modern individual is strangely sinless. And the expression "sin" is vanishing fast like "virgin" and "adolescent" because the real world is satisfied with boys and girls and habits. I shall join the sermon of my opponent with my own antistrophe on the topic of sin. Yes, sin has disappeared, I shall confirm; but whither?

This then, is my antistrophe: "Happy the days when the words I spoke were important, and when the acts which I enacted were mine. The great name of sin rests on the assumption that I can act and that it matters what I say. Sin is the contradiction between words spoken by me, and my own acts. Wherever the acts are not mine and my speech is verbiage without effect, sin becomes impossible. This, we have seen, has happened by our division of the areas of production and consumption. Under scientific management, the work is not my own; it means nothing in my life. Under the shades of the suburb's sidewalks, my words don't matter much. As long as my words made law in my work, the interlacing of my thoughts, words, and acts, decided over their being either good or evil. But nowadays, an advertising agency makes the young writer proclaim the latest hair tonic an eighth world wonder; why hold this against him? These words are not his own. On the other hand, when the same man comes home and writes doggerel for his wife's entertainment it does not make the slightest difference whether he makes "hell" rhyme with "bell," or "God" with "nod," it is a mere game of sets of words.[1]

"We have untied the interaction of words and acts; my acts are now no longer mine, and my words have ceased to be important."

And, my antistrophe goes on, "the soul of the commuter on the highway does not cry out for repentance but for vitality and communion. Where, then, is sin? Whither has it gone?" Let this be answered by the 'epode': "Sin has become collective. The same doctor or manufacturer or mechanic or teacher who is so tame and good and overwrought that he has neither time nor opportunity to sin, belongs to one or more sinning groups. He belongs to a professional group, block, and lobby. They sin for him. And at

[1] See above p. 7.

home, he and his wife fall victim to all the drives in the community."

Now see the contradiction: on the highway we all look down on the pettiness of our jobs or of the "drives" in the neighborhood. But just the same we have this job or drive boosted up by a secretary to astronomical heights. It becomes a white elephant, our work or the quota. And in watching these social pressure groups, we discover the nature of sin which individually, we hardly do understand. The clever thing about the sins of the Farm Bloc and the Medical Society is that they can be committed without breaking our laws. For sin is not a crime of the penal code, although most people seem to think so. Sins and crimes are quite different in nature. Long before an act or an omission becomes defined as a crime, it may be gross sin. And something defined as crime by the law may have ceased to be sin. Our law codes certainly travel in the same direction as sins, trying to transform them into crimes. But sin is always far ahead of them. Hence, a new nature of sin is not defined in the penal code. To the contrary, our laws urge this sin upon us. The only trouble is that this new nature of sin saps our vitality and dwarfs us. It destroys our own true nature.

Now, whenever the nature of sin changed, the nature of Christianity changed too. It is a reasonable deduction from experience to say that the new sin behind suburb and factory cries for a new conception of Christianity.

As always, Christianity in the future must carry on its mission through contagious example. What can take the place of the parsonage or of the monastery in the coming age of pressure-group sins? New forms of fellowship are required. For men and women from the most varied forms of residence and occupation, climate and faith, will have to free each other from the sterile isolation of factory and suburb and will have to laugh off their representation by lobbies. The leisurely life of suburban kindness and the rough and tumble struggle downtown, both, must be made to submit to one human equation. A new communion must come to life. But with such a prediction, we are grating on the ears of the practical man. The trends are all against us. Real estate has invested in suburbs. Production promises the era of plenty through the factory system. To say that "Christianity must do so and so" in the future is an empty phrase as long as we do not show how there can be made room in the future for anything which goes against the trend. Professor Walter A. Jessup frankly told me just before his death in an amazing conversation (with a son of William James, and myself), on the Moral Equivalent of War: "We have invested many millions of dollars in one direction and now this is the trend. And you think that simply because you are right, you can change this trend?" He expressed the practical man's disgust with a hollow idealism which, while life is going actually in one direction materially every day, at the same time proclaims standards which point in exactly the opposite direction.

Interim America is a fact; the factory is a fact. And therefore, to the practical man, these facts predict the future. We, therefore, shall have bigger and better suburbs, and more and more mass production.

But the practical man is impractical about the future. He simply puts his grandfather's beliefs into practice. The practical man, though he often does not know it, embodies a philosophy of the past. For this reason, he does not know the secret of the future.

The real substance of this book turns against the idealists as well as against the practical man by considering a future which differs from the past in quality. That which simply goes on from the past as a trend is not "future" in the full sense of this term. It simply travels on an extension visa from the past. In human history the break with the past is the condition of any future. The relation of any past and any future is never made by a trend, but always by a victory over trends. On the other hand, the idealist is only the fellow-traveller of the trend. He opposes his will to the trend, and no trend has ever been influenced by human will. Ideals are crushed. And idealists are rushed in the very direction which they deny.

However, there is a third attitude. The record of our era is unanimous in this respect. The future does not consist of the extension of existing trends, nor of ideological opposition to them. The future must be created.

In fact while the civilian mind produces and talks, the future has been created and the country has been refounded for him by our soldiers. All the neat map-making of the social order, with suburb, the factory, the solitary souls on the highway, and the massive blocs in Washington, omitted some other localities—like Iwo Jima, Okinawa, the battlefield of the Bulge, the bridge-head at Remagen, the break-through in Normandy and the 453 men missing over Schweinfurt after the air raid.

Isn't that strange? Is war an accident? Are battlefields parts of our geography exactly as much as the Stock Exchange in Wall street or the Pasadena Golf Course?

How could the vestryman of Hyde Park, New York, the busiest man in Washington, D. C., become Commander-in-Chief of eleven million citizen-soldiers, very much against his and the country's will?

Secession from Our Era

Indeed, war seems an accident in our system of thought. Battle-fields are not part of the "environment" of our educational vision. Our systems of thought do not ask and do not answer the question: Why is war indispensable? I have to say "indispensable" to get them to respond at all. "Indispensable?" they growl and are horrified. Unless peace is employed to create the future, wars are indispensable. The last fifty years have run the nation by factories and education, and were ignorant of the creation of future. Thereby, they have pushed the nation upon battlefields and have seceded from our Christian Era. Through our whole era, man had known that wars were indispensable without the daily creation of a future. For this era had been started by a man who said that he brought a sword and that there would be terrible wars and that he was the prince of peace.

Hence, we may surmise that we seceded from our or his era during the last fifty years. And this is what I believe.

I ask the reader to recognize this deliberate secession from our era in the following review of the last half-century; I call this secession the Interim. For nothing was settled definitely. People seceded from the fundamentals without putting anything in their place. Unless we recognize this interim as a secession we shall have neither the desire nor the power to return into our era. Yet, without your and my desire to continue our era, we are bound to kill each other by word and deed. Our peace will depend on our common goal. The revitalization of our era might be such a goal for all men of good will while all other goals cannot fail to divide us.

But of course, our fathers and grandfathers and we ourselves were not simply fools. We had reason to secede from the era. Before criticizing the secession, we should try to understand why the way of life which people had called Christian before 1890 became ineffective afterwards. Suburb and factory made the Christian "Set-up" a mere set-up. And nobody can worship a "set-up," as his ancestors did who believed in God, in one Catholic Church and the Communion of Saints. It is no use casting stones at the immediate past unless we first know to which "set-up" we shall not and cannot return.

No Child Is Father to the Man

The Christian set-up of the past no longer works because it was meant to make every mother an image of the Church and every father an image of government. The modern suburb makes every girl an image of the Arts, and the factory every boy an image of the Sciences. The centuries of Christian Reform, 1500 to 1900, concentrated on Church and State; we concentrate on the Arts and Sciences. Both currents invaded the homes and the natures of men and women, inspiring them as mothers and fathers, as daughters and sons. But while the Christian Reform asked the members of the family to be mothers and fathers first of all, the modern stress is on boys and girls, men and women. Church and State thought of us as parents and children; the Arts and Sciences think of us as individuals.

If the reader will allow me one more word on the achievement of the centuries of Christian Reform, this may pay us dividends for our march into the future.

The centuries of Christian Reform embrace the whole life of Christians, of Roman Catholics as well as of so-called Protestants and Sects: in fact, a step taken by the Church of Rome at the beginning of the whole period, right after 1500, may be used as an illumination for the point that concerns us here. And the illustration is as striking as Luther's own reforms.

Forgetting all theological squabbles, we are looking for the new way of life which all Christians after 1500 endeavored to institute: after 1500, the Church of Rome began to lay far more stress on the cult of St. Joseph and on the conception of the Holy Family. This went parallel with the return into the world of hundreds of thousands of nuns and monks—into a world in which they no longer had any clannish ties. When these highly individualized people married, they carried into the new homes something utterly different from the old type of marriage in which the parents had engaged their children to each other in the cradle. These new homes were shot through with a personal experience wholly unknown to the clan marriage. And this kind of union of two real persons was made the basis of the model home, the model Christian household, in every Christian village and parish of the Reform.

Thereby, every father became aware of his priestly role in his own household as an image of the whole congregation. And the centuries of Christian Reform won a new field of human activity from paganism to Christianity. Down to 1500, the "family" was without Christian ritual. The family ritual was prescribed by the economic heredity. The farmer's son was a farmer, the tailor's son a tailor. In the so-called Middle Ages before the Reform, parents were as incompetent in matters of religion as today. The clergy was suspicious of the pagan superstitions which held sway in the homes of the people. Monasteries and cathedrals were the centers from which to check the *un-Christian* traditions of the common man. The carnival, maypoles, witchcraft, fairy tales of the average household were stark pre-Christian as late as 1600, and, as the *Golden Bough* has shown, even much later. Sir James G. Frazer could write that neither the Roman Empire nor the Christian Church had as much as scratched the surface of the life of the common people even to this day.

But the centuries of the Christian Reform at least began to trust the households of laymen. They did entrust the families with part of the task which, before, the clergy alone had carried out. For example, medieval men were haunted by ghosts and demons; and these were survivals of pre-Roman times. Only inside the consecrated church buildings would a man before the year 1500 feel quite safe from them. The Reform went after these remnants of the spirits in house and barn, yard and field and highway. Luther's fight with the devil and his marriage were of one piece. And the Bishop of the Roman Church (of Rottenburg in Wuertemberg) who in 1925 gratefully remembered in a pastoral letter the daily reading of the Bible before breakfast to him during his boyhood paid tribute to this new and more intimate approach to the Christian life of every day. For every family now was cemented into a spiritual unit while before it was purely hereditary and economic. By the reading of Scripture, the singing of hymns, the common prayer at meals in the native tongue, in the homes of lay families, these homes gained a new power: they could now preserve their holds over its members despite their choosing new professions. The free choice of the professions which has spread all over the world during the last four hundred years, and which we take pretty much for granted, is the corollary to an increase of power of this same family. For, now a son who became a lawyer while his father remained the farmer still could recognize his father as his spiritual elder. The central truths of life the son had learned from his father. The family loyalty now outgrew the material identity of father's and son's activities. They could recognize each other in the spirit.

Modern parents are losing this rank rapidly in the eyes of their children. These are marched off to school and summer camp and are indoctrinated by the spirit of the times. Before the Industrial Revolution, the father went down on his knees in the presence of his children; he sang, read, spoke his faith and since his work, too, was done within sight, his faith and his work interlaced and thereby the term of a Christian home became apparent by word and deed. On the children there was impressed the paradox that they might advance in the ways of the world far beyond the parents and still owe them their first elevation to the highway of the full spirit.

The children could not forget what they are made to forget in our new institutions, that the child begins from scratch, as a little animal. And that no progress is feasible before the child has reached at least its parent's level. He who first lifts a child up to the heights of duty and devotion may be of any social rank. Yet, will he be the real father of the man. The nineteenth-century verse, "The Child is Father to the Man," must be implemented by its opposite: those are the parents of a child who enable the animal in us to become the person. No child is father to the man. Father and mother are the people who call us by our name and make us act and speak, in the power of this name; as their love bestows this name on us we feel that we own it securely and we feel in place.

Physical semination has absolutely nothing to do with fatherhood. Offspring and sonhood and daughterhood are quite separate.

It is all-important that the reader should see before him these four centuries of Christian family life regardless of any denominational bias.[1]

Here lay the socio-economic *reality* of the Reformation, a field in which the Christian's inward freedom could incarnate itself in daily life, in which living faith became works. A subject owed implicit obedience to his prince, but he owed no one save God an account of his actions as head of a household and follower of a calling.

In those days the household was the typical economic unit of production as well as consumption, and not just a dormitory and a meal ticket as it tends to be today. If a man was a craftsman, for example, he would have his workshop there and be surrounded by his apprentices, who also shared his table and joined in family prayers. Children would grow up within this complete little world of daily common song and prayer and food and play and work, and from it derive the most solid part of their education; whereas today they learn almost everything outside the home, at school or in the street. The head of such a household was the typical Christian personality bred by the Protestant way of life, and to him its message was primarily addressed. He attained maturity through being intimately responsible for the lives in his household, ruling and teaching them.

Such a setting combined work and worship, and that is the nerve of all genuine religious life. In daily prayers the head of the family acted as household priest, and the Word that reached the rest through him was illumined for all by the human context of work and fellowship. Bible and hymn and prayer spoke to the heart because they were not spoken in a vacuum.

By breaking with the special sanctity of the visible Church,

[1] See the author's *Das Alter der Kirche* (with Joseph Wittig), pp. 677 ff., 805 ff., and his *Out of Revolution,* p. 427.

Luther made room for the Christian spirit to work in house and workshop as it had never done before.

By transplanting the sacrament of the Word into every household, with the father officiating as a priest, the Centuries of the Reform christianized what had previously been simply a part of the natural world, going its own way since time immemorial. But it did not achieve this by agitation for an ideological program. It transformed the life of all, as Christianity has always done, by living a contagious example.

If we turn to our own day, we can see at a glance that the Christian householder has lost his footing in daily experience. The whole realm of moral freedom, which balanced the outer realm of law, has given way to the hard laws of the industrial system. Man no longer earns his living in a private vocation but in an industrial function. The household is no longer an economic unit; the modern individual no longer ripens into a person through household responsibility; work and worship are divorced. Thanks to the factory and its implications, man's labor is separated from his right to teach, once the supreme value of a master's earthly life.

If one side of the Protestant scale of values has vanished, the other has become top-heavy. As the economic sphere ceases to be a realm of individual freedom, the State threatens to become an all-engulfing leviathan. In former days, Christendom achieved a unique liberty for men, unknown in other cultures, by maintaining the duality of Church and State: every earthly city had to admit at least one building in its midst which was not of national origin; men saw two worlds, one national and the other divine, when they moved from State House to Meeting House, and the choice between the two allegiances prevented their enslavement by either.

The very word "State" was invented to designate a territorial power which lacks the right to create a local cult. Even the most tyrannical State could have only an established Church, not an established religion of Vitzliputzli or Wotan. The plurality of many States in contrast to the universality of the Church has been the specifically Christian contribution to political life. If there were only one State we should be unable to breathe freely. Outside Christianity, "States" were annexes of the temple; they should be called "temple-states," never States. "State" is territorial order minus the divine order.

In the old days the family as economic unit was the foundation of Church and State alike. Modern conditions have disintegrated the family economy, and in its place the State is tempted to become a super-family which feeds everybody. In so far as it succeeds, it inevitably absorbs the Church too, because there are no longer any independent private economies to support the Church against the State. Thus, we arrive at the totalitarian systems of Germany and Russia, which fuse the three bodies politic, Church, State, and Family, into one. If we planned a World State, it would turn out to bear the same features of economic regimentation and political self-righteousness, and it would soon be headed by a tribal chieftain whom the people would worship because he fed them. As we move toward wider and wider economic unification of the world, we must see to it that economic boundaries are not allowed to coincide with political ones lest freedom vanish. And all our educational activities must stress the diversity of the powers which rule our lives on this earth, as against the close-knit tribalism of the economic super-state.

The foregoing pages indicate why any attempt merely to reaffirm the old Protestant values is doomed to fail. The day of self-contained autonomous personality is over because its economic foundations in reality have crumbled. The modern individual—externally a homeless, shiftless, noncommittal nomad, internally a jig-saw puzzle of nervous conflicts—is the very opposite of the Christian patriarchs to whom after 1500 the gospel was addressed. He is far too weak to stand alone. He cannot justify himself by faith, for he is a natural unbeliever—not simply in religious matters, but in relation to himself and the basic instincts and decisions of ordinary life. To try to convert him in the traditional manner and ask him to begin with a confession of sin would be a hopeless proceeding. Not until we take the burden of loneliness from him, and restore his natural powers of belief through a new experience of living with his fellowmen in shared hope, can we expect a rebirth of Christian faith in him. The preliminary experience of hope rather than the central experience of faith must take the lead in the new era. Thus, the nature of sin has changed. When Christianity began, sin isolated men. Today it binds them more and more under the tutelage of society. The great sinners of our times are not individuals but groups. Individuals are rather self-denying; but the groups composed of them lust for power, need power, exercise power. We, as citizens of our countries, have some reason to recognize the religious meaning of these world armies to which we belong directly or indirectly. For the world is a camping army. The last child is mobilized at least for the scrap drive. Is perhaps war the place, the home, the hell where we belong when we remove the gracious curtain of suburb and factory?

In any case, the war community and the warring communities have to be included *into our thinking of our own nature.* In the foreground, we have seemed to live by arts and sciences, by education and production. But we are called into life and we are called upon to die, and who does this calling?

Many a good man has loathed dishonesty and divided loyalty. They have become deniers of State as well as Church by Pacifism. They wanted to be honest; and they saw the contradiction. They seceded from our era which surmised that war was unavoidable and peace intermittent. We have satisfied them that we do not aspire to a return to Romanism or Puritanism. We have conceded to them the obsolescence of the previous Christian "set-up." But, now, the seceders from our era cannot call it unfair when they themselves come up for attack. They gave a horrible answer to a terrible dilemma. Granted the dilemma, they still became deserters. And they tried to make the upholstery of the suburb so thick that the rumbling of war and revolution could not be heard through the velvet curtains, the carpets and rugs of progressive education.

Our Invasion by China

At this moment, 1940 to 1945, belligerency and pacifism have scaled new heights of efficiency, with rangers and commandos and with conscientious objectors' camps. The slaughter is wholesale, and the defiance of war is well organized, too.

Innumerable good people are physically engaged in the war and mentally haunted by their pacifist temperament. What a conflict for a nation with an unbroken record of virile fighting! But how familiar to China where a soldier was contemptible for more than a thousand years. At present, however, China fights her first enthusiastic national war, whereas Americans in great numbers regard enthusiasm about war as despicable. They even despise themselves that they should be part and parcel of a world in which people still shoot at each other. The most pessimistic and Darwinian poet of the last decades, Robinson Jeffers, despises this American involvement in war. In his latest book of verse, cruel and harsh as it is,[1] he calls America a perishing empire and adds that he had thought her to be too good for this kind of destiny. His example proves that contempt for war goes far beyond the districts of organized pacifism in America. It is in this form quite unknown in Europe where war was dreaded, hated, cursed, but never despised.

Is it possible that the East and the West have exchanged roles?

I do not mean the conscious exchange of mere objects as in trade or of interesting items in art or thought, or even the noteworthy attempts of the Theosophical Society to draw on Buddha, Laotse, Confucius, for our inspiration, or the growing popular

[1] *Be Angry with the Sun*, New York, 1943.

literature on China. They go with trade, missions, engineering and teaching. They do not shake the foundations of our society but are contributions to it. The process which allows us to say that "The East invades us," does not carry the label "Made in the Orient." Pacifism, for instance, has spread on the crutches of humanitarianism or it is backed up by the Sermon on the Mount (though I yet have to discover one word of pacifism in this). I suggest that the Theosophical Society has not imported into America one per cent of the Oriental thinking which has been introduced by pragmatism.

John Dewey

The pragmatist John Dewey, the patron saint of progressive education, has emancipated the mentality of our suburbs from any subservience to Church or State. He has become the Confucius, the educational sage, of the Western World. His rise to power over our educational system is impressive. And it is all the more impressive since the principles of his own upbringing, and of the convictions which his life embodies, belong to the era of Christian Reform, while his activities and his influence belong to Interim America and to the Secession from our era.

Born in 1859, Dewey grew up in Vermont, under the full impact of the Christian heritage. Parents still educated their children in the fear of the Lord and in their own faith, with gusto, and a war was fought, the Civil War, for this passionate faith. Pioneers founded communities by the dozen every day. Congregations trained people from all ways of life in doing a bit of "horse shedding" before and after Church [1] and to expedite thereby the democratic process of confidential humming and eternal vigilance. There was bred into him the discipline of the centuries of reform: selfless brotherly love and the devotion of the whole man to his life work. Like an artisan or old craftsman of which he always

[1] See below p. 203.

reminds me, John Dewey never has undergone the depersonalizing influences of watered labor, of the scatterbrain environment, of the split between residence and business district. I, who have suffered from these ills, can well see that they did not sear him. My objection to John Dewey is that he takes his healthy heritage for granted, that he thinks these qualities to be man's Nature while they are the fruits of 1900 years of our era, and that he goes on from there as though nothing could jeopardize this assumed "Nature" of Man. Dewey has never a word of gratitude for the powers which gave him the strength and the unity and the wholeness. The thirtieth year of his life coincided with the closing of the frontier. Shortly thereafter the University of Chicago was founded. And in John Dewey this university called a man who recognized clearly that the sectarianism of pioneering groups, strong in their group faith with the denominational schooling and ministry, was doomed. The vast forty-eight states needed social integration of all the individuals regardless of color, race, and creed. And so, on his own fundus of Christian standards implicitly lived, John Dewey has erected a complete system of agnostic ethics and morality.

Now, this exactly was the greatness of the system of Confucius, who also was silent about the gods.

The radical aspect of Chinese thought has come to us through Dewey, anonymously, for even in his letters from China to his children [2] he does not recognize the kinship, but in great force and with the persuasiveness of the plain. The ideal society is conceived by him and his followers—and these practically are the teachers of America at this moment—as a

scientific
democratic
depersonalizing
cooperative
functional

mechanism, in which all the individuals who agree to it are held

[2] New York, 1920.

together by what they call social intelligence.[3] John Dewey feels deeply that his method is something new. When Hitler began to threaten his world, Dewey exclaimed, at the end of his book, *Liberalism and Social Action,*[4] "Social intelligence has found itself after millions of years of errancy as a method and it will not be lost forever in the darkness of night." This strangely quantitative oratory of the "millions of years"—common with the Pharaohs of Egypt—is the only pompousness which he will allow. Unfortunately, the sentence is void of any meaning. Otherwise he shuns emphasis. Hence for all those truths which only come to life when we feel them as new qualities, for his own heritage of fervent beliefs as listed above, he never has one word to say because personal sacrifice, worship, devotion, exuberance have no representation in his over-plain style. *Dewey and his followers are silent about their own motives.* They must be silent about the gods since they have cleansed their language from all emphatic elements. ("Millions of years," a mere quantity, stands for God.) This lack is found in Confucius, too. He left religion alone, as a petrified forest. Of Confucius it has been said: "To the honor of the human race it should be mentioned that nowhere but in China has a complete bore like Kongfutse been able to become the classic model of humanity."[5] The writer of this sentence was right as well as wrong. Dewey made and makes a deep impression on our times from Turkey to China, and for the same reason as Confucius: both make for boredom, but they make the boredom of depersonalization, of the "cog-in-the-wheel" existence, respectable. That they are able to be impersonal makes them venerable to people who find themselves in an impersonal machine.

Argument is useless against success. The invasion of our West

[3] In 1945, a friend of mine, a Deweyite, admonished us to restate "The *spiritual* values" of the Liberal Arts College. He made a motion to this effect. In his speech to support the motion, he began: "The educational *mechanism* of a college . . ." Nobody protested his contradiction in terms.

[4] New York, 1935, p. 93.

[5] Franz Rosenzweig, *Der Stern der Erloesung,* 2nd edition, Frankfurt, 1930, p. 98.

by Confucius is a fact. Our homelands are overrun by classic China. Let us look through the verbiage of pragmatism and education. What kind of a society is served by Dewey and who is his god? Dewey himself is simply a Christian Liberal who declines to talk about his faith. But his followers hold this belief:

1. Society is God and otherwise there is no god who sends us into the world by calling us by our names.
2. Therefore, human speech is merely a tool, not an inspiration; a set of words, not a baptism of fire.
3. Society includes all men regardless of their evil character. Everybody can be educated or re-educated. The body politic needs no self-purification.
4. The *ipse dixit* of authority is always out of place. Conflicts can be solved by discussions between equals.

This was the perfect philosophy for that America which emerged in 1890. This America, protected by the British Navy, had moved its frontier three thousand miles to the West during a century in which bigger was the same as better and in which no foreign policy was necessary. This incredible situation of no dangers abroad and of mere rolling along in space as the proof of progress ceased. The children of the pioneers still heard the fairy tales of those days but many of them lived now as cogs on the wheel of industry. They had to be taught that they, too, might lead the good life.

Hence, Dewey's success was well deserved. Some such adaptation of the Confucian pattern was needed after we settled down inside one explored world. The grandeur of Confucius had consisted in exactly the same trait. He was impersonal, functional, silent about God, unemphatic, democratic in education, and he came when the China of the hundred tribes had been welded into one empire. Confucius could hold that politics was education, since by that time everybody was inside the Chinese wall of one empire.

Dewey and Confucius came when man emerged from the elementary struggle against chaos, when anarchy was retreating, when man and beast and jungle became civilized. Their dogma that man is a function inside some definite society corresponds to the actual march of their contemporaries in exactly this direction. This beehive idea was well on its way to becoming a dogma. Whether apes or bees or ants or schools of fishes were investigated, they all were held up to us for imitation. How dogmatic people had become, I learned in 1940 at a conference of the educational advisers to the Civilian Conservation Corps—the famous CCC. Under general consent, we were asked to take down the following definition of a citizen: "A citizen is a man who is profitably employed." In vain, did I protest that a citizen is a man who can either found or, in an emergency, refound his city or civilization. These convinced functionalists thought I was joking. In protest, we founded Camp William James with the blessing of President Roosevelt as a leadership training center for citizen soldiers.[6] In the war, we have had to entrust to untold millions the task of refounding the United States. This is new history. But the mind is always far behind events. The masses of educated people would not be shocked by the definition given in 1940, the definition of citizenship in terms of "profitable employment." Their own sons may have died on the battlefield for a new order. And still, their educational vision will have no room for heroism and the quality of founders. Our boys themselves, in their hurry, will ask for jobs. But the blindness of educators and soldiers to their own actual behavior does not erase the fact from our slate that the civilians were saved by soldiers. All we may concede, then, is that a man can be treated as an ant or bee with considerable success in peace times.

We conclude that if thinking had no other function than to explain to man his own bend and trend, Master Confucius Dewey well might be our social saint.

[6] See pp. 27 ff.

Unfortunately, thought is not consecrated unless it resists trends. The truth is something bigger than that which most people are satisfied with. Often, great truth is hated and crucified. This fact refutes pragmatism. That we are not only inside society but also outside of it, ahead of it, behind it, is unthinkable or at least undesirable for Dewey. "Integration," to him, is God. But in a bad society, it is my duty to disintegrate her still further by taking up arms. The Cross says just this. At times we are inside but at others we have to suffer the fate of outcasts. We may have to hold on to old values when our society is drunk with speed and then we appear to be lagging like the fundamentalists. We may have to be ahead of our times, and again we shall be unhappy. The Cross explains war and revolution and decay and disintegration and explains why some sacrifice must bridge the gaps which man's abuse of his freedom always rips open.

Free men must shift their allegiance from solidarity and functioning "inside," to rebellion, to reverence, to sacrifice, according to the evils which have to be resisted most urgently.

In other words, we ever draw anew the lines between the inside and the outside, tradition and progress. For instance, when we decide that we must go to war, we are made uncertain, by acts of our enemies, about the old Adam in man and the new Adam to be created.

Every war makes an epoch because the warring parties try to push one specific part of our nature into hell. War is not fought by individuals but by moulds in which human nature is produced. In war, the enemy presents us with an order which threatens some aspect of our own development. The threat may come from their being defenders of an obsolete or of a too radically new order. We had no diplomatic relations with Russia as long as she pretended to be the only power already representing the future. And we broke with Germany when, in her counter-revolution, she turned the clock back to barbaric ages with which this country no longer had any connection. Wars divide the past and the future.

The opposite is true of peace. In peace times our commerce, production, exploration, push the border of society outward into the world of nature. In peace times, we doubt the character of every material factor in research, experiment, colonization. In war, the nature of man himself is dubious.

Peace and war together represent the cross of reality to which we are nailed, changing natures in a changing world. Hence, we send obsolete phases of social order to hell—war *is* hell—and we usher in new elements of nature, like electricity and radio, into our homes when we are at peace. Both times we act at the risk of human lives. It is not true that the Industrial Revolution did not cost lives. Peace as the struggle against nature involves risk. And the civil wars of mankind are costly in individual victims.

Neither of these struggles can disappear. Only, we may distribute the energies which change man more evenly; we may invent for man that which the explosion motor constitutes in nature; a moral equivalent for one great destruction might be found if every individual went to war personally in his own right. The Cross has always asked man to live as a warrior. But the incessant change in human nature is as indispensable as the change in industry.

All this is unacceptable to Confucius or Dewey. Their belief is in functioning inside a world where man is what he is and discusses changes with others as though no lunacy or degeneration or wickedness might exclude people from the discussion. To them it is a fact that we are already inside the universe as our home. This is irreconcilable with the acceptance of the two struggles represented by war and peace. Dewey and Confucius do not admit that in war we are created into a new period of history, and that in peace we draw new frontiers between the world rejected and the world domesticated by us. For they hold that nothing and nobody is outside. They smile indulgently at the heroism needed for the struggles. St. George, who slays the dragon, is to them a myth. Birds in cages, waterfalls in gardens, and—the climax of

Chinese culture—dragons on boudoir tables: nature is tamed. Even the chaos is included in society as the open spaces in New York are included by Park Commissioner Moses. "Western Ranches," with everything in western style, are advertised in the Catskills; this is a domesticated, profitable wilderness. This wilderness has lost its serious character of an infinite challenge. And with its infinity disappears the full risk which alone makes us attain our full stature, our second and third wind. A chaos which shall give us our full size must still hold terror, may drive us panicky, and catastrophes of nature—human or cosmic—must overawe us. This civil war, in which the abyss of our own darkness surrounds us, is smiled at as youthful error, as impractical and unwise.

Confucius and Dewey are very wise, very old, very kind and patient, very sure of being on the inside. Hence, prudence, justice, temperance, industry, self-control are their virtues. Cannot the murderer be improved, the wicked be enlightened, the wars abolished? And revolutions can be avoided. Since man, as they are convinced, can be sure of this, he need not get excited when catastrophes do befall him. They need not make us unhappy *since they need not to be.* We may overlook them by anticipating the certainty of being inside everything. To them progress is ingress. They mean by it the constant entrance of more and more people into the inside order already familiar. Progress is not the revolutionary beginning of a tradition hitherto unknown but the extension of known qualities. Progress is painless and not the heartrending conflict of previous progress now hardened into tradition and future tradition initiated as progress. To the man who believes that we are creatures, our own accomplishments of yesterday stand in the way of the next accomplishment because the old traditions are sanctified by sacrifices made. But Dewey says that intelligence for millions of years was led astray and has now found itself. Within the frame of millions of years, it is childish to weep over any loss of country, loyalty, love of old; we may keep smiling and this indeed is what we are told.

Dewey cannot be refuted since he represents the needs of his age. From 1890 to 1940, America had to get inside herself, so to speak. The wilderness did become Yellowstone Park. The Grand Canyon was civilized. America hung out her shingle—at home.

Nevertheless, it is an Interim America of which Dewey was the midwife. And the man whose middle-age philosophy of pragmatism Dewey unfolded, William James, knew that it was an Interim. For, on Interim America lies a mortgage: the mortgage of inherited beliefs. The brotherhood of man, free discussion between good fellows, trust of the young in the wisdom of credits and marks and courses in colleges under pragmatic leaders, hope in a rational solution of evil, this whole belief that God is immanent in good society, all these tenets were earned by heroes and make sense only because they created democracy and founded the inside in which they may be practiced. Religion and war brought men inside and this is the mortgage now for which we must pay interest by further changes in the quality of man and world. Which power shall get future man "inside"? Creeds must be imparted to the new born. They must believe that teachers are to be listened to, parents are to be respected, laws obeyed, long before they can know. There is a revolution on for the last forty years since the Japanese broke into the Western World at Port Arthur in 1904 and after the sailors mutinied on the *Potemkin* in 1905. This revolution proves that not everybody thinks he is inside and that others who are inside are in peril of being cast out.

This refutes the tenets of Deweyism, of one scientific

silently functioning
all inclusive
cooperative
impersonal
painless

order, an order in which nothing vital has to be settled by force; nothing lunatic can ever befall whole nations, no personal decision must save the world from ruin.

For Dewey's tenets, the only guarantee is found in exalted beliefs, faith, hopes, sacrifices, decisions of men and women who struggle daily against chaos. These are the facts—some of them—which upset the pragmatic universe: 1. No youthful nation including America has ever settled vital questions by discussion. St. Augustine said that discussion is for those questions which do not deal with the necessary. We can discuss in a democracy, everything. But we cannot discuss anything with those who reject discussion. 2. The German youth threw out all teaching authority wholesale, and followed an untaught Fuehrer. It denied all intellectual authority which Dewey and Teachers College take for granted. 3. Bolshevism has destroyed millions of victims. 4. Hitler has murdered millions of Jews. 5. America cannot find a rational solution of the Negro question after one hundred years of search. 6. Our armies had to gain the initiative by bold decisions.

These are political lessons. With respect to individuals, too, the lunacy of any paranoiac requires a decision, a very bold decision at times, of the relative who has to bring him to an institution. The lunacy of nations does not require less courageous daring. Also, against the blindness of any one generation, young or old, teaching cannot efface itself. We may make the children believe that they discover the truth themselves; actually we must have authority before we may make them believe even that. Against class hatred, sacrifices alone can help, sacrifices of a completely irrational character, sacrifices which cannot be discussed beforehand but must impress themselves by their symbolical potency. And all the insoluble cruxes like unhappy marriages, race strife, injustice, are not borne by reasoning but by the eternal combination of three irrational qualities: forbearing charity against the perpetrators, flaming defense of the outraged victim, reverence for the inscrutable decree of providence. Our faith in forces greater than man's intelligence, a charity greater than any social intelligence ever warrants, and unbending hope in the victory over the worst fiend, animate those who by their personal decisions and sacrifices enable Confucius or us to cooperate and to live inside of some semblance of order.

Spiritual authority, sacrifice, creative exuberance, aye, ecstasy, sufferings, are creating the frame of reference "inside" of which Dewey's army of teachers alone can work.

Inside this frame of reference, it is true, science, democracy, cooperation, intelligent functioning, pragmatic planning, are all in their place. But it borders on social irresponsibility to take the timberwork of society, the beams of authority, decision, faith, love, worship, for granted while everywhere these beams crack.

Our soldiers, airmen, sailors, volunteers in all walks of life, have flung themselves into the breach left by pragmatism. They are the living bodies who form the timberwork which Dewey took for granted and inside of which he well may keep smiling. You cannot be impersonal when you have to die in person.

Confucius was as light-hearted as Dewey. And we can renounce Dewey to no greater degree than China can abandon Confucius. But Confucius had to be made innocuous. If we wish to survive the state of helplessness created by pragmatism—helplessness against war, anarchy, decay—we need an antidote by which Interim America may be integrated into the real world of our black hearts and real deserts.

Charles Darwin

Many of my readers will resent the expressions used in the last sentence: black hearts and real deserts. As a friend expressed it: in America, everybody goes to heaven at long last. The complete success of Dewey's philosophy shows itself most clearly in the fact that my criticism may be—perhaps—acceptable, but that my excitement over "black hearts" seems quite out of place. These terms are left to stump speakers. Far beyond its content, pragmatism has conquered as a style. Great truth in the modern world can only be treated without emphasis. I have heard colleagues talk of

God as though they talked of a pair of shoes. The slimy style of indifference and superiority has conquered even those who defend positions outside Deweyism. Of black hearts only he will speak who trembles lest his own heart be found wanting. The speaker who feels like drowning will shout. Our intellectuals are always above their problem, on the *terra firma* outside the ocean of risk.

Therefore it would be no use to continue at this point our analysis of Interim America by intellectual criticism. When I said "black hearts," I lost face with the rational critic. The critic will shrug his shoulders because I am not scientific. I therefore invite the reader to a second round. The second idol of our time, taking even higher rank than Dewey's educational creed, is information. Intellectual curiosity is officially cultivated by all our institutions of higher learning.[1]

Information is the mortal enemy of science when information is sought by curiosity.

For, curiosity leads to a picture of the world which is as distorted as the Dewey-Confucius picture of society. Confucius said it was man's divine destiny to find his function in the smooth-running society. The curious mind sees the outside world as void of any meaning, as the battlefield on which the survival of the fittest is decided.

The curious minds are Darwinians and always have been since the Hindoos conceived of the worlds as innumerable sinking and ascending whirls of struggle.

The only thing they can see—and it is the essence of mere curiosity that it separates "seeing" and isolates the staring of the eye from all other insights or evaluations—is cosmic dust whirled around for millions of years before the creation of man.[2] In the process, the fog of dust incidentally took on various shapes which

[1] John U. Nef's brilliant criticism, *The United States and Civilisation*, Chicago, 1942, should be consulted on this point.

[2] John Dewey, "After Millions of Years of Errancy" in *Liberalism and Social Action*, 1935, p. 93. See the full quotation above on p. 45.

by mere chance, under the laws of probability, began to make sense.

It needs a special statement to shake our habitual complacency about the picture of the world, the so-called world view which in 1859, with Darwin's book, became fashionable. For it often is overlooked that this world view was totally different from the Platonic order of nature in which our natural scientists had believed from the Renaissance. In 1859 the universe ceased to be orderly. Plato was replaced. The Darwinian vision of life is that of a jungle of ceaseless strife. By now, this evolutionary scheme has penetrated. It is sold on the market place today. It is called the scientific picture of the world. It is, however, only the scientists' assumption about the world. The scientist makes the assumption that nothing is given but observable facts outside of our minds. Attachments are sacrificed to enable him to make his observations with complete detachment. Once this assumption is made, we can't observe anything but incessant movement outside. Life processes which are viewed with detachment present themselves as motions. It is, therefore, not true that Darwinianism has proved that the world *is* ruthless struggle. But it is true that when we give "science" free rein, the world cannot help *appearing* as jungle.

As a tendency, one among many, science has pushed observation to its limits: that Mussolini had a movie shot of Ciano's execution, that we may see our troops landing on the beaches of Normandy, are triumphs of cold-blooded observation. In these instances, we know that the events do not reveal their whole significance to the camera. We supply the moral evaluation. However, the victory of the evolutionary theory meant that this moral evaluation lost its status as an equal to the perception of sense data. We were required to restrict ourselves to the observable fact and our children were not told any more that these data were a fraction of the whole truth. The world of the scientists was recommended as the whole world.

Plato had sought to "look into" the world of beauty and goodness and truth. But this was less logical than to profess that our senses perceive nothing but quantities of size, of weight, of extension, of movement. Observation can never prove the unity of man, nature, universe.

"I think the universe is all spots and jumps, without unity, without continuity, without coherence or orderliness or any of the properties that govern love. Indeed there is little but prejudice and habit to be said for the view that there is one world at all." After eighty years of "pure" science, Bertrand Russell could formulate its world view in the foregoing classic manner. Science since Darwin abandoned unity; John Dewey abandoned suffering as our basis of understanding the world. Compare the words of Oscar Wilde: "Suffering is really a revelation. One discerns things one never discerned before." For the reason of unity, we had made all our history since Christ one common enterprise for all men who were converted to this Oneness. And for the reason of revelation through suffering, we had built up a hierarchy of values: according to the degree a man had suffered, we listened to what he had to reveal.

Darwin and Dewey persuaded us of the opposite. The less we suffered, the better. And the less we tried to convert ourselves away from ourselves, the better would the universe fulfill its purpose.

We now may sum up the astonishing power of the modern mind. This mind has a twofold capacity: it will not get excited or pained over anything because it thinks that to be civilized means to do nothing violent. We may know everything without getting excited. But the same mind will perceive the world as a jungle of strife and struggle and greed and blind passions.

We already know the kind of surroundings in which modern man has developed this double feature of extreme self-control and extreme scepticism. The creative ecstasies of men were smiled out of existence, and the beautiful meanings of the universe were deciphered as wave lengths. Simply by living in suburb and factory the modern man is daily fortified in his inoffensive, pragmatic Confucius style of living and smiling and working and whispering and pitying the follies of others.

To this man, the future always comes as a complete surprise. How else can it be as the future is the fruit of passionate, dogmatic, devoted, eloquent living? The war, for modern man, was a shock. How uncivilized. Bolshevism was a shock. Good ends but what violence. Hitler was a shock. A madman, and were we not all sane and intelligent and reasonable? This modern man strikes me as the queerest combination of the best-informed and the most surprised human being. The public knows everything and does not understand anything that happens. For, the facts which they call knowledge deal with living and standards of living. But things happen not by living but by birth and death. "Living" is but one half of life, the repetitive and predictable part. The other half is the agonizing creation and the creative agony of dying and being born.

He who wishes to be a little bit less surprised by the world's fits and tantrums, a bit less unprepared for the next crisis, may now be willing to face the simple question: How is Future created? How can it be created? When does mere living become less important than the coming to life?

Not before this question is admitted by your mind, will you have left the suburb's frame of reference behind. And not before you begin to fear for Life's return, will you meet the original question of Christianity.

PART TWO: WHEN TIME IS OUT OF JOINT

"The most significant characteristic of modern civilization is the sacrifice of the future for the present, and all the power of science has been prostituted to this purpose."

William James (1842–1910)

III

THE CREATION OF FUTURE

The Conquest of Paganism—The Anticipation of Death—The Meaning of History—Progress: Christian or Modern—Science and the Christian Era—The Intermittence of Faith

A question about the future of Christianity would be out of order. "The Future and Christianity" is no casual combination of words like "the future of motoring" or "the future of Europe." Christianity is the founder and trustee of the future, the very process of finding and securing it, and without the Christian spirit there is no real future for man.

Future means novelty, surprise; it means outgrowing past habits and attainments. When a job, a movement, an institution promises nothing but treadmill repetition of a given routine in thought and action, we say correctly, "There is no future in it."

In apparent doubt whether there is still any future in Christianity, people have been demanding in recent years that we save Christianity from destruction—along with civilization and some neighboring treasure islands. But "saving" Christianity is unnecessary, undesirable, impossible, because it is anti-Christian. Christianity says that he who tries to save his soul shall lose it. Our supreme need is not to save what we smugly presume to have, but to revive what we have almost lost. The real question is: Do we have a future? Then, we would have to be Christians.

At the center of the Christian creed is faith in death and resurrection. Christians believe in an end of the world, not only once but again and again. This and this alone is the power which enables us to die to our old habits and ideals, get out of our old ruts, leave our dead selves behind and take the first step into a genuine future.[1] That is why Christianity and future are synonymous.

By the time Hitler came to power the modern world had well-nigh forgotten what Christianity means. So many of its gifts had unconsciously permeated our lives that we took them for granted and ignored the giver. The conflict with pagans made early Christians vividly aware of what they stood for; but by 1850 there were not enough confessed pagans left to keep our hearts awake to the conflict—except on remote mission fields, where the contemptuous term "natives" implied that they were not to be taken seriously as a threat to Christendom. Meanwhile a disguised paganism flourished at home in academic traditions and popular absorption with material improvements. But now that naked paganism has burst forth again, we not only can but must recover the real meaning of Christianity if we are to survive.

The Conquest of Paganism

Nazi race theories and practices should help to revive in us a memory long dimmed: Christianity came into a world of divided loyalties—races, classes, tribes, nations, empires, all living to themselves alone. It did not simply erase these loyalties; that would have plunged men into nihilism and cancelled the previous work of creation, and Jesus came not to deny but to fulfill. Rather, by its gift of a real future, Christianity implanted in the very midst of men's loyalties a power which, reaching back from the end of time, drew them step by step into unity.

Paganism thus meant—and means—disunity, dividedness of

[1] When, early in 1942, our automobile factories were made over to produce implements of war, *Time* remarked that the industry "had literally died and was being reborn." The whole story is a Christian parable in modern dress, warning that men must take care to die in time, lest a worse death befall them.

mankind. This is true historically as well as geographically. Pagan histories are many, not one; each begins somewhere *within* time, for instance with the founding of Rome or with the Olympic Games in 776 B.C., and ends likewise: the god Chronos devours all his children. So pagan thought almost universally pictures human life as a decline from a golden age in the past toward ultimate destruction in the future. And beyond that it can imagine nothing but meaningless repetition of the same cycle to all eternity.[1] The Greeks did not believe in progress.[2]

Cyclical thinking is a real obsession of the pagan mind.[3] The Babylonian Great Year and its echoes in Hindu, Buddhist, Platonic, and Stoic teachings; the doctrine of inevitable rotation in the forms of government, given classic formulation by Polybius; the culture cycles of Vico and Spengler; the Mexican myths; the Germanic "twilight of the gods" which recurs at regular intervals;

[1] An exception in favor of Zoroastrianism was urged in the days when it was the learned fashion to disparage the uniqueness of Christianity and Judaism: cf. the discussion of Zoroastrianism in Hastings' *Encyclopedia of Religion and Ethics,* Art, "Ages of the World." But more recent scholarship has upset the premises on which this argument was based. Zoroaster lived in the sixth century B.C., not the tenth or eleventh as formerly supposed. The oldest Zoroastrian text expressing a view of history akin to the Jewish and Christian views was not composed until 650 A.D., at a time when, under the stress of Islam, Zoroastrians would naturally have become more receptive to Jewish and Christian ideas; it can, therefore, provide no foundation for the claim that Zoroastrianism created a non-cyclic view of history independently—still less that it *lived* such a view, as the Jews and Christians did. The only early sources of Zoroastrianism, the *Gathas,* simply give the usual mythical account of the four ages of man, like Hesiod, and say nothing of a middle or an end of history. Cf. the memoirs by Herzfeld and Lehmann-Haupt in *Oriental Studies in Honor of Corsetji Eradiji Parry,* Oxford University Press, 1933. The copious *History of Zoroastrianism* by its priest M. N. Dhalla, New York, 1938, is quite unhistorical. Consult, J. Hertel, in *Abhandlungen Saechsische AdW.* Leipzig 40 (1929), 192 f. Also see Maria W. Smith, *Studies in the Syntax of the Gathas of Zarathushtra,* Philadelphia, 1929, p. 18.

[2] A. Nock, *Conversion,* 1933, p. 113.

[3] For a penetrating treatment of the Greek thought on cycles, see Rodolfo Mondolfo (now in Argentine), Studi sopra L' Infinito nel Pensiero dei Greci, *Memorie dell' Istituto di Bologna, Classe di Scienze Morali,* III[a] serie, vol. VI (1931/2) pp. 67–116, esp. 73.

Hitler's brushing aside of "whole solar constellations" of history which he proclaimed to be over—all these are examples. Such thinking embodies the best virtues of the heathen: it faces the world with prudence and courage; it is grounded in facts of experience. But it is faithless, loveless, hopeless thinking, and therefore it lacks future. The medieval Song of the Nibelungen ends with the outcry that all love ends in torment and mourning.

Indeed the cycle is the very type of futureless existence, chained forever to a wheel of senseless repetition, and it is no accident that the earliest known source of cyclic thinking was Babylonian astrology. Paganism puts its faith in the automatism of the solar calendar and borrows for its stone heart the duration that astral bodies have, mere blind rotation in circles, ellipses and epicycles.

The only remedy the pagan knows for his sense of doom is to veil it in myths. We hear much of myths nowadays, and their deliberate revival is a sure sign of the resurgence of paganism. Paganism is best understood, I think, as primitive man's response to the fear of death. All men are born into some particular bond of loyalty to family, race, country. But all finite forms must die, and if nothing can lift us beyond these accidents of birth then we must die wholly when they do. The pagan is stuck in the narrow plot of earth to which his birth roots him, and his soul is therefore haunted by inexorable doom.

A myth is a form of mental life which pretends to be deathless; its kernel is always a fixing of the mind on some transient thing which thereby is immortalized. Nothing on earth is good or forever. The myth pretends it to be. In this pagan fragmentation of mankind by myths every community was enclosed in a private time and space. Every myth, from Osiris in Egypt to Odin in Sweden, tried to establish an immediate relation between its possessors and the universe in order to mark off their particular place or ethnic group from the rest. In the eighth century, the Pope was amazed to find that the kings of Lindfairne were satisfied with tracing their ancestry to the god Odin, beginning about A.D. 340!

Myths arose to conceal death in the past as well as in the future. Any founder of a city jealously cut the roots which connected him with the past. Romulus had to be king; so Remus was killed, because no man can be a king in the eyes of his brother. The tribes and cities of antiquity had lost common memories because blood guilt lay about their origins. Their myths accordingly were built on a phase of experience which was repressed and left nameless, an ineffable gap—the Greeks called it ἄρρητον, unspeakable. All secular societies have a skeleton in their closet. Even family genealogies usually omit the unpleasant ancestors and tell fairy tales in their stead.

Christianity, on the other hand, took the unpleasantness for granted: in place of a pedigree from a mythical ancestor it put original sin inherited from Adam. And resolutely, it began in the midst of time, not in a mythical fog. Against all deathless myths and hopeless cycles the price of a living future is to admit death in our lives and overcome it. This is the supreme gift of Christianity; it showed that the fear of death need not force man into the narrow circle of any given community. In place of pagan dividedness it created a universal pedigree for man that transcends all partial ends and beginnings, and measures history from the end of time.

But the Christian era would not have had the bright courage to march toward the end if Israel had not prepared the way, declaring war on mythology by establishing the unity of man's beginning. The Bible opens with a cry of triumph: "In the beginning God created the heaven and the earth." These words were spoken into a world in which the celestial gods had sanctified the divisions of lands on earth by their various myths for each locality, a world in which the separation of heaven and earth, of land and land, nation and nation, was the accepted reality. Against the thousands of elohims, inspiring mythical heroes, One is God. But the Jews did not make their own founders into mythic heroes; they kept them human and inconspicuous, surrounding them with stories of their conversations and dealings with other men. Piercing the veil of partial, pagan beginnings, they laid bare the chain of unspeakable crimes—like the murder of Abel by Cain—which had torn the unity of mankind; and behind all these they found the One God, who did not share the man-made divisions. In Him the end of humankind, to live as one in peace, became known as the oneness already guaranteed in the creation of Adam.

Small wonder, then, that Christians in Germany today are persecuted in the shadow cast by the persecution of the Jews. The myth-weavers know their first enemy. The Jews are living witnesses to the truth which has to be suppressed whenever a myth is to be woven. Perhaps one day men will fabricate a myth about the Red-Indian character of all Americans. If so, the Jews will again have to suffer as they suffer today from the Nordic race complex.

Jesus created man's future by building on the work of Israel. That work had been to establish the unity of heaven and earth, man and woman, brother and brother, father and son. Jesus completed this unified orientation of human history by opening up a new dimension: Creation of a new man by letting the pagan and the Jew survive themselves. That is why he was the perfect man, the first complete human being. He overcame man's dividedness by living once for all the specific law of the human kind, namely, that man can progress from fragmentariness to completeness only by surviving the death of his old Adam, his old allegiances, and beginning new ones. Homer, Pericles, Caesar were great men, certainly; but not one of them survived himself completely, not one shed his nationality, clan or city in so exemplary a way that this very process became the theme of his whole life and made others succeed him in this conversion. Now Jesus did just that, and thereby proved that every end could and should be turned into a new beginning, that even absolute failure and death could be made fertile. Herewith the last frontier of the soul was conquered, and its complete realm could now begin to evolve. By overcoming our pagan dread of dying spiritually, Jesus opened in all of us avenues of contact between ourselves and everybody else. Death became a carrier of life *between* souls.[4]

The Anticipation of Death

Because he was the first to turn mankind's direction toward unity, Jesus is the center of history.[1] He is Alpha and Omega, beginning and end: all past and all future meet in him. He was not merely prophet of things to come, like John the Baptist. Neither was he an idealist, like Plato. He was the first "final" man, the first who lived *from the end of time* back into his own age.

Chesterton expressed the paradoxical nature of the Christian time concept inimitably when he wrote, in *The Ballad of the White Horse,* "And the end of the world was long ago." The Christian has the end of the world, his world, behind him; beginning and end have changed places. Pagan natural man begins with birth and lives forward through time toward death; the Christian lives in the opposite direction, from the end of life into a new beginning. In surviving death he finds the first day of creation again before him. He emerges from the grave of his old self into the openness of a real future.[2]

Rufus Jones, in writing of a modern Christian, has explained

[4] See pp. 147, 190.

[1] Cf. Paul Tillich, *The Interpretation of History,* New York, 1936; C. H. Dodd, *History and the Gospel,* New York, 1938; also, *The Apostolic Preaching, with an Appendix on Eschatology and History,* London, 1939. Today people take the unity of human history so much for granted—as if it were simply there, like space—that they are apt to dismiss as baseless exaggeration the notion that any event could be its center. In Christian eyes, however, that Jesus is the center of history is the one statement on which no man after him can go back without plunging his world into utter darkness.

[2] "The End of the World," from now on, should become a technical term, to express the special viewpoint in the treatment of men, that the end is, as it were, at hand. See my essay, "The Church at the End of the World," in the volume *Credo Ecclesiam,* Ed. H. Ehrenberg, 1930, Guetersloh, 161 ff.

what it means to live from the end of time: "He did not propose to postpone the practice of the principles of the kingdom until it had finally come in its final triumph. If that course were pursued there would never be a kingdom. The way to bring it is to start courageously to be the kingdom so far as the person can reveal it. Instead of postponing it to a heavenly sphere or to a millennial dawn he boldly undertook to begin living the way of the kingdom."[3]

Living the kingdom, bringing it back from the end of time and embodying some of it here and now, is the process by which man, ever since Jesus, consciously participates in his own creation. Man is initiated into his destiny. He has acquired partnership in God's deepest wisdom: when to let go, when to say farewell, when to end a chapter of evolution. In the flowering of the great pagan cultures he had shown himself a master of brilliantly creative beginnings; through Christianity he has become master of creative endings, of the termination of himself and all his enterprises. Able now to say *both* no and yes, to die in part and survive in part, he is made *whole* and enters the full freedom of the children of God.

He that would save his life shall lose it, and he who loses his life for Christ's sake shall find it: death has paradoxically become the key to everlasting life. By learning to anticipate the inevitable end which the pagan fights off, man has robbed death of its paralyzing doom. Anticipating the worst, he can bury his dead in time. A pagan was ready enough to die physically—for his family, temple, guild, nation or race—but these he held to be immortal and therefore without flaw. He could not admit the necessity of letting them die when the time had come; hence all went down together.

Men create future when they are more than doubtful about the stability of society as it is, and feel that the end of the world is ever imminent. By freely anticipating the death of some part of

[3] *The Hibbert Journal,* XXIII, 39.

their minds, ideals, old allegiances, they conquer the compulsory total death which hunts pagans down like nemesis. So, for example, "in anticipating the Anti-Christ the mediaeval Church watched for the slightest symptom of decay. By anticipating the final threat, any form of society can attain immortality." "The anticipation of a Last Judgment looming over our own civilization is the best remedy against its inevitable downfall."[4]

Belief in an end of the world, or "eschatology," is thus the very essence of Christianity. Yet, until recently, the modern world had virtually forgotten about it. While lecturing at the Harvard Divinity School a few years ago, I asked each person in the room if he believed in a Last Judgment. Everyone laughed. Belief in Last Things was left to jesters like Chesterton.[5]

So-called "liberal" theology inherited a "natural Christianity," shorn of eschatology, from the eighteenth-century Enlightenment, and its own interests centered around the "philosophy" of religion and research in the life of Jesus. Only in the fifty years since 1892 did theology gradually recover its abandoned eschatological position, at least with regard to Jesus himself and the early church.[6] But leading scholars like Kirsopp Lake thereupon concluded in all honesty that original Christianity was forever divorced from reasonable modern man: for how could a reasonable man believe in an end of the world?

Meanwhile, however, Europe has "realized" eschatology as the stark truth of everyday life. In describing the fall of France, a

[4] Eugen Rosenstock-Huessy, *Out of Revolution,* New York, 1938, p. 561. Cf. Rosenstock and Wittig, *Das Alter der Kirche,* 3 vols., Berlin, 1927, I, 84 ff.

[5] So circumspect a religious observer as von Hügel in "The Apocalyptic Element in the Teaching of Jesus" (*Essays and Addresses,* p. 132), in 1919, was unaware that Nietzsche, Marx, and others were rising to power because of this neglect. He dryly remarks, "The doctrine of the End of the World seems to exercise but little influence." The truth was that this doctrine had broken away, become independent, and inspired Communists and Fascists, because in Christendom, it had degenerated into the Jehovah Witness type. And so, the end came swiftly!

[6] Cf. Frederick S. Grant, "Realized Eschatology," *Christendom,* Spring, 1941.

foreign correspondent wrote, "When you see a great nation disintegrate, you feel that the end of the world has come." The following Easter I received a historic document from a Catholic historian of the Church, Joseph Wittig. It was only a brief letter, asking me to look up Rouet de Jouvenel, *Enchiridion Patristicum,* Nos. 10, 832, 1771, and adding that these are the texts of actual concern to the peoples of Europe. They turned out to be *Didache* 16, 3; Cyril's Catecheses 15, 11; and Augustine, *De civit. dei* 20, 19, 4: the most solemn and violent descriptions of the Last Judgment and the Anti-Christ at the end of times!

So this historian lives right now, in present reality, through what Grant's essay presented to American "professors of the crucifixion"—in Kierkegaard's ironic phrase—as a vision of nineteen hundred years ago. The truth of eschatology is not a theoretical proposition to be rediscovered scientifically and put on our desks in the form of a book. It is an ever-threatening event to be reconquered on and by faith. We have to love the world because it is always at its wits' end. "The corpse of a nation which has committed suicide," General Templar has described Germany. Is this still not enough "End of the World," for Reason?

The overthrow of Christian eschatology by the Enlightenment had tremendous repercussions. No people can live without faith in the ultimate victory of something. So while theology slept, the laity betook itself to other sources of Last Things. What else could a layman do during the erratic brainstorms of the scholars? Man cannot live on the latest scientific news. He needs complete faith, hope, love. Accordingly, while liberal theology ignored the existence of such radical forces in human life, men like Karl Marx and Friedrich Nietzsche kept the flames of eschatology alive. Marx preached the eschatology of the Old Testament in secular terms, by shouting the infinite demands of social ethics into a finite bourgeois world. Nietzsche, whatever his teachings, lived an infinite faith, a mad faith like that of the New Testament—mad in the eyes of contemporary churchmen themselves.

The essence of eschatology is its infinity. It asks complete surrender to something outside the existing order of things. In this way it cleaves the identity between you and the world. The world has a fate; you have not. The world dies because it is calculable; you rise if you are incalculable. The world is at an end, is yesterday, but you may be a beginning, a tomorrow.

The first coming of Christ, therefore, receives meaning only from his second coming. Christianity never existed at all, it is an illusion, if it did not initiate the movement towards the end of time. The last saying of the New Testament—with the exception of the final benediction—expresses the connection of first and second coming beautifully. It is a prayer: "Come, Lord Jesus." When this prayer was uttered, the final story of Man had been started, and had been told through two generations; yet the Bible ends as if everything were still to come. That means that what has happened and everything that is going to happen are all of a piece, and neither is complete without the other.[7]

The Meaning of History

Through its creation of future, Christianity has endowed man, individually and collectively, with the power of having a life history. Meaningful history depends upon having one beginning, one middle, and one end. If our data are not oriented by single pillars of time in this way, history becomes a mere catalogue of changes, "1066 and all that." In the cyclic, pagan view of history there is nothing new under the sun; everything we do has hap-

[7] Theologians have made a great pother about the early expectation, and subsequent delay, of the second coming. The debate is pointless. For one who lives *from* the end of time, the combined expectation *and* delay of Christ's return is the contradiction on which the Christian lives (St. Peter II, 3, 8–10), a tension which is the paradoxical essence of Christianity. By anticipating death we actually postpone it, and thereby generate a unique historical process which is the Christian story of salvation. Von Hügel, *Essays and Addresses,* 1924, 132 ff., and my essay, "The Church at the End of the World," in *Credo Ecclesiam,* 1930, 161 ff., deal with this fact.

pened before, will happen again; nothing of permanent value is achieved; there is only change, without beginning or end. Christianity, on the contrary, has shown "how man can be eternal in the moment, how he can act *once for all*."[1] As a French scholar has written, "The unsurmountable abyss between Greek and Christian thought is the Christian rehabilitation of the unique and temporal event. The moral order is general and abstract to every philosophical or Greek mind. In Christianity the time of every human existence receives a superior quality in its smallest fragments."[2]

Man gives his acts an eternal, i.e. a "once-for-ever" meaning, by throwing his whole personality on the side of life that should now come forward, at each moment of his march through time. But he can select what should come forward, what will make a moment unique, only because one end of time like a magnet draws his heart at each step into the future. The uniqueness of the present derives from the uniqueness of the end. Hence only if history is one can our present-day acts have a once-for-ever meaning.

People nowadays imagine that man and his history simply *are* one, but all the facts are against them. Unity is not given, it is not a natural fact, but a common task of some ninety-nine generations to date.[3] And it can be destroyed any minute by anyone who sets out to do so, in a world which has forgotten that it depends wholly on resolve.

Purely secular histories never achieve unity. They offer us hundreds of familiar fragments—the history of art, or of economics, or of America, or of the modern theater—but the meaning of all these partial histories will vanish at once if their author cannot connect his story with the more comprehensive one which transcends it. For example, neither "modern" nor "theater" makes

[1] *Das Alter der Kirche*, I, 108.

[2] Jean Guitton, *Le temps et l'éternité chez Plotin et Saint Augustin*, Paris, 1933, p. 359.

[3] In this light the often disparaged first chapter of the New Testament becomes electric with meaning.

sense apart from the relation of modern to medieval, and of the theater to Greece and the mystery plays of the Church. Or, if secular history tries to be encyclopedic, it seems an inclusive frame of reference by going back to the cave man—but in vain, because the primitive races have no urge to cooperate with the rest of the world, let alone merge.

The meaning of Jesus as the center of history is that man had been split into such a variety of specimens that the unity of the species was imperilled, and that consequently the lowliest stratum of man—not Caesar Augustus but the child in the manger—had to be made the foundation of a universal unity. Everything which our modern optimists, from Emerson to Marx and from Bellamy to Streit, can adduce in support of one general significance or unified task for mankind, is taken from the Christian era.[4]

The future of Christianity and the future in Christianity are both abandoned by millions today. That Nazis, Fascists, Communists and Japanese deny the Christian orientation of history is ominous enough. But what is truly menacing is to see the Christian era deserted unthinkingly by educated people in our own midst. In the spring of 1941, a poem was read at a club meeting in my small town in Vermont, stating that B.C. and A.D. made no difference after all: there was no such thing as a Christian era![5] When such a doctrine can be proclaimed in Vermont, things must have gone pretty far. At the same meeting a guest speaker asserted that civilization was obviously at an end, but that was not very bad: had not the Dark Ages prevailed for many a

[4] Every Revolution, since Joachim of Floris in 1200, stormed against the Christian Era. Nietzsche dated the final era on September 30, 1888. My book, *Out of Revolution, Autobiography of Western Man,* 1938, is written around this problem of one era for all, with special eras within it.

[5] It was the "battle-fatigue" of Christian theology itself which surrendered the Christian era to the various revolutions. The first to do so seems to have been Franz Overbeck, in Basel. Against him, the *Journal of Religion,* April, 1945, has printed a sample of my "Reconquest of Our Era." Overbeck's position in the seventies of the last century by now has penetrated the masses. It signifies the capitulation of theology before "science"; and is part of the suicide of Europe.

century, and then a glorious Renaissance burst forth? The speaker forgot to add that man had survived the Dark Ages by his faith in the future, in an end of time, a Last Judgment, a final coming of the Word made flesh, and that this glowing faith had brought about all rebirth from generation to generation, in Franciscans, Protestants, Puritans, perfectionists, and even in the so-greatly-admired Renaissance itself.

Unasked, unchallenged, undefeated outwardly, the poet and the speaker carelessly threw away the pearl of their faith and hope. They stepped outside their own civilization with a light-hearted, "Well, it seems to be all over," and invited us to wait a few hundred years in utter darkness. Such an attitude is so arbitrary that it shakes all confidence in the meaning of history. It is hard enough to assume, with Protestants, that some ten centuries since Christ from Justinian to the Reformation were nullified by corruption and superstition. But if now we are to throw the whole two thousand years of Christianity overboard, we must simply lose orientation in time altogether and wander in circles like a man lost in the woods. A humanity without beginning or end falls prey to the senseless cycle of Spenglerian ups and downs, or Sorokin's fluctuations, or Pareto's alternating residues. Civilization and dark ages and renaissance chase each other. We begin nowhere and end where we started. If two thousand years have erred, we can hardly look to history for progress at all.

Progress: Christian or Modern?

Strangely enough, the word "progress" is apt to sum up a modern reader's most ready objections to the argument of these pages. Has there not been a wavering but undeniable line of progress since the dawn of history? Has it not obviously been the work of man's intelligence, devising better and better means of utilizing his environment? And is not this same mother wit our best guarantee of hope for the future?

Progress and future are indeed inseparable, but their order of dependence is just the reverse. Precisely because Christianity created future, progress is the gift of the Christian era,[1] and it vanishes in proportion as we secede from that era. Of course there were particular instances of improvement in man's estate before Christ, but they remained sporadic, for they were at the mercy of the cyclic character of pagan history, which swallows all its children again so that nothing finally adds up. And only since Christianity unified man's history from the end of time are these pre-Christian achievements of the race being rescued from the twilight of the gods which was their doom. What, for instance, would have become of Greek science and philosophy had Rome simply declined and fallen like Babylon, with no Church to preserve its relics and initiate that recapture of ancient learning which has been one of our glories since the twelfth century?

The idea of progress was not invented in 1789 or 1492. Jesus promised that his followers would do greater works than he had done (Jn. 14:12). The Church Fathers championed progress as the Christian view in opposition to the pagan belief in cycles of fate, with the golden age lying in the past; they proclaimed the resurrection of life and love after and through suffering, whereby God himself made progress in the hearts of the faithful.[2] In the twelfth century, Joachim of Floris prophesied visible, earthly progress beyond the Church for the following century, and in this

[1] "Shall there be no progress of religion in the Church of Christ? By all means the greatest progress. Who could be so jealous against men, so spiteful against God that he try to prohibit this? However, the progress must be one which can be called a progress of our faith and not a change." "The decisions of the Christian religion shall follow rightly these laws of how to make progress." Migne, *Patrologia Latina,* 50, 667 (Vincent of Lerinum, A.D. 434).

[2] Material now to be found in Hugo Rahner, "Die Gottesgeburt in den Herzen der Gläubigen nach den Kirchenvätern," *Zeitschrift für Katholische Theologie,* 1935. Probably the first explicit discussion of progress is in Vincent of Lerinum's *Commonitorium,* written in A.D. 434, but the idea is central, though less explicit, in the first great Christian philosophy of history, St. Augustine's *City of God.*

way he heralded all the social reforms and revolutions of our own millennium.[3] But his conception of progress beyond the Church depended by implication upon the existence of the Church, and thus his position remained Christian.[4] Any regress or cycle of a Great Year was explicitly combatted in the Middle Ages.[5]

The distinctively modern idea of progress is hardly older than the eighteenth century, when men like Condorcet, in his *Les progrès de l'esprit humain,*[6] cut loose from the preceding centuries of religious continuity and set up a purely secular humanitarian ideal.[7] The human spirit replaced the Holy Spirit. Emancipation from Christian traditions seemed at the time to promise unbounded possibilities—but the lack of guarantees for any such assumption has haunted all the secular philosophies of history from that day to this.

The secularization of progress only began with Condorcet. He still conceived it in spiritual, if human, terms. French *esprit* is, after all, a very special flower; it can prove its worth, in gaiety of courage, even amid a decline of material conditions. The French of 1789 were well aware that the steps forward which they called "progresses," were pluralistic and that therefore there were many spirits held together by one single spirit. The trouble today is that this distinction is forgotten. The people who write on progress today do not even mention the astounding fact that Condorcet, through the whole of his book, never once used the term progress

[3] Cf. *Out of Revolution,* pp. 586 f., 699.

[4] A beautiful application of the Christian progress to medicine may be found in *Paracelsus* (1494–1541) ed. Sudhoff XI (1928), 26.

[5] "*Non est regressus secundum naturam.* De Reprobatione Magni Anni." *Isis* 31 (1939), p. 71.

[6] The full title betrays the newness of approach: *Esquisse d'un tableau historique des progrès de l'esprit humain,* 1792.

[7] Cf. J. B. Bury, *The Idea of Progress,* London, 1920, and the Romanes Lecture with the same title for 1920 by Dean Inge. The same author has a chapter on "Progress" in his *The Fall of the Idols,* London, 1940. Also, J. Chevalier, *En Quoi Consiste le Progrès de l'Humanité?* Paris, 1930.

in the singular. It always is *"les progrès,"* on the title page as well as in the text. To this plural of improvements, nobody can have any objections. Bombs get better all the time. But this improvement does not determine progress at all. The One progress of all of us is secured only if the bombs are, though improved, yet *not* used. Of this NOT-using of our own gadgets, Condorcet did not speak because he took it for granted that we all agreed on this goal. He wished to apply and to extend the established principle of One progress in Church and State, to the Arts and Sciences. This, and this alone, was the topic of his book. It was his conviction that progress, after having advanced the heart and the mind of the person, now could be made *multiple.* Whereas, before, the pilgrim made progress in a stagnating world, the French conceived of our power to impart this progress to our environment, to the world.

And it was for this simple reason of *imparting* a known quality to an external field, that his pen would always use the multiplication *"les progrès,"* meaning all the sciences and all the arts. *"Le génie,"* he wrote, *"semble avoir plus que doublé ses forces"* (p. 151). Genius will have more than doubled his energies.

The English language has defied this French conception of multiple progress extended to new fields. The distinction between the progress of the soul as instituted by the Christian era, and *les progrès,* multiplied by applying the idea to the new fields of arts and sciences, was obliterated by an ambiguity in English which is not rare. The English translators of Condorcet, and the Great World Exhibition in the Crystal Palace of London, and the Chicago Century of Progress, all used the singular, and thereby mixed the religious original and the technical applications into one unholy welter.

At the end of this period, our perception is so dulled that we usually do not care for this fundamental difference between singular and plural. I am afraid the reader himself may scoff at my distinction as pedantic. But can he overlook that all "progress" in torpedoing, gunning, demolishing, are progresses in special fields and that they may prevent the man in the center of all these advances from progressing himself? Progresses do not ensure progress. They may accompany or embellish it. But progress must first be ascertained before we can apply it to the many technical advances. The great idea of human progress is not guaranteed by 101,000 progresses in special sciences or gadgets since they have led to the quickest and most intensive destruction of a whole civilization in our own time. If I wish to understand the progress from the feudal state to the modern state, it is no use to look at the states of Ethiopia, Nepal, Paraguay, and Liberia, although they all call themselves modern. I must know from another source that though they are given the privileges of modern states, they really do not disclose this progress to me. They are mere applications of a principle established in the center of modern history, and to these territories at the periphery the principle was merely extended.

Here is a simple example for the principle of progress: in antiquity, the individual gods regressed. The whole of antiquity suffered from the cry: bigger and better gods. Barely was a temple for one god built, that a new national disaster made them spend millions for another, newer, god's temple. And the new gods were always quite ruthless against the old throwing them down into Tartaros. This incessant "peristaltic" was anything but progress. It was a wild-goose chase. A definite change of mind was the prerequisite for real progress in this matter of the gods. The world came to rest only after God was recognized as single and unique once and for all times.

An example nearer home is marriage. The Moslem is allowed to marry two or more wives. This prevents the wife's progress. She does not know if she will remain his wife in the full sense of this term. She, therefore, has to fear actual regress. Therefore, the Moslem marriage is not progressive. There is no release of power for new tasks, either for her or him. He is still chasing the idea of a prettier wife. Hopes and fears about the final character of their alliance play havoc with their marital state.

The two examples reveal the laws on which progress rests. Progress must be explicit. Cycles happen to us as the seasons of the year. But progress calls for a commitment by our own explicit saying so. Unless we do away with the bachelor state we cannot get progress to the married state. That is the difference between progress and cycles—the cycle is an external myth at which we stare, and progress an act of our own creative faith. A newcomer to the United States rewrites his whole past, by this act. Take an European who in Europe dreamed of a certain future, a career, a house to build, etc. Later, he comes to the United States. By this step, his dreams of the future now become past. And this is the best description of progress—that even the future, envisaged yesterday, now is an element of the past. His visions of the future as entertained in Europe now are ploughed under as fertilizer for his American field. Progress depends on our power to give to the aspect which yesterday seemed far-away future, the name "past," ourselves.[8]

An explicit christening of the act, an explicit burying of the past, a definite commitment, and a unique response, are prerequisites of progress. As long as people have not *said so,* they may sleep, eat, work together, and yet not be married at all. They have not cut out the possibilities of doing otherwise. We now have gained a poignant insight into the real history of progress: from Condorcet to the Exhibition in the Crystal Palace in 1850, the progresses of the arts and sciences were considered extensions of the whole man's progress to further fields of application. By 1850, the applications were the only progress considered; the center collapsed.

This century after 1850 was the first to invent a regular method

[8] This insight was well expressed by a Professor of Geneva, Switzerland, in a spirited message to his American friends in 1940: "Greetings from this continent of Europe which has a glorious future behind it."

of promoting inventions, and thence came the idea of organized, automatic progress, guaranteed solely by the inventive intelligence of men. The original Christian view made progress depend upon frail but living human hearts consenting to die and become birthplaces of God; the deathless and lifeless machinery of modern "progresses" logically rejects the heart as an undependable nuisance. The constructor of a mechanical heart posed as a hero for millions of Americans.

Now we know already that when an aspect of human life claims to be deathless it becomes a myth. The favorite symbol of the myth of automatic progress has been a straight line, representing unbroken advance in one direction with no definite beginning or end. But just as a lost man tries to walk straight ahead but really goes in a circle, so would-be linear progress, rejecting the orientation toward beginning and end supplied by the Christian's compass, falls unwarily into the trap of circular recurrence which is the pagan's curse. Belief in automatic progress accordingly stops progress.

It would indeed be a mistake to consider all repetition bad. Life itself rests on a certain balance between recurrent and novel processes; the former are our fixed capital investment, the latter our free range of choice, selection, change, at any given moment. Unless the achievements of the past were continually reproduced along with the fresh creations of the present, there would be mere mutation without cumulative growth of any kind.[9]

But the natural tendency of life when left to itself is to relax from initiative to routine, and thereby to upset the balance between past and future, recurrence and innovation. That is why the automatic conception of progress is fallacious. Each group in society by sheer inertia tends to go on doing and demanding more and more of whatever its heart is set upon—shorter hours, higher profits, professional privileges, sectional advantages, established methods. But "more of the same" means getting in a rut, a vicious

[9] Cf. *Out of Revolution*, pp. 464 f.

circle, for quantitative expansion means qualitative repetition. Ruts divide us from each other and cut us off from the future. And when life has lost unity and future, when it is disintegrated and imprisoned in the past, it is dead.[10]

That civilization has actually moved steadily onward and upward according to the mechanic formula is too transparent a myth for any realistic observation of history. So in compromising with the evidence of grave recessions, Benedetto Croce proposed that we conceive history as a mounting spiral, in which declines occur, but only to be followed by a yet higher rise. But spiral progress is still automatic progress as it does not depend on you or me creating it. It shuns the Cross which leads through our hearts without any predictable shape of the curve whatever. The spiral has been accepted by many members of the academic professions as the ultimate in understanding. "Life travels upward in spirals," we are told by John Dewey.[11] "All evolution proceeds in an ascending spiral," is another recent statement by a good man.[12] These utterances are good proof for the old adage that the world is governed with incredibly little brain. For, this solemnly advocated "symbol" of the spiral does not fulfill the purpose of its own advocates in any appreciable measure.[13] They must never have analyzed it. After all, it was selected as their symbol because they had before them the Christian idea of progress and the pagan idea of cycles and the historical or personal experiences of dark ages, wars, depressions, crimes, etc. Set-backs occur; advances occur; life recurs incessantly. These are our three facts.

[10] It is interesting to see the idea of secular progress repeat the characteristic traits of paganism: dividedness and cyclic repetition.

[11] This sentence is his motto to the *Living Thoughts of Thomas Jefferson*, New York, 1940.

[12] Julius Stenzel, *Studien zur Platonischen Dialektik*, Leipzig, 1931, p. 171.

[13] Here is an example from religious literature: "The spiritual life has been compared to a spiral staircase on which one keeps coming round to the same spot at greater heights and depths." In the duplication, "heights" as well as "depths" the inadequacy of the comparison stands exposed. The quotation is from Maisie Spens, *Those Things Which Cannot Be Shaken*, London, 1944, p. 39.

Does the spiral convey these three facts? I do not see it. A crime, a paranoia of a whole nation, turns the clock back, and the fall is so deep that we are compelled to reinstate a minimum of decency, much less than we had before. In the process of restoring this lost level of common decency, we may rise higher and finally progress to new heights but this cannot happen unless we first have admitted the deep fall.

Progress, then, includes the following steps: 1. A certain level of common decency is accepted as "natural" for some time. 2. A fall into barbarism, a suspension of all standards by one individual or group shocks us. Standards hitherto considered safe are threatened. 3. We reconsider our human state. Unable to understand such a deep fall, we try to delve deeper into the secret of our nature. We find some leak in our former conception of justice. 4. The next peace after the fall reflects a more complete insight into man's true nature. It organizes us in such a manner that we will fall less deep next time.

Progress, then, could be expressed in a negative fashion. It means to become more and more the true human which our maker calls into being and not to fall away or to fall down on this response. I believe in progress in the sense that I believe that every century of our era has fallen less and less completely away and that man has become more and more natural, more fully all he was meant to be, from the beginning.

While "evolution" makes us lift ourselves by our own bootstraps, progress makes us stay more and more in the palm of our maker, and makes fewer and fewer fall less and less out of his hand.

The symbol of the spiral is useless in its snake-like recoil because it tries to compromise between a downward and an upward vision. It feigns to reconcile them and in fact does an injustice to both. It *omits* the very experiences which led to the search for any symbol.

These are the objections to the spiral: 1. The greatest height of our destiny is already ours when we use the term progress, as we otherwise could not measure the individual event by a standard. But the spiral goes up into an empty space and is not comparable to any known fact or value. Space itself has no "height," in any qualitative sense of this term. 2. The facts of history which led to the spiral idea do show actual losses of level, actual falls or relapses. The spiral pretends that no such loss of level ever is observable. Thereby it abolishes our vigilance. 3. The spiral is a comfort for the sceptical bystander of history who has decided to look at the spectacle from the outside and does not wish to participate in the agony and triumph of history himself, a kind of Santayana. Such a mind wants to have a formula. 4. The spiral, by suggesting to the many that they can look at the spectacle from the outside, makes for the next fall; for the lack of participation by the sceptics weakens progress.

Man is not made to "know" this process of progress; he solely is allowed to believe in it. The arch vice of the serpent is to confuse that which we can know and that which we believe. The spiral is this very serpent in its taxidermic state, so to speak. The choice of this meaningless symbol by the onlooker mind goes to prove that we are willing to pay any price for the pride of being mere spectators in the big show of history. Under no circumstances is history a spiral. Under no circumstances is man a spectator of history.

We can now see why man's life must be neither linear nor spiral but crucial. The future does not stay open automatically; it has to be re-opened by your own inward death and renewal. Not steady movement in one direction but continual re-direction, breaking through old ruts, is the formula for progress. All routine, all secondary forms of life, all the organs of our body even, decay when they do not serve and are not keyed up again by the growth of a new leaf, the bursting of one new blossom, by the one step into the unknown and improbable which we experience when we ask ourselves where our heart really is. Christianity is the power to open and to close cycles; hence it is not cyclical itself, but is able to contain many cycles and periods, spirals and lines.

Science and the Christian Era

The foregoing discussion can be illustrated by the sciences, which would generally be cited as the most triumphant examples of modern progress. Progress is indeed the life blood of science. But science has replaced magic and superstition in our era only by inheriting from Christianity its faith in progress and its power to fight against the vicious circle of mental habits for an open future, the power to change our minds through suffering.

Not only laymen but all too many experts think of scientific progress in fallacious linear terms, as if it were simply a matter of applying the good old methods to more and more data. "Doubt within your science, never doubt your science," is a prominent college president's ironic recipe for a successful academic career. But the best scientist is not merely a man who looks for answers; he is one who revises his questions, too, in the light of new experience, new emotion, new faith. That is why innovators like Darwin, Freud or Einstein have to fight against stubborn and often bitter opposition from orthodox scientists in their own fields. Perhaps the greatest founder of modern science, Paracelsus, was so persecuted by his Humanist enemies that even to this day most scholars believe he was only a quack.[1] Therefore, he said: "The truth begets hatred."

A myth of purely scientific progress has deluded scientists into thinking that sciences can advance without regard to the society of which they are a part, and even that their particular science can move ahead without paying any heed to the philosophy of science as a whole. Here again the linear conception of progress works itself out into a pagan hell of dividedness, as increasing specialization threatens to make the modern mind a tower of Babel. The truth is the exact opposite: each science depends upon the others,

[1] Cf. *Das Alter der Kirche,* II, 729 ff.

and science as a whole depends upon the rest of society, for support and for that rejuvenation which saves us from routine. Surely the events of recent decades in Europe should be sufficiently clear writing on the wall to impress this on the dullest minds. If the common faith which integrates the scientist into society is not kept alive, society will not stand up for the scientist.[2]

Specialists and experts today owe their very existence to several centuries in which faith in and good will towards science were generated throughout occidental society. At least half the energies of Western thought had to be spent on the perpetual welding together of all contemporaries by a common philosophy, a pervasive belief that all men lived in one nature governed by universal laws. Until the public was disciplined by some degree of unanimity, until a new philosophy taught the public to respect science, the new academic exploration of nature had little chance of success. Otherwise there would have been little cooperation, or support of particular scientific experiments, or selection of important questions. Sciences without philosophy are like spokes without a hub: the wheel must break. And break it does before our very eyes in Europe. Having lost their proper center, the sciences are crushed and perverted by dictators.

Welding the centrifugal sciences together with a centripetal philosophy was the work of men who suffered in order to make people sit up and have reverence and confidence and patience with science, even when the scientist made colossal blunders or let us wait for centuries. From Descartes to Dewey, the worlds of psychology, geography, economics, history, chemistry and the rest were kept together by philosophers who told every member of society, expert and layman alike, what nature, man, and science were, and how all three should interact in building the future. Good will and cooperation towards a goal have to be generated and regenerated.

Failure to do this adequately in recent times underlies the great

[2] See the chapter on "Hitler and Israel" from my book *The Fruit of Our Lips,* as printed by the *Journal of Religion,* 1945.

convulsions which are upon us today, and for them the renascent paganism in our sciences shares responsibility. Scholars have been complacently sawing off the trunk of Revelation on which their science was but a branch. By refusing to acknowledge their indebtedness to the Christian era for one future, one time common to all men, they lose orientation. Sciences do not give orientation; they presuppose it. The pillars of time are erected by lived lives, not by theories.

The most dramatic instance, in my own memory, of a scientist's secession from the Christian era was James Breasted, famed Egyptologist and most amicable of men, speaking before the American Historical Association in 1934.[3] "Thank God we are through with the four thousand years of revelation," he declared, meaning Israel and Christianity; Franklin D. Roosevelt could now line up directly with the great Pharaohs of Egypt for social progress.

Breasted stands for a host of distinguished scholars who from sheer love of the great discoveries in their own fields have insisted that these were the center of history. His eulogy of Egypt for its "social idealism" and its founding the "age of character" shows that he has not cared to understand what it was in Egyptian idolatry that had to be overcome by revelation. The vice of paganism is not too little but rather too much character and too much human sacrifice in honor of society! The Egyptians were the first to organize a territory—an immortal achievement; but the price they paid was to identify rule on earth with the laws of heaven: Pharaoh was not a king in our sense of the word, but "the House of Ra," the sun god. The seers of Israel saw that life in the desert was preferable to this law of the sun.

As the sciences liquidate the last residue of their Christian basis, they inevitably fall prey to mental death in the form of a vicious

[3] Cf. *American Historical Magazine*, XL, 427, and *The Rationalist Annual*, London, 1935. Also the same author, *The Dawn of Conscience*, New York, 1933, pp. xv ff.

circle. Criticism of the Homeric poems is back to the days before Wolff: Bassett and other sober minds have returned to the thesis of the unity of Homer, which to the dying hero of Greek philology, Wilamowitz-Moellendorf, was anathema as late as 1927. History is back to the chronicles since it became "social" history: it narrates mere sequences of events and customs; there are no true periods. Conscientiousness forbids to have ever a fully new story begin. And none is fulfilled. Historians who insist on being merely scientific do not ask and cannot ask how faith makes epoch, how it ends and how it starts; for this we learn exclusively from our own faith in the future. And all living history connects the past with the future. But the mere past created by scientific history considers the past not as the corollary of our future, but as the cause of the present. The past of our future would have an end; the past of our present has no end. It literally is endless and the only form to describe endlessness is a circle. Every vicious circle is vicious because it does not include its own overflow, its enigma. The unsolved problems of history alone are capable of organizing the endless material about the solved ones.

The neatest circle of all, properly enough, has been demonstrated in Biblical criticism itself. In 1906, Albert Schweitzer published a history of research in the Life of Jesus from the time of the first investigation in 1770 to his own days [4] in which he showed that scholarship had come full circle: every possible thesis had been held, rejected, replaced, until finally Wrede asked the same questions with which Reimarus had begun. A great mind like Schweitzer's saw that Christendom could expect no further light from continuing the same meaningless round. Instead of studying the Life of Jesus, he rediscovered the Death of Christ and went to the Congo as a medical missionary.

[4] *The Quest of the Historical Jesus,* London, 1922. One of the earliest theses of the critical century was the late date of the Gospel of St. John. It was "unscientific" to believe anything else. Opening the *Journal of Biblical Literature* of 1945 I find the circle there complete too with an essay on the early date of John's Gospel.

Through Schweitzer we may assess the significance of the decision between progress and vicious circle. A human being who finds his mental activities caught in a pagan rotation will react by a violent jump. Our colleges cannot afford to let any science fall into such a rut, because it would destroy the student's loyalty. Cynicism, violence, exodus must be the soul's answer to such silly games. Soul erosion has already resulted.

Another science imperilled by the vicious circle, although you would expect it least, is economics. As economics deals with the ever-changing material processes which link us to the earth, change is in the center of its thought. We cannot eat the same loaf of bread twice. Hard as it is to believe that such a science of incessant change could itself tend to become circular, much evidence points in this direction. In an attack of mental fatigue, many economists publicly and conversationally tell us: "The pendulum has swung back; we are back to mercantilism; we are back to economics as a part of moral philosophy." The sweep of 160 years of progress in economic theory is dying down. Only a new starting point for the economic theory would hinder this relapse into the cycle. And this is the mental revolution, the death and resurrection on which all progress in science, as in any field, depends. The starting point is obvious. The last decades have seen large treatises on the theory of unemployment, but all were written still as appendages or excrescences of the economic theory in general. In Taussig's textbook of economics, *Principles of Economics,* unemployment at first had not even a chapter of its own.[5] The same is, by the way, true of Marxian economics. Gradually, this question of unemployment, swelling up to larger and larger dimensions, has become the sore spot of the present manner of reasoning. In the last chapter, we shall come to practical conclusions about this crisis of economic theory. At this point, it suffices

[5] The recent *Theory of Unemployment* by Arthur Cecil Pigou, London, 1933, still is a footnote of the classical theory only grown into a sizable monograph. But it has no new foundations.

for our orientation that this science also is threatened by vicious repetition, in the place of true progress.

The most depressing feature I see is the fact that the men in these fields do not get excited over the situation. They think that it is all a difference of terms or expressions and that it does not matter how you call or organize your thought. My sermon on rethinking is lost in the padded walls of their good conscience, but the vitality of their science is lost, too. Nothing which you yourself consider unimportant will make a dent. Without the scientist's feeling that truth is of the utmost concern, truth ceases to be of concern, in the mores of the people. If the scientist says: we now go back to 1750, he abolishes the progress of science which has made science a treasure of the nations. If we now shall have mercantilism again, obviously the cause which led Adam Smith to reject mercantilism in his day and to advocate free trade will become operative soon. In this recurrent cycle, there would be no place for science. It would be the same blind movement once more and all over again. Thus, economics as a science commits suicide with the remark, "We are back."

Friends of science may be tempted to evade the challenge of these pages by interpreting them as a hostile, and therefore bigoted, attack on science. But the attack is really not on science but on the pagan abuse of science. It is love of science that makes me speak against its diseases and for a society in which science can progress. Progress is impossible in a society which has lost orientation.

The Intermittence of Faith

There is a final objection which is familiar to all of us. If things are so bad today, does that not mean that Christianity itself is bankrupt and therefore refuted? Yes, Christianity is bankrupt today. But not refuted. Christianity has repeatedly been bankrupt. When it goes bankrupt, it begins over again; therein rests its power.

The story of Christianity, both in the lives of individual Christians and in the life of humanity, is a perpetual reenactment of the death and resurrection of its Founder. Only by his great outcry, "My God, my God, why hast thou forsaken me?" did Jesus become our brother. All of us are bankrupt at times; by giving up the power of his spirit for this one moment he created his equality and unanimity with all men. One thousand years later, Anselm of Canterbury founded the new science of theology with a kindred appeal to God: "What shall thy servant do, exiled so far away from thee?" [1] And in the recent past, that great Christian sage, Baron von Hügel, never wearied of proclaiming that faith is an intermittent process. Christianity is based on the discovery that our minds are as mortal as the cells of our bodies. Faith cannot live unless it remains intermittent: that bitter truth admits death where it belongs in our belief, as a bringer of new life.

So every Christian community or movement is the result of tears shed in common, of a bankruptcy faced in the fellowship of hearts that have survived defeat. What new forms of death and resurrection the present age demands of us I shall attempt, very tentatively, to discuss in later chapters. The potential Christians of the future will not follow any known pattern of Christian life, and I tremble at the task of speaking of them—these new types of Atlas who will have to support heaven on earth again.

But the general relation between Christianity and the future is a sort of "mediterranean" problem that lies between the familiar shores of every Christian soul, and I have not added a word to the teachings of the Fathers on the subject. The vision that God's time, which is both end and beginning, inspires and survives many beginnings and many ends of man's endeavors gives us

[1] *Quid faciet, quid faciet, iste tuus longinquus exul? Quid faciet servus tuus longe projectus a facie tua?" Proslogion* I. Compare the complaint on the Absence of God, *Meditatio* XX, and on the Quest and Rediscovery of God, *Meditatio* XXI.

the power to begin anew. Today as every day, his Spirit demands from us an answer to this question: What is as yet unfinished, uncreated, unprecedented, uncompromised in the vicious circle of our thinking? And we shall always find that the future of Christianity is present here and now as long as two or three Christians believe in it, and answer. And they answer, these poor timeful creatures, by contracting time to a point of most fruitful faith and love, and in this contraction, the suddenness of the end of the world and the endlessness of a first beginning are coupled and bear witness to the timelessness of our origin and our destiny.

IV

THE CREED OF THE LIVING GOD

How God Is Known—Adults and the Creed—The Divinity of Christ—Let Us Make Man

"God is dead!" cried Friedrich Nietzsche. The clergy of our departmentalized religion—living as they did in a world which no longer feared being forsaken by God—dismissed this statement as insane blasphemy; but it was a true accusation of them and their age, and probably no one between 1870 and 1917 did more than Nietzsche to resuscitate God in the hearts of men. That epoch had forgotten mankind's ancient tradition of the God that died and rose again, was killed by his worshippers that he might be reborn, or was crucified that he might raise us all.

Man's faith in the death and resurrection of God runs like a red thread through the ages, linking the primitives in Frazer's *Golden Bough* to the most enlightened service in a Protestant Church. Before Christ, the gods were thought to die in the twilight of fate, or in a frenzy of tribal ecstasy, like Adonis or Tamuz or Osiris. But Christianity, beginning with the Crucifixion, then in the Catholic Mass and the Protestant Service of the Word, showed that God dies from the unclean hands and minds and lips of those who may partake in his resurrection. The whole meaning of Jesus' forgiveness was that we remain God's children despite the fact that we all do kill Him in our hearts at times.

How God Is Known

God becomes known to us in all the powers which triumph over death, and from the earliest times men have called any such power divine. Using this definition as a guide, let us survey the growing knowledge of God.

When men lived in tribes, they saw a god in the power that kept a tribe together after the death of all its present members. This power became known especially when warriors gave their lives for the tribe and victims were sacrificed. At this level, God is identified with the spirits of the tribe's ancestors, and He overcomes death by simple denial: the ancestors aren't "really" dead, but have merely migrated to a happy hunting ground.

Then came the pagan cities and empires. To them God became known as eternal cosmic order revealed by the stars and imitated by the stone walls and temples and pyramids built for its worship. One of the oldest terms in the Egyptian tradition is "millions of years," whereas primitive men cannot count with precision beyond a hundred or a thousand. At this level, God overcomes the facts of death not by denying them but by going around them, ignoring them: the sun-god and his temple enjoy deathless duration.

The Jews discovered God as the power who, having created the celestial order as well as the earth, could enable His people to discount the passing of all visible things and wait for His future coming as Messiah. Here death is neither denied nor ignored, but it still has only a negative significance. It is something to be endured.

The climax in conquering death, and therefore in man's knowledge of God, was the crucifixion and resurrection of Christ. By him, at last, death was included as a positive factor within life and was thereby finally and completely overcome: death became the gateway to the future, to new life.[1] Moreover Jesus had given up

[1] The endeavor of the Reitzenstein School has been to reduce the Crucifixion to one of the innumerable mystery cults of antiquity in which gods were slain, just as other schools have investigated the psychic cases in our hospitals for an "explanation" of our faith. It is of course the other way round. We are all embryonic Christians, but incomplete and often warped or stopped halfway. The mystery cults, indeed, were stirred up by any group's plight that genius and inspiration come and go, that the God in our bosom and the unanimity of our nation do come and go in inexplicable vicissitudes. The mystery cults divined that all "movements"

his mind, his spirit, his inspiration, as well as his body, yet he survived. Now the tribal spirits ceased to linger on, and the walls of cities and whole civilizations could fall with impunity, for God was victorious over men's minds as well as over the objects in heaven and earth: all death had lost its sting.

The Living God thus revealed by Jesus must be forever distinguished from the merely conceptual God of philosophers. Most atheists deny God because they look for Him in the wrong way. He is not an object but a person, and He has not a concept but a name. To approach Him as an object of theoretical discussion is to defeat the quest from the start. Nothing but the world of space is given in this manner. Nobody can look at God as an object. God looks at us and has looked at us before we open our eyes or our mouths. He is the power which makes us speak. He puts words of life on our lips.

If the Divine becomes known in our lives as the power of conquering death, it is something that can only happen to us in this or that particular moment of time; it is known as an *event,* never as an essence or a thing. And it can happen to us only in the midst of living, *after* death in some form—bereavement, nervous breakdown, loss of hopes—has come upon us. Hence Christianity has no God in the sense of Aristotle or Plato or a modern deist [2] who frames a concept of Him as prime mover, world soul, or first cause. We have no other authority for our faith in God but

---

died. The titanic struggles of the sons of God ended in exhaustion. The mysteries initiated the faithful into this stupendous enigma of an end of their particular world. But there was not the missionary element by which the faithful were required to seek their own Cross and to continue the story indefinitely. The myth enclosed them in a finite frame which could not grow into universality. When Jesus was crucified very profanely, after a trial in court, he took all his believers with him outside the myth on the open roads which led and lead them to the ends of the real world, in space as well as in time. The difference is summed up in Hebrews, 13:13.

[2] Nietzsche felt sure that he had refuted "God." Yet, in 1886, he wrote: "Refuted is the moral God only," and that is the God who neither speaks nor inspires, but is merely an idea like Voltaire's moral God.

the living soul of man, which attained fulfillment in the resurrection of the first perfect man. Imperfectly, however, every child believes in a saving grace from its first day in life, much more than it believes in self.

The typical philosopher starts with the world of space and therefore never really gets outside it. God, for Aristotle, may be a logical necessity, but He can never be an experienced and telling reality because philosophy tries to be timeless. The prime mover knows nothing and provides nothing with regard to you or me.

Aristotle, however, had a better sense of the Divine than modern philosophers, for he was a Greek, and the Greeks had given divine honors to the human heroes who had founded their cities. Once, for every man and nation, comes the experience of power to decide and to create and to build up values. Aristotle gave to his prime mover only the abstract existence of "thinking about thought," but he shared in a culture which deified speaking, ruling, legislating Man.[3] In our era, a ruthless division of labor has left the defense of the divine events in history to the clergy, and philosophers have stressed mainly the undivine logical and mechanical processes.

When Thomas Aquinas claimed to harmonize Aristotle with the Christian tradition, a Latin Averroist, Siger of Brabant, showed that it was impossible. Siger was murdered for his bold stand against the academic idols of his day, and since then the Western mind, for Catholics and Humanists alike, has retained a dogmatic acceptance of Aristotle's "reason" as man's "natural" mode of knowing God and life's supreme values. Such natural reason is really immature reason, like the philosophizing of a child prodigy who thinks before he has lived. A child has to think in external, physical terms about God or science or royalty, for example, because he has not yet lived long enough to identify

[3] Aristotle is reported to have twice offered sacrifices to friends as gods (O. Hamelin, *Système d'Aristôte,* Paris, 1920, p. 12). Here, then, are his "gods who speak"!

himself, through sympathy, with the more mature phases of human experience. The Living God cannot be met on the level of natural reason because by definition He crosses our path in the midst of life, long after we have tried to think the world into a system. The young are backed by God; only the mature must face Him.

That power which compels us to answer a question of life and death—and "any part of the world, sun, earthquake, crisis, revolution, can become a god when we feel that it is a power urging this question upon us"—is always our God; "the power which makes the atheist fight for atheism is *his* God." Neither the question nor our answer need be verbal. "God's questions come to us through the meek yet irresistible forces of heart and soul," and they demand our devotion, not lip service.[4] An utterly godless person would have to be one who never acknowledged any such power above himself and therefore pretended in effect to be his own maker; in short, to be all of god himself. We know God primarily because we know that we are not gods but would like to be.[5]

Modern man is not so much godless as polytheistic, and therefore pagan. His life is split between many gods—or "values," as it has become fashionable to call them. "Art, science, sex, greed, socialism, speed—these gods of our age devour the lives of their worshippers completely." "There are many questions and many answers. But none of the multiplex deities . . . can enslave all the elements of our being . . . Science is too severe a god for children. Venus abdicates her authority over old age. Socialism annoys the man of sixty, and greed is hardly conceivable to a young person. The gods pass. When the individual realizes their passing, their unceasing change, he is converted to God—the living God who invites us to obey the *'unum necessarium,'* the one thing necessary and timely at every moment. This man dis-

[4] *Out of Revolution,* pp. 723, 725.

[5] Theages, in Plato's dialogue, says that every man wishes to be a god.

covers his complete liberty . . . because the God of our future and our beginning is superior to the gods he has put around us in the short periods of our conscious efforts." [6]

Jesus completed the revelation of the living God because he created true future. God is alive only if he is as much beyond the flux of time toward the future as he is beyond the same flux in the past. "In the beginning was the Word," but the Word illumined the beginning only because it hailed from the end. God's Word is always spoken from the future back into the times, calling us out of the past to incarnate the one thing needful in the unique present.

When people consider God as having been our maker in the past only, and abandon eschatology and a belief in God's future, their belief in God's presence disappears too. So Nietzsche, finding a Christianity devoid of faith in Last Things, rightly shouted, "God is dead." Nietzsche tried to be God and take over the future himself, but his life committed him, despite himself, to a faith in something larger. He, just as much as any mechanist, had to believe in the unity of the material world which would sustain him, in the unity of mankind which would need all the goals and methods he advocated, in the collaboration of sister, mother, friends, printers, readers, and the whole cloud of witnesses who now work to carry his words around. These assumptions show that no one can open his mouth in this world of ours without implying belief in an identity of meaning: for the world as created in the past, for the end of time as inviting us to bring it about, and for the present opportunity of fellowship to realize that end. And faith in this identity of meaning, for death, birth and consciousness, *i.e.,* for end, beginning, and our own present in between, *is* faith in the living God, who gives new commands from moment to moment, yet is one from eternity to eternity. He alone can satisfy man's deepest need, to lead a meaningful life.

[6] *Out of Revolution,* pp. 725, 727. Cf. *Das Alter der Kirche,* I, 103 f.; II, 713–717.

Adults and the Creed

The above triune faith is none other than that formulated in the Athanasian Creed, and therefore I believe the Creed simply true. Its three articles guarantee our trust in the unity of creation from the beginning (God the Father made *all* things in heaven and on earth), our liberty to die to our old selves (given us by God's Son, who implanted the Divine itself in human life by living as a man, and dying, yet rising again), and the inspiration of the Holy Spirit which enables us to commune with posterity and start fellowship here and now.

In our day it is the fashion to disparage creeds in religion, and even theologians speak apologetically about them. That is because an intellectually slothful ministry prefers Pacifism or the Social Gospel to the Gospel, and our theologians, forgetting Jn. 14:17,[1] treat the Creed in purely worldly manner, as if it were a theorem in pagan philosophy and not the stream which carried their own lives.

The Christian Dogma is not an intellectual formula but a record and promise of life. It does not propose ideas for our minds to master; it tells actual events which can master and transform *us* as they did the first Christians. It is not a mere topic of thought but the presupposition of sanity. It is the Christian *"a priori,"* the Table of Categories under which the faithful live.

The first Christians experienced radically new processes which of course were said to be non-existent by the Arthur Brisbanes of their day. The Christians knew that the "world" in us—that part of humanity or of ourselves which lagged behind this new step in the evolution of the race—would either never acknowledge the new experiences or would forget them time and again (Heb. 5:11—6:7). So the only protection was to invite the nations of this world to admit these truths as at least lying ahead of them in

[1] "That Spirit of Truth whom the world cannot receive because it is unable to see Him or to know of Him."

experience. This was achieved by converting the Gentiles en masse. Baptism did not open the eyes of individuals, but it did orient their search in the direction which would lead them to rediscover the vital experiences of the first Christians. Each generation had, and still has, to be introduced to the whole painful process of rediscovery.

Hence the Church has acted like an immense sponge, sucking up all childish approaches toward understanding, and deterring no one who was of good faith and on the road and still alive. No pagan, native, primitive first step was rebuked as long as group or individual remained in communion with the complete truth and its guardian, the Church. As a result, rationalists—who are a large part of the "world" in our day—are able to see this sponge character of the Church, but not the central truths toward which it drew the pre-Christian approximations which it absorbed. So rationalists reduce Christianity to a mere patchwork of prior sources, and identify a literal adult belief in the Creed with this or that childish stage in its understanding.

Truth, however, is only in those experiences that can be expressed by various ages in various ways. Even in mathematics the same truth recurs in new applications and in very different forms of statement. So legends like Santa Claus are not lies when told to children that they may understand the workings of the Spirit among us—as long as the legend waits to be told again, in appropriate terms, to the adolescent, the man, the father, the community leader. *To omit the legendary form of truth is to suppress truth.* As a human being, I need the legend, the myth, the ritual, the poem, the theorem, the prophecy, the witness, the sermon, every one of them. The four Gospels give a model example of this rule that one truth must be expressed in different ways for different times of life, and that the whole truth is conveyed only on several such levels together. The Gospels express an identical truth in four different phases of the life of the Church—something that had to be true for Matthew, who tried to prove it to the Jews; for Mark, who lived with Peter; for Luke, who taught the future generations; and for John, who wrote after the fall of Jerusalem, when the Word, the Torah, was no longer enshrined in the visible Temple of Solomon, and men could therefore understand why "the Word had to become flesh."

Now the Church has always allowed the childish to see things childishly, and has forbidden clever people to sneer at a child's belief. But it has with equal energy forbidden children to dabble with the adult understanding of the Creed. One day Woodrow Wilson's youngest daughter overheard her father say, "Hell is a state of mind." She ran downstairs and told her sisters, "Father has lost his faith." It is natural for children to think that Heaven and Hell are places in space, because they can only picture in external terms what they have not yet experienced. But Wilson's remark was strictly orthodox, and by no means an instance of modernist fudging. Jesus said both that his kingdom is not of this world, and that it is in our hearts. And Origen wrote before A.D. 250: "I have commented on this [prayer] 'Our Father who art in Heaven,' in order to abolish the low opinion of God held by those who place him locally in the heavens. Nobody is permitted to say that God dwells in a physical place." [2] And if "God in Heaven" does not mean something in space, neither by implication does "the Devil in Hell."

The confusion of childish and adult ways of understanding the Creed has been aggravated by the predominant emphasis given to the child in the Church since the Reformation. In the sixteenth century the Church had become so worldly, so like a secular State, that Luther threw the Catholic Church-State over to the worldly side of life and erected a realm of Christian conscience beyond the authority of either Pope or Prince. After this revolution the Church renewed herself, in both Protestant and Catholic confessions, by developing the religious education of the young, under the leadership of such men as Melanchthon and the Jesuits. From that day to this the school—Sunday School, Parochial

[2] Cf. Rouet de Jouvenel, *Enchiridion Patristicum,* No. 472.

School, Church College—has been the part of Church activities that really mattered, while adults have grown silent within the Church because their energies were invested outside, in politics, business, and professions.[3] No wonder, then, that adults today feel dwarfed by interpretations of the Creed which were shaped historically to fit the needs of children.

Since the Living God comes to us in the midst of living, after death has come upon us, in the form of some crucial experience,[4] let us try to orient our understanding of the Creed in terms of adult experience. Most people in middle life have known responsibility by creating life in others, as parents; defending the life of others, as mothers or soldiers; inspiring life in others, as writers, teachers, friends; or improving skills for others, as mechanics, scientists, executives. Each of these experiences involves some kind of break with "the world" as it is, followed by a new beginning. A man has to leave his parents to cleave to the wife of his choice. An administrator has to scrap standard routines and revered rules of business practice when he makes an important innovation in his work—as we see amply illustrated in the war effort today. A good parent or teacher has to discard much mental lumber and reshape his perspectives under the stress of having to select what is vitally important for the new generation in his care. And at times every parent or leader has to forget himself and fight for his flock as a lioness fights for her cubs.

The Christian Dogma simply generalizes these experiences of maturity into principles which apply not only to the way an individual reaches his climax in life but to all climaxes in the universe. Since we know new beginnings in our own lives, we can understand that God made heaven and earth in the beginning, that the whole universe had one creative origin rather than coming about by chaotic accident or from opposing deities as Sun-worshippers would have us believe. Knowing struggle for

[3] Cf. the author's *Politische Reden,* Berlin, 1929, pp. 44 ff.

[4] Eros is, as the Greeks knew, our first meeting with death. A man who loves begins to die.

the life of others, we can understand how God loves us. Because our own soul has had to escape the prison of convention and precedent, we realize that a soul can survive any of its social embodiments. Having had to forget and to select in order to teach, we know that the Word has power to give life and take life in our students. And we can believe in the Last Judgment because we have seen last judgments passed on Proust's France, Rasputin's Russia, Wilhelm II's Germany, and President Harding's America. The belief required of a Christian, in sum, is that his manhood knows more than his childhood about the fundamental processes of living. Philosophy may overlook beginning and end. A man who has planted a tree, won a battle, begotten a child, must posit the fact of a new creation in the center. To him, it is as certain as 2 and 2 equals 4. He knows that the question "Why?" for a creative or heroic act is a childish question.

The Divinity of Christ

Perhaps a personal confession is permissible here. I had always hoped to be a Christian. But twenty years ago I felt that I was undergoing a real crucifixion. I was deprived of all my powers, virtually paralyzed, yet I came to life again, a changed man. What saved me was that I could look back to the supreme event of Jesus' life and recognize my small eclipse in his great suffering. That enabled me to wait in complete faith for resurrection to follow crucifixion in my own experience. Ever since then it has seemed foolish to doubt the historical reality of the original Crucifixion and Resurrection.

The Crucifixion is the fountainhead of all my values, the great divide whence flow the processes most real to my inner life, and my primary response to our tradition is one of gratitude to the source of my own frame of reference in everyday life. Hence our chronology of B.C. and A.D. makes sense to me. Something new came into being then, not a man as part of the world but The Man who gives meaning to the world, to heaven and hell, bodies and spirits. When a bride receives her husband's name, a new realm is created to which all her acts are credited. Likewise, in His name we enter a realm of freedom unknown to mere heirs.

Every value in human history is first set on high by one single event which lends its name and gives meaning to later events. Every "a" has to be preceded by a creative "the."[5] We have seen many movements called "crusades"—for example, America's entry into the war in 1917—but they derive their name, if it is properly given, from the First Crusade, which burst upon the Occident as a new conception and wrought profound changes in our subsequent modes of living.

The faithlessness of modern men, clergy included, comes most of all from ignoring this principle. Speech has lost its vital, creative, costly character. They do not see the blood of millions that must be shed to place certain values on the throne of life. They use words to propagandize or advertise, and do not even say "thank you" to the martyrs who lifted these words as sacred values above the crowd. They think one can abstract a definition of a crusade, for instance, by looking over fifty-seven crusades and taking an average. But how is one to select his sample crusades unless one already knows what a crusade is? In the world of things, a whole may be built out of many details, but values are not produced that way. The one unique event must precede the many. Therefore crucifixion (or last judgment)[6] and resur-

[5] See Robert Browning, Tiburzio's last speech in "Luria":

> "A people is but the attempt of many
> To rise to the completer life of one;
> And those who live as models for the mass
> Are singly of more value than they all."

[6] In the Crucifixion, with the accompanying darkness, rending of the curtain in the Temple, etc., that which is to happen finally has happened once already; and for the faithful the second coming of Christ as Judge really began with his first coming. The Crucifixion judges us all, because we know that we would have behaved like Pilate or Gamaliel or Peter or Judas or the soldiers. The Last Judgment will make known publicly what those who have died with their First Brother already experience daily, that our Maker remains our Judge.

rection would not be known as everyday occurrences in our lives if they had not happened once for all, with terrific majesty.

It is for such reasons, it seems to me, that Jesus' divinity must be sustained.[7] Jesus the man would simply mean one man among many, a kind, likable man perhaps, but "a" man only. But inasmuch as he is the norm, the way, the truth, and the life to be developed by us beyond the state in which we find ourselves, it is impossible to call him "a" man. He is "my maker," the first who was neither Greek nor Jew nor Scythe, but complete and perfect humanity, and each of the rest of us, if we are not simply jealous like Nietzsche, must be content with being his men. If we presume to judge, criticize, assess Jesus, of course we make him a man. But he is the measure by which we must judge ourselves; his life gives meaning to ours; and, to sustain the stage of human perfection which he achieved, the word "man" would have been quite inadequate in a world in which any Caesar was a god.

The Creed finds men today in an attitude opposite to that of those for whom it was first formulated. Let us put side by side the two equally puzzling facts about the Creed, one negative, one positive:

Negative—The Creed finds men today in an attitude opposite to that of those for whom it was first formulated. The very success of Christianity has made disappear the creeds and cults against which the dogma defended us victoriously.

Positive—The Creed says with perfect truth that there has appeared the final man, the man from the end of all times, Jesus, and that he interprets now all the events happening before this end, in the light of this end.

Every word of the Creed is true; yet it has become ununderstandable in so far as it has come true. One more word about the Divinity of Christ. The reader may perhaps go so far as to admit Jesus' inspiration, but why "divine"? The full answer will become

[7] For the political aspect of this dogma, see pages 147, 159, 190, 240.

clear in the chapters of the second part.[8] Let him here kindly be satisfied with this logical distinction: we call him the perfect man because he himself was full of the right spirit. Many men, however, were full of the spirit. But besides being inspired himself, he also, and he alone, gave and left us the right spirit as a community possession and opened the inspirations of the separate individuals and nations to each other. As the creator of our own spirit, he has divinity.

I am fully conscious of the hollowness of these remarks for many good people who have no notions of God. To tell them that Jesus has divinity conveys little. They would first have to realize who God is, by starting with some experience of the Spirit who triumphs over their prejudices. It is the third article of the Creed which will have to form the basis of experience without which no reflection on the dogma is of any use. After all, the Creed reflects active participation in some prayer to God the Father or some sacrifice in the love of the Son. All the Scholastics who reasoned out God were priests or monks who prayed day and night. Their reflections on the trinity came as afterthought to real action and a way of life. One of my students, on the other hand, frankly told me in his examination paper: "I have never prayed and I do not know what prayer is or is intended to do." It is forbidden and would be blasphemous to discuss with this boy the divinity of Christ. He must be plunged into some communal experience of inspired living before we may mention to him the spirit behind all inspirations. I am afraid that we are prone, in our discussions of the Divinity, to gloss over the second commandment not to use God's name in vain. Alas, it is applicable to our vain attempts of "discussing" God with people before they have experienced Him in one of the three ways in which God overwhelms us, as our Maker, as our Victim, and as our Vivifier. This danger to blaspheme places the dogma with us on the opposite front from antiquity.

[8] Pp. 135 f.

The pagans as well as the Jews prayed and sacrificed and experienced rapture. The three actions the modern students pretend to be ignorant of were familiar then. Kings, priests, poets, prophets, the offices regenerated by Jesus were known. Only their union in every man's life was deemed impossible. The modern unemployed, inarticulate, psychoanalyzed cog-in-the-wheel has no ambition to be king, prophet, poet, priest. This ambition will have to be kindled before they understand "divinity." The men of antiquity knew many stories about God or gods, but had never heard of Jesus; so they could be told about Jesus by beginning with God.

Since the Creed was addressed to both Jews and Greeks, it had to deal with the minds of each. The first article sides with Jews against Greeks. Sky and earth are not the domains of separate deities, for in the beginning God created both. The second article sides with the Greeks against Jews to the extent of saying that one man was God. To a Greek, this placed Jesus in the list of sons of God, from Hercules and Achilles to the Divus Julius and Titus of his own day. But as the Christ, the only begotten son of God, Jesus *closed* the list, ended the era in which scattered individuals could receive divine honors. And though this kinship of Jesus to the pagan heroes was enough to make Jews abhor him, the Dogma assured them that at least he was not a hero by blood relations or in any mythical manner: no heroic deed anchored him in this life as it then was. The Spirit of God was upon this child, drawing him to his Cross from the start. His every breath was inspired by the life that had to be given to future mankind: the eternal hope of the Jews for a Messiah, and the perpetual faith of the Greeks in a divine flesh and blood in their midst were to be superseded by the fellowship of those who would share One Divine Spirit and thereby were held in the palm of God's hand and could no longer fall. We do not evolve upward; we fall less downward, after Jesus. That Jesus was *the* son of God means that he was the definite historic eventuation of man's divinity. Christianity transmits the Divine Life to all men who come after him; we are all God's sons; but ours is a plural emanating from his singular, an "a" deriving from his creative "the." As all the grains of sand in an hourglass must pass through the narrow neck where there is room for only one, so the Divine Life had to be focussed completely in one man before it could spread out from him to all. That is why it could happen only once, why only Jesus can be *the* son of God. He united the Divine and the human once for all, and to speak of a second or third Christ would be to deny the essence of his achievement and cancel the unification of mankind which he began. The Anti-Christ attitude is the attempt to do just that. Any Christian may be tempted by a Messiah complex which would make him pretend to be the unique representative of Deity in his generation; so when the Christian fellowship decays an Anti-Christ appears. Nietzsche's "God is dead" leads logically to the German storm troopers who have actually said, "Hitler is Christ."

It is significant that the Apostle who wrestled with the Anti-Christ problem was the one who was Jesus' natural friend and a spiritual eagle. St. John used to say in his old age that the whole gospel was contained in the saying, "Children, love one another." When people asked why, he gave two reasons: "First, because it suffices, and second, because the Lord said it." By acknowledging that his friend was the Lord, and thus submitting voluntarily to the historical sequence which Jesus founded, John overcame the temptation to act as a substitute Christ.

The Dogma of the Incarnation, that in Jesus God became man once for all, is our sole guarantee against the lapse into polytheism, which is always possible, and widespread today. Modern philosophies of value are nearly all polytheistic.[9] Human values are many, and philosophy inevitably reflects their pluralism unless it has a universal standard for the perfect man.

One Man must rightly be called God for all time, or paganism

[9] *E.g.* Nicolai Hartmann, *Ethics,* 3 vols., New York and London, 1932.

will return again and again as often as inspiration lifts men out of the daily groove of the law. Jesus overcame the division of mankind among the sons of gods who had looted the world in antiquity. They had founded cities and empires by murder and rape, war and slavery, usurping the spiritual powers of the masses who worshipped them as heroes. Jesus showed his divinity in just the opposite way, by taking on himself not earthly glory but ignominy and earthly suffering. Thus, instead of exploiting the hero worship of the masses, he emancipated them by sharing his divinity with them. But one condition was attached, the Christian condition that henceforth no individual could become a god on his own account. The communion with God became one for all men together, and in every generation the same coincidence of God and man that started in Jesus is realized by those who keep together in One Spirit. That is the meaning of the Church as the Body of Christ.

Let Us Make Man

Hence the third article of the Creed is the specifically Christian one: from now on the Holy Spirit makes man a partner in his own creation. In the beginning God had said, "Let us make man in our image" (Gen. 1:26). In this light, the Church Fathers interpreted human history as a process of making Man like God. They called it "anthropurgy": as metallurgy refines metal from its ore, anthropurgy wins the true stuff of Man out of his coarse physical substance. Christ, in the center of history, enables us to participate consciously in this man-making process and to study its laws.

One of the greatest of these laws is formulated by the Creed as the resurrection of the body. Only in this way can the higher types of man, once created, be reproduced regularly in human history and thus make permanent progress in the evolution of man. A new soul, a fresh originality of the human heart, thereby survives the man or nation in which it came to birth and incarnates itself in a spiritual succession of typical representatives through the ages. For there are definite new phases of human existence never lived before, which arise at particular birthdates and, if they are genuine, they force themselves upon man's plasticity with such impressiveness that they don the bodies of later men and women in turn, and shape them into the same type.

But this must not be understood as pagan reincarnation or unselective, mechanical repetition. The new embodiment is not a mere copy of, still less identical with, the old one. The body "is sown a natural body; it is raised a spiritual body" (I Cor. 15:44). "The corrupt body does not return in its first nature, for it is not the corrupt seed that returns as grain. But as from the seed of grain there rises the ear, in the same manner there is in our body a *raison d'être,* in the power of which, if it has not been corrupted, the body rises in an incorrupt state."[1] So a human type will rise again only in so far as it is "not corrupt." It has to be purified, and nothing but the pure metal will show in the resurrection.

There are countless illustrations of the resurrection of the body in Christian history. St. Francis, for example, died without offspring, but Franciscan humanity has flourished ever since, and not only in his Order. The Franciscan way of life, immortally portrayed in *The Imitation of Christ,* became daily bread for the lives of countless Christians of all denominations, even the most radical Protestants. The Franciscan type guided the political life of medieval Italian cities. The "Third Order" spread over all Europe and counted among its members even the Habsburg emperors, who, in death, humbly deposed their titles before the majesty of the Franciscan spirit.[2] Finally, in Abraham Lincoln,

[1] Rouet de Jouvenel, *op. cit.,* No. 528 = Origen, *Contra Celsum* (A.D. 248) 5, 22.

[2] Cf. *Out of Revolution,* pp. 507 f.

Francis of Assisi celebrated his secular resurrection in America. When Lincoln, as President and Commander-in-Chief of a victorious army, walked into Richmond in 1865, on foot, without escort, St. Francis had conquered the powers of this earth. In Siberia, in Egypt, people would whisper that old Abe, a new type of man, had appeared in the world.[3] Here, ruler and servant were blended into one. Such men are epoch-making in the history of the human species. The relation of Lincoln to St. Francis was unconscious. It was not imitation but genuine succession, revealing the power of a soul that had tried to come into the flesh ever since St. Francis set the example.

In like fashion, Christian astronomers, chemists, doctors, preachers, missionaries, painters, masons have populated the earth. Anticipating a Last Judgment over our corruptible flesh, they have come into the flesh out of the Spirit, achieving a tempestuous resurrection from the dead in the name of the new life. The Chaldean astrologers of antiquity came to life as modern astronomers. The Hippocratean doctor, in whose tradition Socrates asked that a cock be sacrificed at his death, came to life as the modern scientific doctor, in the name of the Living God, uncorrupted by local prejudice.[4] In the light of the central dogma of a final resurrection, we have seen many partial resurrections accomplished, and this and nothing else is the Great Economy of our destiny.

Christian anthropurgy, then, has gone on and continues to go on before our very eyes. These visible processes are the projection of our faith on this earth; they anticipate and foreshadow the ultimates of our Creed. The communion around us in the name of the Son we called the Church, and because we believed in the Son we found ourselves growing up in a Christian world. The communion around us in the name of the Father we called

[3] Cf. Roy P. Basler, *The Lincoln Legend,* Boston, 1935.

[4] On this complete transformation, cf. Victor von Weizsäcker, "Bilden und Helfen (Hippokrates und Paracelsus)," in *Die Schildgenossen* VI (1926), 477 ff.

Nature, and because we believed in the Father we investigated all things in heaven and earth which He had made.

In short, the story of man since Christ has been the application of the Athanasian Creed to everyday life. This story makes it clear that the Creed is not a statement of bare facts but a command given at baptism. The Creed describes essentially three things—God's trust in man, God's liberty, God's creativity [5]—and enjoins us to accept the conditions under which we may make Man by sharing these Divine attributes.

For nineteen centuries, the outstanding contributors to the life we live have believed and enacted the commands of the Creed. They have believed themselves capable of creating trustworthiness, have hopefully cherished their creative powers, and have acted as free men. In so living, they have worshipped the Father as the guarantor of their trust, the Son as the guarantor of their liberty, and the Spirit as the guarantor of their creativity.

Thus our whole civilized inheritance has been made by men in the image of the Trinity, and we may see that image in such everyday things as pilots, whom we trust with our lives, doctors, who employ the latest creations of medical science, and teachers, who enjoy liberty to influence children in ways that would never happen if we merely let nature take its course. Correspondingly, we also witness what happens as modern society forsakes the

[5] These are the powers of faith, love, and hope, which bridge the abysses inside of "Man" whom we little men have to represent through the ages. It is essential to realize that they come from God rather than the human will. The Greek and Hebrew words for faith mean God's faithfulness and trust. Our belief is but the poor reflex of God's faithfulness to all of us together. William James' unfortunate phrase of "the Will to Believe," ushered in the revolt of the masses because it deprived our faith of its prop. The masses are plunged into night when faith is made dependent on human will, instead of meaning that God holds us in the palm of his hand. Similarly love and its liberty are too often confused with will, even by theologians. Love and will have as little to do with each other as a wedding ring with a cannon. Will is not free, for it must struggle for life; but love is free, because it can choose death. The history of this wrong doctrine of humanism which classifies "love" with "will," from the sources, is given in my *Industrierecht*, Breslau, 1926.

Divine attributes for their opposites, mistrust, mechanization, fatalism: men are killed in wars, disintegrated by mechanical repetition, enslaved by dictators.

Therefore the people who destroy Christianity by degrading Jesus into a nice man saying niceties and doing good deeds in Palestine simply do not use their five senses. Otherwise they would discover that under certain conditions they have trustworthiness, creativity and liberty, and that under others they do not. That is the heart of the Christian Creed.

V

THE ECONOMY OF SALVATION

The Three Epochs—Inspired Succession—The Rebirth of Meaning—Carnality versus Incarnation—Christianity Incognito—The Death and Resurrection of the Word

How few still believe that the past two thousand years have really been a story of man's salvation! The average layman, or even theologian, will speak with admiration of the life and teachings of Jesus, but appears to think that God has more or less abdicated since then. Yet unless we do believe that Christ began a life process which has continually transformed us and the world we live in, true faith is dead.

This modern predicament doubtless has several causes, some of which have already been mentioned. Belief in Christian history depends upon belief in an end of the world towards which that history is oriented. But our theologians have progressively abandoned such belief, until today a naive communist or fascist is a better eschatologist than they. Moreover, the modern world has been shaped largely by the Protestant spirit, and Protestantism justified its protest against the Papacy by charging that Christendom had been in the hands of Anti-Christ for a thousand years—the very term "Middle Ages" or "Dark Ages" was invented for this purpose. Therefore most moderns are unconsciously predisposed to think that vast stretches of history since Christ have been so corrupt as to be null and void for Christian purposes.

Now the Protestant charges, like the report of Mark Twain's death, were grossly exaggerated—every great revolution exaggerates—but corruption there undoubtedly has been, in many forms, and sometimes in the most revered places. Dante describes popes in hell. There is nothing unorthodox in that; men are still free to sin. But classical idealism, and belief in automatic progress, perhaps, have made men interpret the tragedies in Christian history as a refutation of Christianity, as if it must be either ideally perfect or non-existent. And since the world in our time is hardly a picture of salvation, despair drives many to join in the sarcasm of Nietzsche: "If Jesus of Nazareth did want to redeem humanity, can he not have failed, perhaps?" To say that Christianity has never been tried is at best a forlorn reply.

But if we realize that our faith is intermittent by establishment, that Christianity does not abolish sin and death but overcomes them, and that in the tenth and fifteenth centuries Christendom was as bankrupt as it is today, yet emerged reborn—then we can turn to history with fresh eyes for the story of salvation that has actually been happening.

The Three Epochs

That story by its very nature must be, not a recondite discovery of scholars, but something so simple that any school-boy can understand it. It can be stated in one sentence. The story of salvation on earth is the advance of the singular against the plural. Salvation came into a world of many gods, many lands, many peoples. Over against each of these it sets up a singular: one God, one world, one humankind.

Correspondingly, the story comprises three great epochs. In the first, one God triumphs over the many false gods. This process fills the first millennium of our era, and its outcome is the Christian Church. Therefore church history is the interesting and important aspect of the first thousand years A.D. In the second epoch one earth is won from the plural of unconnected countries and undiscovered lands; no Chinese walls remain effective. This is the point at which we stand today: geographically, technically, statistically, the earth is finally one, and so indeed is the whole world of nature, thanks to modern science which Christendom created. The master institutions of the second millennium are, first the Papacy as a worldly power, then the system of territorial states which grew from under its wings.[1] Therefore world history or political history is the theme of this period.

Today we are living through the agonies of transition to the third epoch. We have yet to establish Man, the great singular of humanity, in one household, over the plurality of races, classes and age groups. This will be the center of struggle in the future, and already we have seen the outbreak of youth movements and Townsendites, class war and race war. They pose the questions which the third millennium will have to answer. The Totalitarian State is a mistaken attempt to solve the new problems by using the old means created by and for the second millennium. The very convulsiveness of totalitarianism is a sign of weakness; its disciples scream loudly because they secretly fear that their idol is already dead. The State is on the defensive because it is inadequate for the needs of the coming age. The theme of future history will be not territorial or political but social: it will be the story of man's creation.

Once having grasped this sequence of three major epochs, we can see that each epoch corresponds to an article of the Creed, and therefore that the story of salvation enacts the Creed in human history. The three articles deal respectively with (1) Creation, (2) Redemption, (3) Revelation. History realizes them in a different order: Article two made epoch first. Later, article one was realized. And now, we are turning to article three.

In the first millennium, the Church was wholly concerned with being the Body of Christ. Accordingly, the heart of the Church was the second article of the Creed: Jesus the true Christ, his father the true God, the spirit of his Church the Holy Spirit; he who believed this was saved. The Church was the communion of the redeemed.

[1] Cf. *Out of Revolution,* passim.

The second millennium restored creation to its Creator. After the Christian soul had found its dwelling place in God, the external world could be purged of all ungodliness: the whole earth was organized in a system of territorial states, and nature herself became a realm of universal law and order—magic, demons, capricious agencies were banned. Thus even modern science is a process within the story of salvation, and through its unification of nature the first article of the Creed has become a living possession of man.

The next thousand years may be expected, consequently, to concentrate on the third article, namely to wrestle with the task of revealing God in society. The double concern of this epoch will be the revivification of all dead branches of the single human race, and the reinspiration of all mechanized portions of the single human life. Since the successive stages of an individual's biography and the shifting demands of industrialized society both involve us in a repeated change of roles, the breath of life must be allowed to take hold of us again and again with original renewing power, lest whole drab stretches of life and of mankind remain uninspired.[2] The history of the Church and the history of the world will have to be matched by a history of all mankind. And who is man? The being which can be inspired.

Inspired Succession—The Rebirth of Meaning

Throughout all its epochs, however, the story of salvation is one process: mission and conversion, the perpetual transmission of the life of the First Christian to new men. This process constitutes the miracle of Christianity: it is reproduction without heredity. Hereditary Christianity has existed, of course, but it is a concession to the ways of the world, and at bottom a contradiction in terms. Christianity proper stands between philosophy and the

[2] See Chapter VIII. This correlation of epochs with articles of the Creed is of course only a matter of emphasis, not of exclusion. All truths of our faith were as completely given in the coming of Christ as they will be at the last moment of time.

older religions. Philosophy exists by leisurely conversation rather than conversion; it does not require a steady reproduction of its convictions, any line of organized succession through the ages. One Platonist may live in A.D. 550, three in 1700, a dozen in 1942. Even Socrates, the saint and martyr of philosophy, founded only some esoteric and quite opposite schools. It matters little to philosophy that it has no unbroken tradition. Pagan and Jewish religions, on the other hand, did perpetuate themselves, but by heredity; they were not interested in converts. For reproduction by natural birth, Christianity substituted participation in death. It admitted a breakdown, an intermission of faith, between generations,[1] but it believed in the spark which jumps from missionary to convert, across the chasm of men's free and independent existence.

The fertility of the spirit was Jesus' problem, how to make it eternally reproductive, self-perpetuating. His answer was the Christian paradox of success through failure. As he hung on the Cross he experienced the most utter and complete failure man could undergo, yet he has become the most successful man in history, and successful in the deepest sense of inspiring an endless *succession* of followers. If he had been a success in his own lifetime, his disciples would have become mere imitators. Even if he had so much as protested on the Cross, they would have been vindictive. As it was, he voluntarily gave back his spirit into his Father's hands, and thereby it was able to rise again in his disciples, because they felt that they were now in his stead. Thus Jesus posited that the intermission of inspiration is the condition for its perpetual transmission from man to man.

He showed the same creative renunciation in other lesser ways. If he had written a book, his disciples would have thought it more important to be professors; instead, he founded the Church. He

[1] Marcus Aurelius, the "best" emperor according to philosophical standards, had been adopted by his predecessor. Pricing his philosophy above his spiritual origin, he permitted his own flesh and blood to succeed, and this ruined the Empire.

saw that, as man, he should not monopolize the powers of insight, of prophecy, of wisdom. He overcame the temptations of genius to rule the world by his sword, or his tongue, or his mind, and thereby he created a dynasty of geniuses instead. For the saints are exactly that, a dynasty of geniuses who are more concerned with the perpetual flow of spirit to all than with their private exaltation and self-expression. Jesus reversed the natural direction of genius, which strives toward self-creation; he ignited in every soul which succeeds him the eternal power to become creative in turn. By choosing a limit for his own genius, he showed that the spirit will return to others in due season as long as no one usurps it too long and too exclusively.

True spiritual succession does more than perpetuate. It spreads and deepens. The Church believed in her own existence only through the fact of mission and conversion. She came into existence at Pentecost, when the Spirit poured forth upon the apostles. When they misunderstood the new rule of succession and dreamed of a family bishopric under Jesus' brother in Jerusalem, Paul, who was unrelated to Jesus in the flesh, renewed the Church by going out to preach to the Gentiles. So after the original twelve and the five thousand of the first Church, there followed the innumerable Churches all over the earth, and after the priests laymen too received the full Spirit.

Christian conversion always involves four things: (1) breaking with an old way of living, ceasing to identify ourselves with the world as it is because it holds our body or our mind too closely—this is the meaning of Christian otherworldliness, of the self-denial Christ required from his followers; (2) discovering the power to get our second wind in life and enter into a new allegiance; (3) verifying this experience by mingling with a new group of people, formerly overlooked or even despised, who now enable us to strengthen experience into habit;[2] and (4) recogniz-

[2] America was practical Christianity as long as millions of immigrants experienced a change of allegiance from an Old World to a New World, as long as tears shed in the Old World backed up as seed the harvest of joyful experiences in the New.

ing that the power and the fellowship stem from the Founder of our faith. Christianity continues to exist only as long as new groups are constantly forming around the lasting memory of Christ. It is not enough to imitate Christ; it is also necessary to accept this example as the Founder's free and deliberate gift.

But though the meaning of mission and conversion is ever the same, they have taken on different forms with the course of time. In the Church of the first thousand years—still preserved in the East—men died to the world of false gods and demons. The supreme exemplars of this form of mission were martyrs and monks or hermits. A martyr, as the name itself indicates, was a witness; by his refusal to worship Caesar's statue or shout the equivalent of "Heil Hitler," he testified to the Living God against the idols of the market place. A hermit fought the spirits of these deities within the mind of man, the temptations to diabolical demonism. St. Anthony, for instance, wrestled with the titan and giant, the magician and sorcerer in himself.[3] In this way man's supernatural enemies were subdued; the spiritual demons of a wrong astrological and magic heaven became members of one fellowship under God. As a result, one drop of asceticism has entered the life stream of us all. Compared to the men of antiquity, we all have something of the monk in our work, sex life, diet, sports and amusements.

After martyrs and monks had driven the demons out of the sky, the second millennium fought the local powers of earth to establish one Christian world, "God's world." Crusader and Pilgrim were the representative embodiments of this new form of mission. The right of pilgrimage and crusade was the first eman-

[3] We shall never understand the miracles of the New Testament as long as we do not appreciate the demonic obsessions of the pagan mind. They were real processes in a man-made heaven. Magic and sorcery tempted individuals to play god and manipulate the cosmos at will. Jesus overcame these temptations in the wilderness. Later he performed very few miracles—only enough to show that he too could do things of this kind, thereby proving that his disdain for signs and miracles was genuine, not sour grapes.

cipation of Western men from local blood and economic ties.[4] And from that day to this, as the Church of the Reformers stepped beside the Church of the Crusaders, and Bunyan's Pilgrims sanctified the Western waves and settled the New World, ever new forms of crusade and pilgrimage have fought the inertia of home and possessions and earthly rule by sustaining a constant movement into some larger world, some Holy land or Commonwealth, "beyond." In consequence, some quality of spiritual pilgrimage has permeated life for all of us.

Each form of mission and conversion both prepares the way for, and is renewed by, its successor. Christianity had to conquer the false gods before it could conquer the false, *i.e.* divided, earth. But the spirit moves on, and old forms of life can stay alive only as long as new ones unburden them from the stagnation that comes with repetition. Toward the end of the first millennium true spiritual growth of the Church gave way to sheer quantitative expansion, as kings converted peoples by fire and sword and whole tribes accepted Christianity merely at the command of their chieftains. This meant that the next millennium had to fight the paganism which consequently remained in men and institutions that had become nominally Christian, and in lands that had lapsed again from Christianity. Hence crusades and reformations had to supplement the older forms. Today crusaders and reformers are commonplace; they have cheapened their role by dabbling with insignificant problems. They will remain with us, for no Christian way of life is wholly destroyed by time; but they cry for renewal by fresh incarnations of the spirit.

Carnality versus Incarnation

Mission and conversion will continue as long as the soul loses her path and needs regeneration, but we may expect that in the

[4] Cf. *Out of Revolution*, pp. 543 ff.

coming millennium they will occur in a more intimately human way than before. The temptations of our time do not arise from heavenly demonism or earthly provincialism. They come from soul erosion. Our life is haunted by boredom and neurosis; it is disintegrated by a mechanized society, and by a mechanizing science which makes man a mere derivation of antecedent causes. Hence we are tempted to worship crude vitality, sensationalism, life at any price.[1]

What have the traditional patterns of reformation or conversion to offer such people? There is nothing to convert them *from*. They are too weak. The cure which is most loudly and seductively preached is vitalism or tribalism, the cult of man's carnality which idolizes his origins in class, race, creed, color or nation. Perhaps we can take our cue from the phenomenal spread of this cult, for we shall have to compete with it.

Christianity always has to compete with quacks who offer easy, deceptive short cuts to salvation. The early Church, in converting the Gentiles, was rivalled by the Gnostics with alarming success. Gnostics substituted diversion of the brain for conversion of the heart; you merely thought out a cosmic system and were spared the trouble of obeying an historical Revelation. Gnostics held that truth was alive anyway and need only be known, whereas the Christian knew that it had to be lived by *him*. In the second millennium, the Crusaders had their quacks in the Vikings, who conquered quickly but did not know what to do with their Greenlands; and the Reformers were almost outdone by the Humanists for a similar reason—Luther by Erasmus, Calvin by Bacon, the model of St. Paul by that of Plato. A Platonist is an idealist; a Christian is crucified to his natural ideals, for only if he gives up his own spirit does he receive it back as with a divine inspiration

[1] Even man's lusts and fears have become respectable today because they testify to his vitality. "Vital, dynamic, powerful, stirring, stimulating, exciting, thrilling, terrific," are the medals which modern man bestows. They are really insults. To call a speaker stimulating, for instance, is a triumph of Pontius Pilate among us. It seems that the truth no longer matters.

that has to be embodied here and now. Humanists thought that life was good anyway; the Reformer knew that he himself had to make good his promises. The quacks of our time are carnalists and tribalists. They promise life eternal if you are a proletarian, or a German, or if you eat Vitamin B1. They hold that life is beautiful anyway; the Christian knows that life relapses into savagery unless we ourselves make it the incarnation of a new creative Word.

Note the sequence: Gnostics taught that life had truth without need of historic Revelation; Humanists thought that life was good without the Crucifixion; carnalists hold that life is beautiful without the Incarnation. All quacks thus use essentially the same trick, and therefore it is no wonder that tribalists are defeating humanists with their own weapons today. For four centuries the worshippers of Classical Civilization have done their best to dispense with Christianity. Clinging to their conviction that life is good without Revelation, without the Cross, they have enthroned the myth of humanity in the place of God and deserted the Christian era. My colleagues in the classics still read Xenophon instead of St. Paul, and Caesar instead of St. Augustine, with their students. Though they have next to no students of Latin and Greek; yet do they not see how funny they are. Naturally, without Christian orientation their selection of classical models appears completely arbitrary, hence impotent to defend itself against tribalists who go still further back for their models—to the cruelties of Nineveh and the dances of Bali.

We can overcome the new hordes who make vitality their god only with a sword whose steel contains no alloy of Gnosticism or Humanism. That sword must be forged by the whole man—the creature, not merely the thinker. In the sweat of our brow and the chores of industrial society we must find a place for renewing spirit, for the divine origin of man. Incarnation must supersede carnality. The Tribalist is vital at the expense of some other tribe. The Christian seeks a comprehensive incarnation of man in all his branches, through common work and suffering. Our next form of conversion must promise the birth of the great human family.

The contrast between carnality and incarnation is only a new form of the perennial dualism between worldliness and other-worldliness which lies at the heart of Christian conversion. In recent times this dualism has often been misunderstood as mere negation. Nietzsche, for example, identified Christianity with nihilism, sheer denial of life—yet he gave a secular version of the real Christian other-worldliness in his vision of super-manliness and the perpetual self-overcoming of life.

This confusion about Christianity is largely due to the persistence of pagan or childish modes of understanding the Creed. Even the customary terms, "other-worldly," "supernatural," reflect this. Thinking primarily in spatial terms, the child's mind pictures heaven as another world existing "above" this one. But as the very essence of Christianity is historical—it is the story of man's salvation—so to be a Christian is to think primarily in the language of time rather than of space, as shown by the favorite biblical phrase, "the world to come." Christianity created true future, as we have seen. Christian other-worldliness actually consists of "the powers of the world to come" (Heb. 6:5) breaking in upon the world as it has already come to be.

In the same way, the supernatural should not be thought of as a magical force somehow competing with electricity or gravitation in the world of space, but as the power to transcend the past by stepping into an open future. Nature moves in recurrent cycles and downward trends; she is not free to say No and rise above her entropy and inertia. But man is the animal who is more than nature because he can go against his nature: *Ecce homo.* His heart can arrest social habits and physical causes as they impinge upon human life; it can make the future grow by taking the first step into it. Pagans proceed on precedent, but Christians remain unpredictable: they *pre*cede.

Jesus came not to negate life but to give it more abundantly. Christianity is not a decadent worship of death for its own sake, but the discovery that including death within life is the secret of the fullest life.[2] Even the extremest types of Christian other-worldliness, ascetic hermits and monks, have lived this truth. By giving up a part of the world before they died bodily, they placed death in the middle of life as an encouragement. They proved that death is an essential element of living, in fact its sharpest ingredient. But there are more forms of other-worldliness as well.[3] Any father, manager, or teacher has to practice resignation and let the young learn by doing things he could do better himself; for he knows that one day he must die and they must take his place. The New Testament is full of such heroic resignation; Jesus voluntarily forewent saying many truths that the second or third generation needed to discover for themselves. All such acts from the beyond stem not from our instinct of life but from our wisdom of death. Man as an animal organism lives forward from birth toward death, but, as a soul who knows beforehand that he will die, he molds his life looking backward from its end.

Perhaps another reason why the older forms of other-worldliness have been misunderstood is that new forms are needed today. As man has been progressively de-naturalized by two thousand years of Christianity, less sharp and obvious total contrasts are required. The first Christians confronted an utterly non-Christian world; only by holding themselves aloof from it and predicting its speedy cataclysmic end could they make their own message effective. So saints and martyrs emigrated *from* this world altogether. In the second millennium, pilgrims and crusaders travelled *through* a world that already was or had been partly Christian but needed to be reconquered, reformed, lifted beyond tribal and local ties. In the third epoch, beginning today, Christians must immigrate *into* our workaday world, there to incarnate the spirit

[2] Cf. *Das Alter der Kirche,* I, 83–91.

[3] Cf. the author's *Soziologie,* Berlin, 1925, pp. 197 ff.

in unpredictable forms. For the daily life of men has become so unnatural, so un-naive and worried and splintered and tortured, and at the same time so mixed with bits and fragments of by-gone Christian times, that the old ways of contrasting worldly and unworldly life are inappropriate. It is unnecessary to deny this world: chaos denies itself. Modern man is crucified already. The salvation he needs is inspiration for his daily toil and leisure. For us the difference between worldliness and other-worldliness is that between the finite forms already created by the past and the infinite breath of the spirit which blows in upon us from the open future. The other world is in this world as man's destiny, man's meaning.

Christianity Incognito

Finding Christian and pagan, believer and unbeliever, no longer separate from each other as at first, but side by side within every soul, we are challenged to achieve a further innovation in the evolution of Christianity. No one can claim to be one hundred per cent Christian or one hundred per cent pagan. Convert and converter will have to live on united in one and the same person, like the two movements of our respiration, like a constant dying and coming to life again of our faith.

Under such circumstances we shall have to admit that human souls are incalculable in their various needs, and the forms of conversion will be correspondingly varied. We can see this most strikingly in the fact that several clergymen of deep spiritual insight are already realizing that some persons actually need to be converted *from* the Church. A friend of mine had a woman in his parish who busied herself so much with reading theology and converting people, and became so immersed in religious activities generally, that she made a nuisance of herself. One day he had a serious talk with her and told her that religion had become a cancer in her system. "Cut it out!" he suddenly shouted. She was dumfounded, of course, but obeyed his orders, left the Church, secularized her life completely, and became an enterprising horsewoman who was liked everywhere. My friend explained that as long as she had used one single traditionally religious term, it turned in her mouth into a weapon of criticism or attack against her neighbors; she found peace by weeding out the whole Church vocabulary. Organized religion had to be reduced to a minimum with her so as to re-evoke religion in her. And as she bowed to the minister's authority, he acted for the living Church, in this case, which has many mansions.

Such illustrations could be multiplied. That we can understand conversions and tendencies away from us is a new event in the history of Christianity. It shows that our world is felt to be a Christian, unified world far beyond the pale of official Christianity; my friend would not have sent his parishioner out of the Church if that had meant condemning her to utter paganism or Judaism. Seeds of Christianity are now germinating in secular forms of life as much as in church pews, and some souls will need to step away from the light of full Christian consciousness and live at the periphery where only the indirect results of Christianity surround them. In renouncing noisy confessionalism they may add new professions of faith.

This means that we must sacrifice our denominational labels. Since believer and unbeliever are inside each of us, even the name of pagan or Christian runs the risk of excluding a soul that is really God's, or including the pagan that dwells in our own breast. But Christianity has always meant sacrifice. The early Church demanded that all men give up their private, clannish or national names on entering the Church, for the love of Christ: his was the only name that could be mentioned inside the Church for the first thousand years; everything was done in his Name alone. The power of names has become so weak today that we can scarcely realize with what awe men sacrificed their identity as Gentiles to become the people of his Name. A new sacrifice was made in the Church of the Reformation: here men abandoned the certainties of visible cathedrals and relics and the sacral order of priesthood; in the dark night of a secular world they threw themselves upon faith in God.

Today we are called on to sacrifice the pride of being certain that we are Christians at all. "I hope to believe," is all that the most orthodox may stammer in the perplexity and confusion of a machine-age society. So the love of Christ and faith in God must be strengthened today by hope for the Spirit.

A third Christianity, the Christianity of Hope, is beginning with what has rightly been called the Good Friday of Christianity. Good Friday is the very center of our faith, but modern churches, drunk with "civilization" and feeling safe and smug, failed to evolve their own Good Friday voluntarily: their conventional preaching against selfishness spoke less eloquently than their selfish actions as vested interests. So we are surrounded today by the horrors of an actual Good Friday in Europe and Russia, where Christianity is denied or cynically manipulated. Hence our reasonable service must be to initiate the faithless masses into a new hope, for hope is our natural point of contact with them. Faith may be gone; hope gives us time to wait for faith's return. Unless people hope, they will not be patient enough to listen.

Though I believe that the Church is a divine creation and that the Athanasian Creed is true, I also believe that in the future, Church and Creed can be given a new lease on life only by services that are nameless or incognito. The inspirations of the Holy Spirit will not remain inside the walls of the visible or preaching Church. A third form, the listening Church, will have to unburden the older modes of worship by assembling the faithful to live out their hopes through working and suffering together in unlabelled, undenominational groups, thereby to wait and listen for the inbreak of a new consolation which shall redeem modern life from its curse of disintegration and mechanization. By this penance we may hope to rescue our hymns and Creeds and historic Churches from destruction in times to come. Christianity itself may rise from the dead if it now discards its own self-centeredness.

The Death and Resurrection of the Word

The wearing out of the old names, the old words, the old language, is the most widely and deeply felt fact in the crisis through which Christianity is passing, and that is why we must give them up today. A great Swiss Jesuit writer has even gone so far as to declare, "The word 'God' is so spent that we do not intend to haggle with Nietzsche on its behalf."[1] That would be nameless Christianity indeed.

The question of Christian language is not a superficial matter of propaganda techniques. Christianity holds that the Word is man's matrix.[2] We rightly speak of our "mother tongue" rather than our "mother's tongue," for language itself is maternal, the womb of time in which man has been created and is constantly being re-created: nearly every word we use has a history running back thousands of years, yet all genuine speech remakes both listener and speaker—a fact which propagandists ignore, thinking that they can catch men without being caught themselves. Idealism, materialism, realism are hopelessly embarrassed by the place of language in man's creation; they hate it because it makes our mind itself into a creature. But theology begins neither with things nor ideas but with the Word: Holy, Holy, Holy, and the voices that judge, pray, sing, name, bless and curse. The account of creation tells how God brought order into the "waste and void" through speech: "And God said, Let there be light . . ." All

[1] Hans Urs von Balthasar, *Die Apokalypse der Deutschen Seele,* 3 vols., Salzburg and Leipzig, 1939, II, p. 379. Also see above pp. 7–10.

[2] It is impossible to give more on this point in this book. I know that this is inadequate and can only say apologetically that a book of considerably greater length than this one, on the origins of language and its restoration by the Word, is awaiting publication; although I am told that it is impossible to publish it, I have not given up hope.

things were made by the Word, and came out of it. In the beginning there was neither mind nor matter. In the beginning was the Word. St. John was properly the first Christian theologian because he was overwhelmed by the spokenness of all meaningful happening.

The language of the secular mind is either universal and abstract, like mathematics, or concrete and particular, like Southern dialect. "Two times two is four" is for all men, but it is abstract: "Maryland, my Maryland" is concrete but not for all men. But the language of the Christian soul is at the same time universal, unifying, and yet personal, bestowing concrete singleness of purpose on speaker and listener.[3] The soul awakes only when it is addressed in a language which combines universal validity and the concreteness of a here-and-now situation. All the sayings of Jesus were quite simple, but they became important forever because they were spoken at the right moment, "when the time was fulfilled." He died for all men, but he did it here and now, wholeheartedly, with words spoken to his neighbor for this and no other occasion.

It was Jesus' mission to restore the relation of word and act on all fronts of life. His commands, his lyrics, his concise formulations of natural laws, are perfect examples of the different moods in which reality can be expressed. Observe, above all, his last words: "It is finished." He does not make speeches from the Cross, as modern political martyrs have done. He does not go on record with a statement for the papers. Here is no mind observing matter, no soul subjectively seeking another soul, nor yet a gospel being preached. Something usually not even mentioned is the meaning of this sentence: that words are acts, and that these acts are phases of the life process itself. In completing its course, life

[3] If this is to some extent reminiscent of Hegel, it is because Hegel in turn developed his philosophy out of a study of Christian history. As an idealist, however, Hegel completely reversed the Christian meaning of concreteness; God is not found inside our minds or ideas; He speaks to us through the other fellow we try to help. The creative energies of Faith, Hope, and Love are not properties *of* minds but bonds ***between*** men.

is leading finally to utterance. "It is finished" is the last part of the crucifixion. That Jesus, after complete despair, can take up the thread of human history as it has run through Abraham, Moses and the Prophets, and recognize his own death as the historical sequence of the life of the race—this distinguishes his end from that of his two neighbors. Only this tiny sentence of three words makes the event his own experience.

Language cannot be kept alive on ice or in dictionaries. The law of deterioration from inspiration to routine holds for speech as for other phases of life. Every time we speak we either renew or cheapen the words we use. Hence Christian language can be abused like any other, and we hear it abused today by "Christian" fascists, communists, pacifists and snobs. Looking back into the past, we can see that whole streams of Christian language have cooled off into geological stratifications. The languages of saints and martyrs, crusaders and pilgrims, no longer move men's hearts. Neither the ritual of the mass—that flawless creation of the first millennium—nor the sublime language of Canaan in the Protestant Bible suffice to create peace between men today. Yet we also see that when the bread of life has gone stale, it has been refreshed again and again by a new transubstantiation. These transformations of living speech-in-action are the real sacrament of the Spirit, and if we walk humbly under our bankruptcy today, we may hope to hear the Word spoken once more.

The death and resurrection of the Word, the intermittence of the Christian faith, the ebb and renewed flow of its life, must not blind us to the essential unity of the story of salvation. The tree of everlasting life can grow only through successive generations of men reaching their hands to each other in one spirit across the ages. And *each generation has to act differently precisely in order to represent the same thing*. Only so can each become a full partner in the process of Making Man; only so can life be as authentic in the last age as in the first.

In the past century, historical scholarship forgot this basic truth, and therefore to this day it is the learned fashion to neglect the fundamental unanimity of Christians through the centuries, and to concentrate instead on isolating the many layers of its historical expression.[4] Modern men have thought it a crime for the Church to have changed during her two thousand years. St. Paul was called the first deserter;[5] then came the bishops, and on it went from corruption to corruption until, by 1789, rationalists considered the Church completely superfluous.

Yet the role of the Church has been specific, tangible and perpetual, for all that. The meaning of the Christian era is that the time of divided loyalties is coming to an end and the reunion of mankind has begun. In every epoch after Christ another part of creation is finding its home in lasting unity.

[4] A picture of the great unity of the Church during the first three generations is drawn by Lord Charnwood in his charming *According to Saint John*, Boston, 1925. Equally impressive in this respect, E. C. Hoskyns and F. N. Davey, *The Riddle of the New Testament*, New York, 1931.

[5] The same essentially unhistoric method has been applied to Jesus himself, and has led to such fatal antitheses as Life vs. Teachings, "the religion of Jesus" vs. "the religion about Jesus," etc. But if we perceive that the law of unanimity-through-difference applies also to the successive stages of an individual man's life, we no longer try to crucify Jesus on our Procrustean conceptual systems, but see that he lived through a rhythmic succession of "stations"—his "natural" early life as an obedient son, his period of spiritual vision, which we see reflected in his teachings like the Sermon on the Mount, and finally his return from vision to enact his Public Office as Christ. Further, each of these stations has its own appropriate ethic which obviously cannot be valid for the others. The child Jesus could not have fulfilled his duties to his parents if he had practiced the Sermon on the Mount; neither could the later Jesus have fulfilled his mission unless, when the time came, he had practiced yet a third mode of life—the life required of all political efficacy: commanding obedience, being silent at times and angry at times, taking care for the morrow, binding and loosing. We can see also that Jesus himself was always a step ahead of his followers, and that therefore a full understanding of what he had done in his last station could only come to a later generation. In this light we can understand that St. Paul, far from being a traitor to the spirit of Christ, was a true successor. By Hans Ehrenberg, it has been said that Paul lived what Jesus taught, but taught what Jesus lived: that is true specifically for what Jesus lived in his last station, namely crucifixion and resurrection. See further *Das Alter der Kirche*, I, 111–140.

PART THREE: THE BODY OF OUR ERA:

BACKWARD, FORWARD, NOW.

"Quam multi jam dies nostri et patrum nostrorum per hodiernum tuum transierunt."—Augustinus.

"How many of our and our fathers' days have already passed through Thine 'Today.' "

Transition

By now, the practical man may impatiently ask: what can we do? Some of the experiences which might come to him—for this is the Christian way of "doing"—he finds in our last chapter; it deals with our present-day task. But first the reader may have to be shown in Chapters six and seven the frame of reference within which we find ourselves. The child of nature reforms the world blindly. We must ask which is the so-called present time in which we can cooperate? It would be a common time for the reader and myself only if we looked at the same past and the same future. Whether we like it or not, whole centuries of Church history march with us as mortgages. The Church has made enemies. On the other hand, whole continents like Asia wait for us in the future. A Christian forfeits his privilege of revealed truth unless he has a relation to past as well as future. With regard to the future, this peculiar relation should be obvious: a Christian who does not make converts is no Christian. We cannot reform the world except by begetting children of our faith. It is less obvious that the chains of the Christian past are real, too. When Christians act, they cannot simply forget the sins of the past. We keep fellowship with the Church "even though she may have made a mess of things." Our present state, therefore, lies between our group loyalty with the Church, and our brothers and sisters who have a right to hear the glad tidings from us. Lest we stay in the individualistic cloud of our private faith, we must do two things: we must identify ourselves with the sins of the Church; and we must become sensitive to the existence of the non-Christian humanity. This is the undertaking of Chapters six and seven.

Chapter six brings to trial the worst crimes of which the Church might be accused: lack of faith and lack of charity. We shall see that we are all molded by these sins, in our own affirmed character as Westerners. It may sound strange, yet we might say that as Westerners, we rely on these sins. If, however, even these sins of the past can be shown to have borne unexpected fruits, our faith in the era under the Cross should be strengthened. For this would mean that even the Church's failures were not lost; though condemned they were at the same time or later at least, pardoned and put to good use by God. This we may learn from the past, and before we identify ourselves with this past, we shall not know to what extent we ourselves are free to act. These sins determine our amount of freedom, and they explain our duty to collaborate with non-Christians.

Chapter seven opens up the vast future. Beyond the boundaries of existing denominational Christianity with its familiar jurisdictions, the work must proceed. And the Far East presents us most distinctly with a world lost for denominational distinctions within our faith. We stand in need of a meeting with this non-Christian reality because our own situation is unsettled. We have seen that our time bears the features of a mere interim of pragmatic expediency. By including non-Christian elements in the future of our era at this very moment, our true direction may be regained. By excluding the non-Christian world, we would miss our future.

Chapter six says that the worst attacks on our faith, the failures of organized Christianity themselves, may be made to strengthen our faith. Chapter seven says that the most unsurmountable obstacles of our hopes, the opposing religions of the East, can be used to rekindle them. Thus, our own daily task gains perspective.

Unless we draw new strength from failure itself and from obstacles, we shall fail to find the answer to the impatient, "What shall we do?" Curious minds ask arbitrarily any question without ever questioning their own right to ask or their own power to understand and to enact the answer. Faith makes us strong enough to face the whole question and it mobilizes all our resources for our response. The response demanded from us will take new power; to experience anything worthwhile in our own trite and familiar environment is next to impossible. But the impossible must happen. These things near home must come to impress us as being not trite or settled long ago.

The Creation of Future was our riddle, all along. On this Creation of Future, our faith depends. The last chapter (eight) will be the touchstone because it must speak of the things near home, American education, American way of Life, American politics. Before we may be sure that our Creation of Future is more than an academic discussion, the common things near home must regain their splendor. And when do old things regain their lustre? When do facts become interesting? When do words recover their meaning? When they again appear as things to come, as acts to be done, as names to be invoked; when everything, so to speak, has ceased to exist because we feel that our own infinite insistence alone can give it a new lease on life.

VI

O FORTUNATE GUILT! OR LOOKING BACK ON THE CHURCH

Mechanism or Frailty?—The Quadrilateral: Chalcedon, Frankfurt, Florence, Stockholm—First Picture: Lack of Faith—Second Picture: Lack of Charity—Third Picture: The Renaissance of the Human Mind—Fourth Picture: The Readmission of Economics—Church History

Mechanism or Frailty?

The Church has not led a happy life. But life she always had. She had something to live for, heart and soul. This truism I must write down at the start. For, most people think today that all organizations of size, states, corporations, labor unions, all the tremendous powers of our world, are rational, legal, and mechanical and we are asked to enter even bigger organizations: Union Now, or the Classless Society, or the Union of all the Churches, or a fusion of all world religions. They all are logical and systematical. And in their center, there stands a typewriter. However, the only group which is really exciting at any minute and full of surprises because it is fully alive also is perfectly unsystematic, irrational, antilogical, and the poorest organization on earth; it has no bylaws, no annual meeting, and all the attempts by home economists to prescribe for it a regular budget break-down. I mean of course, the family. Compared to its colorful folly, the plans now in the forefront of discussion excel in a distinct paleness. These large organizations would die from mere boredom after twenty-four hours if they were as perfect as their supporters foresee them. When I anticipate the ennui of these schemes, I understand better the sigh of the little woman: "Better a bit of unhappiness than no husband at all." In the center of the family, we do not find a typewriter, but a bed and a stove.

The good people who fill our minds with abstract blueprints honestly believe that nothing more exciting than their legal forms can be expected to grow in the field of social existence. The family in its unquenchable illogicality perturbs them. Eugenists, public educators, recommend artificial conception, state education, medical supervision of weddings, etc. etc. The modern mind is embarrassed by the remnants of the family as an organism in an era of mere organization. The only people to whom our planners accord some residue of zest and fancy are the planners themselves. They may sacrifice a fortune to their hobby plan; the world may call them crazy; the Dies Committee may investigate them. But these planners live passionately just the same, in pursuit of their vision.

They are right in their passion and their systematic plans must, for that reason, be wrong. To live means to be vulnerable and he who must remain vulnerable at any moment cannot expect to be secure and happy in the ordinary sense. Unless he is willing to call his wounds happiness, he must choose between living frailty and tin-canned orderliness.

For this reason, the Church has no more a typewriter at its center than does the family. Her center is an altar. By this, she has remained interesting and alive; *she has admitted her wounds.* In no other way could she prove her aliveness. And a biologist, Rudolf Ehrenberg, for the same reason has defined life as the process by which a corpse is produced as the accomplished fact of a life's career. He who lives can die. A "system" which never lived may linger on forever.

The sloughing off of old stages and the insistence on new ones distinguishes life from mechanism. Even the modest term "existence" literally means a getting out from one form and into another. The weak embryo takes an infinite number of changes in his stride. To live means to do something about assimilating external life and excreting. Even more does it mean a suspense between an old and a new form of existence. Life is never contained in one form but in the slope from the old which is doomed to a new which triumphs over death. Our race long ago conceived of the fact that the threat of death preceded the urge for life. For, while a child may think that its birth precedes its death, its parents should know better. Their love for each other came as the first signal of their individual transiency; when a woman and a man fall in love, they actually both make ready, qua individuals, to abandon ship. And love allows them to make room for the best of their own body outside of themselves and beyond themselves. Any two somebodies who get married acknowledge that as individuals they are mortal, and they open an exit to life, beyond their two corpses.

Of this law of all life, the Church is no exception. Boredom is not the characteristic of Church history. Her struggles follow each other in breathless sequence. The fire on her altar burns and cleanses, from generation to generation.

At present, the Eastern Churches have gone over to the attack. The Orthodox Church, in Russia, the Ukraine, Ruthenia, Rumania, Servia, and even in Greece and Turkey and in the United States of America, advances against the West. Rome as well as Geneva and Wittenberg, or Nonconformism, is weakened. We shall hear strange reproaches from the Eastern Patriarchs against the whole of Western Christendom, in these next years.[1]

What a revolution this is. After the First World War, the Christians of the West tried to come to the rescue of the Oriental

[1] "The Orthodox Church proclaims her curse over the whole of the Occident, Rome as well as the Churches of the Reformation. She shakes the foundation on which both are established, the permanent rivalry of Church and State." This prophecy is developed at length in my *Die Hochzeit des Kriegs und der Revolution,* Würzburg, 1920, pp. 147 ff.

Churches from Ethiopia to Moscow; an ecumenic movement arose. This process may soon be reversed. The Eastern Churches have learned their lesson from the World Revolution of the last forty years while we continue to live in our pre-world war patterns of thought. Who, then, is a Christian? And where, then, is the Church?

For our complacency the new clash comes as a distinct shock. The museum piece "Eastern Church" seemed petrified. If anybody, forty years ago, had told us that soon Rome would not be attacked by modernists or atheists but by the Greek Orthodox, we would have laughed. Nearly always the events of today which we ridicule are the serious events of tomorrow. The attack of the Greeks is serious. And in retrospect, the reader may find it difficult to understand why we should have laughed, ever.

For, one permanent feature of Church history is its jumpiness from one direction of the compass to the opposite. The Church stands in a crucial position and the wind that swells her sail may blow from anywhere at any moment.

The Quadrilateral: Chalcedon, Frankfurt, Florence, Stockholm

The reality of this Cross may be perceived in four pictures of the Church. Like the four gospels, these four pictures form a quadrilateral and convey one truth. As four elements of one truth, we shall depict them. The pictures "occurred" centuries apart, in 450, 850, 1440, 1925. But they illuminate each other in one interaction.

In these pictures, we see the Church—and that is our own life written large—in a crucial situation. Her own body was in process of being crucified. Christians were and are divided today and this we take for granted as far as Protestants and Roman Catholics go. However, the rift goes deeper in the form of the schism between East and West; it transfixes the body of the Church.

You might think of the schism as a textbook question in the history department. But then this war is fatal proof that via the schism you and I very personally are in the grips of the Cross. Here are some facts.

A war has been fought between Russia and the country of Hitler (Germany) and Poland and the papacy. And we were in this conflict. Atheism, Marxism, Racism, Materialism, German idealism, were battle cries in this war.

And as to the background of the actual fighting, who were the most provoking Christians of the nineteenth century? Was it not Leo Tolstoi, and the author of the *Brothers Karamasoff* and *The Great Inquisitor,* Fyodor Dostoyevsky? And was it not the Russian Solovyev who wrote *The Antichrist* in 1890, and dreamed of the reunion of East and West more fervently than even Archbishop Söderblom of Sweden? [1] Was it not Berdyaev, the Eastern Christian, who convinced many Westerners of the New Middle Ages?

We see from these few examples that the Russians have contributed more vehement warriors for and against the Cross during the last one hundred years than any other group. This schismatic branch of the Church was in the thick of the fight. Also, the enemies who persecuted the Eastern Church were more vehement. There was Czarism as well as Bolshevism, with tyrannies of one sort or another. In other words, we are denominationally separated from the areas of the Eastern Orthodox Church, but we receive some of our own battle cries and slogans and "party lines" from these same areas. We can understand Tolstoy and Dostoyevsky and Lenin because they argue for and against the Cross. Can it be made clearer that, though separated, our and their branches of the Church still are interdependent? Yes, it can be made clearer

[1] As it is difficult to find Solovyev's prophecy in English it gives me pleasure to report that it is easily accessible now in a volume where the reader will hardly look for it, in Walter Lowrie's delightful, *SS. Peter and Paul in Rome,* Oxford University Press, 1940, pp. 119–139. For further bibliography see Peter P. Zouboff, *Solovyev on Godmanhood,* Int. University Press, 1945, pp. 227–233.

by a comparison with Japan. The Shinto religion of Japan has no interest for our own future. We know that it has to go if the peace shall end well for us. No; we are only transfixed by the sword which entered the Church through the schism. The samurai sword has threatened us physically, but cannot shake us internally.

But the fact that our own discussion is now carried on between "Eastern" Christians and their idealistic and materialistic opponents, and not between Western minds, of the Roman or Geneva faith, seems providential. For now, the whole Christian position becomes visible as being one and the same against all natural minds. And nobody can say that this or that is merely papal or Lutheran or Puritan or sectarian.

The schism, at this moment, unites the Christians more than it separates them. It becomes a part of every Christian's real existence in the world. That he is a member of one denomination is one thing, that he is a member of Christendom at large is of at least the same momentum. And the schism between East and West by its depth restores the full size of the decision between the Cross and the non-crucial mentalities; compared to the schism, the childishness and small stature of denominational quarrels is too obvious. And a Christian may become a full-grown adult again instead of a Sunday school boy by identifying himself with his schismatic brothers. *Unless he can do this, he has not grown up.*

For this reason the schism should be understood. It can hardly have been for a mean or petty reason that the Church was rent. Perhaps, life itself, because it had to be alive, needed this wound? Stoics may boast of their invulnerability. An honest man should find in his vulnerability his best claim to life.

More than four hundred years had elapsed before the schism inside the Church became a theological fact. These events occurred in about 450 and 850. But they represent acts which you and I probably would repeat today. In the review of the great scenes by which the schism was enacted in the first millennium, the reader may not expect any historical detail. We shall concentrate on two observations which alone matter to us: first, the East missed out in faith against the West and thereby prepared Bolshevism at home; later, the West missed out in charity; and this lack of charity had an equally far-reaching effect on the Western World. When the West, on the eve of the Renaissance, cherished hopes to regain the obedience of the Orthodox Church, these hopes were deceived; not the Greek Churches but Greek antiquity, Plato and Humanism, were harvested from this attempt. Finally, when the Churches of the West and the Patriarchs of the East met, first in 1925 and later in other ecumenic meetings, under the pressure of world-wide catastrophes, the Church of Rome was absent. A second time, unity was not achieved, but the Great Society of common work was advanced by this change of mind of the Churches.

In other words, the four pictures sketched here are not four separate historical events; in our context where the Church stands for the human soul written large, each scene is one fourth of one whole. And the relation of actions separated by many centuries is the stupendous fact which may introduce us to our own life story within our short-lived cycle of seventy years.

Twice, the Church was wounded by lack of faith and charity; twice she tried to heal the wound led by rational, idealistic as well as material, motives. Each time the schism remained. And the success since it was willed rationally benefited not the Church but movements outside the Church. The breach of faith in 451 and the lack of charity in 868 could not be undone by the prudence of later generations. But they could be forgiven.

In our own lives our sins cannot be undone but they can be forgiven. And this is something very different. But I always marvel that this central experience of the guilt which may be turned into a blessing is usually understood as though by some mechanism that which we have done could be treated as though it had not happened. It has happened. The schism did happen. If it could be undone, man could unmake creation. Many good people in their idealism or in their overestimation of power politics think that the reunion of the Churches is right at hand. But is this important? Anybody whose eyes have been opened to the fact that life depends on dying, knows that the resurrection has its severe laws. A wounded heart does not recover in the spiritual world without a change in the visible world. Resurrection never does enthrone the spirit in the same place where it left one body, as though nothing had happened. Something has happened; death has intervened. When I experienced an infinitesimal fraction of resurrection, I learned to my amazement how severe the law was which made it impossible for me to continue among the same people in the same place. It was not that they were not willing to understand. After a while, they saw what had happened and that I had preferred to save the institution by diverting their hatred of their new duties towards me. But that meant that the price which we had paid, was paid. My return remained impossible.

This experience under the microscope of individual life corresponds to the experience of the Eastern and Western Church. They could not simply restore the situation of before 451 and 868. However, they well may hope that the cleavage was forgiven to the extent that some greater unity was achieved, *outside their own disunion*. And so it is indeed. The first reunion, which did not unite the Churches, unified the natural ideas in the mind of man. The second attempt to reunion seems to have power to bring about material unity of our economic organization.

The more one studies the schism, the more life seems to have spread from this wound of the Church into the world at large.

First Picture: Lack of Faith

The Eastern Church has not made history like Rome, Wittenberg, and Geneva. She has triumphed over history like the angels.

And in the monasteries on Mount Athos, from 900 to 1940 (until Hitler came) time stood still and heaven was lived on earth. The moving force of history was excluded: no female, not even hens, were admitted.

Meanwhile, the Western Church tried not to triumph over history but to survive history as suffering mortals. Westerners are repelled by a lack of earthly fight and realization in Orthodox Christendom. How did the Eastern Church become an antic?

By a lack of faith. She insisted on remaining dependent on a part of the pre-Christian order of antiquity. Jealousy provoked the Greeks to insist on the administrative order of the Roman Empire of the Caesars. In Canon 28 of the Council of Chalcedon, A.D. 451, a canon rejected by Rome, the Eastern Church admitted that the Church of St. Peter in Rome was the first Church but added that this order came to pass *because Rome was the capital of the Empire* in the days of Peter. In the meantime, a new capital of the Empire had been established in Constantinople; hence the implications of this Canon 28 for the rights of the New Rome were manifest. If it was true, the Churches took their order from Caesar's empire. The reader is perhaps accustomed to explain by personal motives all history, and here the rivalry of the new capital is manifest. Of course, there would be no history without these personal motives; let us take them for granted. But they never "explain" history because these motives do not change; they are always at work.

The act of Chalcedon was incisive not because of the eternal pettiness of rivalry but because of the argument used. *For the first time in the history of the Church* a prominent feature of its sacred order, the Primacy of Rome, was based *on an external cause.* The whole claim of the Church had been that she was a wholly new creature, not made by the organizational will of men but God-born. For this reason, Jesus had given up his own body and his spirit, lest anything pre-Christian, preceding him, entered the new creature. He had placed himself between the past and the future, and nothing of the man Jesus in the flesh had been allowed to enter the new order of his second body, the Church. People who speak of his sacrifice usually do not understand this. He interposed his whole life, from beginning to end, and not just his last day, between the past and the future so that nothing of his own life was allowed to be carried over. His own whole life was used up in the house cleansing for the new life of the Church, and Paul emphatically distinguished between Jesus' life in the flesh as a part of the old aeon and of the risen Christ as the first inhabitant of the new. It seems next to impossible today to get this proclaimed meaning of his sacrifice across: not the fact that he performed miracles or taught or prophesied, but the astounding feat that he gave up all these powers enabled him to found the next era. In A.D. 451 this secret of his success was jeopardized. The East has never recovered from this defiling argumentation. They remained under the shadow of the Caesars. This branch of the Church longed to keep its casual nexus with a pre-Christian world. But the true Church breaks causation. Every member of the Church supposedly has experienced an act of supreme freedom, an act of breaking away, of breaking the chains of causation. And that Jesus totally freed himself of the old order of things, this alone empowered him to "breathe the spirit" upon the second creation (Jn. 20:22) of man.

The argument of the East in Chalcedon threw the Church back into this very field of force from which she promised redemption.

To this day, the Christian East hovers over the moment of transition from antiquity to our era because one too-material element of antiquity was allowed to enter the bloodstream of the new creation in the East, while the West expelled it from its system. Ever since, the East was weakened against the tyrant's meddling with the Church, while the West was tempted in the opposite direction, *i.e.* to take away from the "Caesars" all dignity. The Roman Popes could see Emperors kiss their foot or hold their stirrup, while the Patriarch of Moscow will write letters to Stalin which smack of servility.

Since the Roman Empire had preceded the birth of the Church, it was as though the Greeks tried to keep the swaddling clothes of the first centuries in perpetuity. They put part of their faith not in the unity achieved by Peter and Paul and the other martyrs, but in that unity which the mere surroundings of the Greek-Egypto-Roman Empire offered. They held that Unity was not completely owed to the spirit of the Church but to environmental factors which in part were pre-Christian. To such an alloy, certainly no new era could be ascribed. Our example of Chalcedon could be supplemented by many other features of the Eastern Church in which the emergence from the pre-Christian world is clearly petrified; for instance the Greek tragedy and the Egyptian economy are still visible behind the ecclesiastical forms. For brevity's sake, we omit them. However, the reader finds in his own day exactly the same problem on hand. Any social group must decide one day which the ultimate basis of its unity shall be. The United Nations and the United States are faced with the same discernment between swaddling-clothes unity or inner unity.

The unity embodied in the Church was not the sort of unity of which the modern mind first thinks—that of a legal corporation, or an organization with central headquarters. It was a unity of inspiration, the power to reach conclusions and act together in inspired moments. Now the power to commune when the Body of Christ is in danger—to achieve unity in action, under the inspiration of the Spirit—is the essence of any belief in the Head of this Body, Christ. Such power is as essential a daily proof of his resurrection as the event of Easter itself. So East and West agreed, in the first millennium, that the "act-ual" communion of all who had given over their souls to Christ was identical with the existence of Christianity.

The most solemn occasions of Christian communion were the "ecumenic," i.e. universal, Church councils, like the great Council of Nicaea which met in A.D. 325. The councils were ecumenic because delegates were invited from every Church in Christendom, and the acts of a council were correspondingly binding for all. The first place at any council was occupied by the Bishop of Rome, as the successor of St. Peter. No conclusion of a Council was valid unless approved by the delegation from Rome. The Patriarch of Constantinople had to be in communion with Rome if he was to be considered orthodox, and the Eastern Emperor sent for the Pope more than once because Greeks deemed this communion essential.

But as the New Rome of the East, Constantinople, began to rival the Italian City, the Eastern Churches began to chafe at the Primacy of Rome, and the matter came to a head at the Council of Chalcedon in A.D. 451. The Greeks did not deny Rome's Primacy directly; instead, they whittled away at its origin. The Greeks implied that Rome owed her rank not to St. Peter's administration and martyrdom but to the fact that in his days Rome had been the capital of the Empire. This whittling away reminds one of modern science, which also reduces every event to an influence, an origin, a motive preceding it as its "cause." If everything had a sufficient cause in the past, obviously freedom and newness would both be misnomers, and the vicious circle of cause and effect would go on for ever and for ever in an enslaved natural world. Since the Church is the unified soul of Man in as far as he is capable of freedom, the modern reader will understand that his own case was argued in Chalcedon. All our acts have a dual aspect, one of freedom, one of causation. The world sees that I marry this girl *"because"*; but I must say to myself that she accepts me *"despite."* Unless a man knows of both interpretations of his acts, he cannot be successfully married. Similarly, St. Peter went to Rome because the Empire had its center on the Capitoline Hill; however, he also braved Rome despite the fact that it was the most dangerous place to tackle. His act made epoch not because of his mixed motives but because he braved the "reasons" which should have *dissuaded* him. Any lawyer knows that precedents are not established by motives but by decisions. Peter's decision created a

Second New Rome. This is shown by the fact that both he and Paul were martyred, and have churches built in their memory, outside the precinct of Caesar's Rome—just as most medieval cathedrals stand outside the ancient pagan precincts of their towns. The Capitoline Hill *had been the center of the Empire,*[1] but Peter was put to death in the Vatican gardens. So the Roman Church was not heir to Imperial Rome but rose against it, in the catacombs outside its walls. When Paul and Peter offered their lives for converting the Romans, they acted in a free response of love, not in a Freudian compulsory reaction to the stimulus, "Roman Empire." To use the term "cause" for Roma as the capital attracting them, and the term "effect," for their sacrifice of life, is insipid.

The sequel to the Council of Chalcedon is an example of the way in which a lack of faith comes back upon ourselves. When the Greeks alleged a legal or natural "reason" for the Primacy of Rome's Church as against the gracious free gift of the apostles, they intended to inherit Rome's rights in the Church or over the Church; for, was not Constantinople the New Rome? And was not the new capital the heiress of the old in matters of Church as well as of State? The final result of this manoeuvre was precisely opposite: from then on, any new capital of any State could turn against Constantinople with the same argument. And this was what happened: Athens, Bukarest, Sofia, Belgrade, claimed independent heads for their Churches on the basis of Canon 28. And they got them. The Eastern Orthodox Church is split into some seventeen Churches today; they all follow national frontiers of purely worldly origin. Rome's Church did not have to imitate these secular events.[2]

[1] . . . *"dum Capitolium scandet cum tacita virgine pontifex."* Horace, *Odes,* III, 30.

[2] The first sentence of the great Gregory VII's classical exposition of the Papacy's rights reads like a refutation of all national theory of the Church: "The Church of Rome was founded by God alone" (supplement: not by an act of politics). For the details see *Die Europaeischen Revolutionen,* Jena, 1931, 132 ff.

Moreover the attitude of Rome enabled the Western Church to be the hibernating larva of civilization when the Roman Empire fell. While the Eastern Church became stagnant, perpetuating the fourth century forever, the Roman Church made ready to march into the future as the Church Militant, free from pre-Christian pagan vestiges. As early as the second century even, Irenaeus wrote of the Church as a completely new ecumenic home intended to receive the peoples of the world and guide them to their destiny beyond all the existing political order. The Church came and grew *in* this world, but by refusing to admit that any of her essential features, including the Primate of Rome, were *of* this world, the Church in the West retained her sovereignty when the Empire crumbled and there was no Constantine to lean on as there had been in the fourth century.

Thus the Western Church could outgrow the ancient world; the East never did, but got moored permanently at the exit of antiquity. "The Eastern Church is only an institution for the other side of the grave; the Western became an institution for this world as well as for the beyond. The Eastern Church, for this reason, remained a sacramental and liturgical home of the soul and did not develop legal and political features. All worldly historical movements passed the Eastern Church by without touching her." [3] "Without knowing something about this unchanged life of the Orthodox Church, it is useless to become excited over the Bolshevik attitude toward religion. This Church never tried to change the world, to teach, to translate, to reform. It is the old church of adoration, attacking nobody, leaving the world alone. The arrow of religion always pointed away from the world and never back into it." [4] Hence Orthodox priests marry before they become priests, and in general the world is left to its old devices as a pre-Christian unsanctified order. Time has stood still in the Eastern Church.

[3] Adolf Harnack, *Sitzungsberichte der Berliner Akademie,* 1913, p. 7.

[4] *Out of Revolution,* p. 42.

Second Picture: Lack of Charity

The "Roemer" in Frankfurt is destroyed with the rest of the city. The one city of Germany which began her career with a big ecclesiastical event, a council, has gone out of existence after 1150 years. But it is not for a sentimental reason that we turn from Chalcedon to Frankfurt. Frankfurt provoked the final schism between East and West. The Greeks had no faith in Rome's consecration by the apostles alone, regardless of the Caesars. After Frankfurt, the West no longer lost much love on the East. The final breach came through a lack of charity on Rome's side. And the first lack of this charity was exhibited conspicuously on the day in Frankfurt in the year 794 when the Orthodoxy of the whole Eastern Church was attacked by the Carolingian clergy of the West. These theologians from Spain, Lombardy, Aquitania, England, Ireland, Burgundy, Gaul, Germany, did not love the East; they dreaded it as the cradle of Islam which encircled them. These Frankish courtiers looked to Charlemagne as the only defender of their faith against the Moslem. The Caesar in faraway Constantinople was a woman, Irene. Fear acts very differently from love in that it will exaggerate differences. This was exactly what happened in Frankfurt. Every bit of difference with the East was written large. Among other items, the Creed was inserted into the Mass as sung in the Royal Chapel (in Rome, this was not done then). And the Creed used by the Franks contained the notorious addition which brought on the schism later. The Creed, in the third article, describes the process by which we are inspired in the right spirit. And while the Greeks and Romans so far had not detailed the manner in which the spirit proceeds, at the Frankish Court the formula was: "who proceeds from the father and the son (*filioque*)." The Son left us the Spirit; so, we may rest assured that the formula was not wrong. But was it right to insert these terms *filioque* into the Creed?

There was no logical objection to inserting *filioque* in the Creed. Even Unitarians have never objected to these words. John's Gospel speaks of the Father and of the Son as sending the Spirit as Comforter alternately. The real basis of the quarrel was not a question of truth but one of charity. The Church of the first millennium, with its massive and martyrized faith, was rent by the Teutonic reformers; they blackmailed the Church of Rome by their zeal and had no patience with the Eastern half of the Church.

Reformers always want to make a clean slate logically complete in every detail: Calvin's *Institutes* and Augustine's *Confessions* are lengthy.[1] But love forbids putting on any fellow Christian any burden of too much belief or too much action. So Athanasius, for example, worried forty years before he was sure that one un-Biblical term might and must be added to the Creed. Modern man hardly appreciates such chastity of the mind. In fact, our school children are taught to poke fun at the iota against which Athanasius fought a lifetime. But in Frankfurt, the unnecessary addition of one little clause busted the Church, as this time the clause was not inserted by a saint but by spiteful warriors.

The men of Frankfurt were violent reformers.[2] They had to weld ten or eleven different tribes[3] into one Church, so they wanted order above everything. The chaste parsimony of dogmatic formulations meant nothing to them. The memories of the agonized struggle for unity in the first five centuries of the

[1] Calvin himself, by the way, resisted the temptations of mere curiosity, and lengthy as his own theology was, it was restricted by him to the necessary. When Socinus pestered him with questions, he wrote: "If you wish to know more, ask somebody else. For you shall never succeed in your quest of making me from eagerness to serve you transgress the boundaries placed on our knowledge by the Lord." (*Opera* ed. Reuss, 1549 Dec. ep. 1323, vol. XIII, 485.)

[2] On this and the deliberate founding of a Ford of the Franks, see *Die Furt der Franken und das Schisma,* Rosenstock-Wittig, *Das Alter der Kirche,* I, 1927, pp. 462–556.

[3] Salic Franks, Ripuarian Franks, Romanized Franks, Burgundians, Aquitanians, Visigoths, Thuringians, Hessians, Bavarians, Frisians, Langobards, Saxons.

Church were not vivid to Northerners. They did not have to cope with innumerable conversions of individual souls through forgiving love, but with many freshly converted tribes to be disciplined in an orderly faith. Between the Franks and the Greeks, the Popes wavered.

For a time the Bishop of Rome tried to live on in the Church as it had been before the Franks domineered in the West. As late as 787 he sent his ambassadors to the Greeks without including, or even inviting, any Franks. The occasion, as it turned out, was the last ecumenic council of Christianity. The Franks made sure of that. They threatened the Pope and condemned the Greeks as heretics.

The Franks could not be ignored in theology after their violent outburst against the Greeks. But what did the Pope do in answer to Frankfurt? He erected two silver plates in St. Peter's Church in Rome on which the Nicene Creed was engraved; in open defiance of the Frankish reformers, their addition "and from the son" was omitted! Rome's refusal to become a party to the innovation then could not have been more marked. This did not prevent the gradual spread of it through the whole kingdom of Charlemagne. By 850, it seems to have been in use all through the Western Churches. In 854, Rome herself capitulated. The protest of 798 was withdrawn. The Franks had mastered the liturgy of the Mother of Churches by swamping all the churches under Rome with the *filioque*. Thus the Church in Rome was the last Western Church which was overwhelmed.

This defeat of Rome by the Franks was exploited by the Patriarch of Constantinòple. He had troubles with Rome. And he seized upon the *filioque* as a heretical and arbitrary innovation which absolved the East from obedience. This opened the historical schism. The break became final in 1054.

The schism was thus the result of a rift not so much between Pope and Patriarch as between the Franks and the ancient tradition. If Rome had been unashamed enough to admit her humiliation by Charlemagne, the schism might have lost much of its sting. Was it pride which forbade the Popes to make this point, though their own records mentioned the protesting silver plates of 798?

The unity of the Christian Church was broken not because Rome and the Greeks believed differently but because the change in the Creed had been made from spite. The soul of Man was torn by lack of love in procedure. Lack of love is behind all serious conflicts. I wonder when the Popes will jettison the method of procedure then used, and thereby do their part for reunion. Why does the Bishop of Rome not admit that his hand was forced by Charlemagne?

Third Picture: The Renaissance of the Human Mind

The scandal of the Church's loss of unity led to many complaints. A reunion was tried often. Twice, things moved really. These two occasions were in Florence and in Stockholm.

In 1439, the Western Church had been suffering from a second schism inside herself for sixty years. The duplication of such a scandal seemed to bury the Church under her ruins. In the East, the Turks were nearing the Dardanelles; in the West, Popes quarrelled with Councils. So the Pope—threatened by a Council, and the Byzantine Emperor—threatened by the Turks—made peace among themselves and declared an end to the schism.

This reunion remained on paper. The days of Florence represented neither the whole West nor the whole East. The Patriarch of Moscow and the Council of Basel never accepted the results. Why then do we mention it at all? The meeting at Florence aroused sympathy between East and West, and its fruits ripened in another field than that of ecclesiastical discipline: the arts and sciences.

The Greeks who fled from the Turks and came to Florence brought with them something more in demand than Christian dogma at that time, namely Plato, and Platonism thus entered the West under the veil of Church collaboration. The man who specially combined the work for reunion with the introduction of Plato was Bessarion, a Greek Bishop who later became a Roman Cardinal. He hailed from the very city of Nicaea whose name conveys so vividly the memory of the schism,[1] and of the original unity.[2] Shortly after the fall of Constantinople, Cosimo de Medici gave Villa Coreggi, near Florence, to Marsilio Ficino, and Ficino opened there the famous Florentine Academy which was the first of its kind in modern times. It became the model of later academies, and through it Plato was introduced into all our universities.

What would our colleges be without the academic spirit of their arts and sciences, which is essentially Platonic? Plato's *Republic,* that college classic, was translated for the first time two years after the Council of Florence, by Decembrio. Plato's *Laws* followed a few years later, at the request of the Pope. In 1516 Erasmus edited the New Testament in Greek.

Moreover the revival of Plato was a major aid to Renaissance thinkers in developing the new sciences which have become the pride of the West. For example, Plato's enthusiasm for mathematics as the clue to the understanding of nature helped to emancipate Western thought from the unmathematical Aristotelian mentality which had dominated the later Middle Ages. And the most fundamental triumph of modern mathematics in its application to nature, the infinitesimal calculus, was already hinted at in 1460 by Nicolas Cusanus; he speculated profoundly on the infinitely great and the infinitely small in a deliberate attempt to fuse scholastic tradition with the new Platonic sources.[3]

[1] It was the Second Council of Nicaea in 787 which infuriated the Franks. See above p. 153.

[2] The First Council of Nicaea, in 325, was the first Council of the whole ecumenic church.

[3] The connection between infinity, traditionally the attribute of God alone, and the new interest in nature, is evident where Cusanus writes *"omnis creatura infinitas finita, quasi deus creatus."* Through Plato's attribution of a sort of "infinity" to matter, Cusanus gained access to the notion of the "apeiron" so important in early Greek philosophy. Cf. especially Plato's *Philebus.*

The Renaissance, though much of its content was pagan, was thus in the long view an event inside Christianity, begun by sparks ignited in a common plight of Eastern and Western Christendom. The millennium of Purgatory created the scientific mind of the West. Some of us still think of this new birth of science as a fight against faith and dogma, but the true relation lies deeper. Sympathy with the most rigid orthodoxy, that of the Eastern Church, lies at the foundations of the Renaissance. Without the schism and its pains, without the yearning for the lost unity of the Church, our academies would not have been built on the synthesis of medieval university traditions with Plato.

The fifteenth century rapprochement of East and West aimed at one thing, but achieved another. It sought a reunion of the soul; it created a renascence of the mind. When the soul lost her unity under the stress of political pressure upon Greek and Frankish Churches, the mind found its opportunity for an unheard and undreamed of unity in science and mathematics. Is there not infinite wisdom in the fact that, though the soul of mankind remained wounded, she enabled the mind to find its true unity through her suffering? The soul remains transfixed, but must not the human heart prove greater than the sword that rends it?

Fourth Picture: The Readmission of Economics

Today, as in 1439, the Churches are in danger. Secularism and Fascism are undermining the Western traditions, Bolshevism the Eastern. And again an effort toward the reunion of East and West has arisen: the Ecumenic Movement. In the East it goes back to Russians like Tchaadiev and Solovyev. In the West it was inaugurated by Nathan Söderblom.

Söderblom was a Swedish professor at my own university of Leipzig; later he was recalled to Sweden as Archbishop of Upsala. I vividly remember talking with him on the train in the summer of 1914. The war was in the air. We all sensed it. Söderblom, great and devoted scholar though he was, burst out in indignation at the passive indifference of his fellow scholars: "All my colleagues go on with their research, like Kierkegaard's 'professors of the crucifixion,' and nobody says anything or does anything against the war!" Thoroughly disgusted with the emasculate mind of scholarship and the stagnation and nationalism of the Churches, that very year he gave up his professorship, became Archbishop, and began working for an Ecumenic Council that was to include the Eastern Patriarchs. Everything that the Ecumenic Movement means today goes back to his exertions from 1914 onward. This one man sacrificed his academic idols in time, when he was still free to act with conviction, not as a mere opportunist. He lived in the faith which he professed on his deathbed: "Now is eternity!"

Söderblom's labors bore their first fruit in 1925 at the Ecumenic Conference in Stockholm. It did not pretend to be a Council, because Rome stayed away, but the Eastern Patriarchs took part. There have been two other ecumenic conferences since then, at Lausanne in 1927, and Oxford in 1937.[1] In addition there is a permanent office in Geneva, and numerous publications have been fostering the spirit of the movement—notably the influential *Christian News-Letter* in England and *Christianity and Crisis* in this country.

The theme of the Stockholm conference was "Life and Work." Söderblom explained this emphasis by telling of an old farmer who had visited him. The farmer had said: "Archbishop, Christendom is entering a new phase. The Church of the Priest has been and is over—Rome. The Church of the Levite has come in its place—Wittenberg and Geneva. Now it is over and the Church of the Good Samaritan is beginning." Impressed, Söderblom tried to form the reunion primarily around social and economic tasks rather than those of dogma and Church government. The later

[1] Significantly, when Hitler invaded Russia in 1941 he held ready an Orthodox bishop, Serafim, who had protested against the Oxford Conference, and ousted the Russian Patriarch who resided in Paris.

conference at Lausanne debated the theological points of dissent, and encountered correspondingly greater difficulties.

Indeed the drive for a new unity of the world is not as promising in the ecclesiastical as in the economic realm. The papacy as a soul trust and science as a brain trust have had their day. Our world seems rather to be looking for a stomach trust, an interplay of various economics. The Bolsheviks have tried to achieve it by revolutionary violence. Beginning in the East, which knew no purgatory, they left heaven and stormed the gates of hell without compromise. But if we must descend into hell, the Master of our souls will not leave us; he will go with us even into the demonic depths of the struggle for survival, into our animal existence as eaters, exploiters, robbers. And though I have little faith in a formal reunion of the Churches, I do believe that only the Ecumenical Christian spirit can build the lock to the gates of hell and coerce the flames which fan our elemental earthly needs.

Looking back on the history of the schism, we can see that it has acted as a mainspring generating a constant movement in the Christian era. That era began with the creation of the Church, the perfect communion of human souls. Without the Church we should not even know what the soul in union with other souls is. This unity is revealed to us in no other way than in the unique process which was called revelation: "They were one heart and one soul." When the communion was torn by the schism, the soul's yearning for unity overflowed beyond the Church and created the cooperation of our minds in the sciences. May we not hope today that the soul's agony will elicit the necessary steps toward a division of labor for our bodies? The schism is not resolved, but it moves the world into other unities beyond that of the Church by acting as a perpetual question demanding new efforts toward an answer.

Unity transcending Church unity has been a tenet of our faith from the beginning. At the end of Revelation, St. John foresaw the New Jerusalem as a healing of the nations without any visible

Church at its center. Today we can realize that the Spirit has actually been at work far beyond the walls of our church buildings and our scientific departments. When the bishops still thought of a reunion of the clergy based on the Creed, scholars worked out a reunion of all minds on the basis of Aristotle and Plato. And now, when scientists still think primarily of a reunion of educated people on the basis of knowledge, workers and farmers are aspiring toward a reunion of all labor on the basis of one great human family. The common meal of all people; this command lies behind the cry: Feed Europe!

But clinging tenaciously to our initial faith in the unity of the soul remains the necessary condition of every step forward. Without a yearning of our souls for peace even economic peace will not come to us. Whenever modern planning has seceded from Christianity, war and slavery have seemed quite normal to the secular mind. So today, economic order without respect for the human soul will mean, and already means, class war, racism, and even the return of bloody sacrifices.[2] The latter, prophesied by the neo-paganism of D. H. Lawrence, has been carried out by Hitler and Stalin. Both were trying to accomplish the next step in the history of mankind, economic unity, without respecting the foundation of soul unity incarnated in the Church. Without Christianity the new economy must become a nightmare world-state which will engulf all liberty and variety of man. The body will not find peace until men realize that the claims of soul and mind cannot be erased. As Italy lost her freedom in the Renaissance after she had succumbed to Humanism without qualifica-

[2] Contemporary neo-savagery comes directly in the wake of the final triumph of natural science over its rival, theology. Man has been conquered by an idol his own mind made: Nature with a capital N. He is an artificially produced African. It seems to be the indescribable attraction of mere grandeur which induces the masses to slaughter human victims in its honor, as in the time of the Aztecs. Man is told that his heartbeat, his personal desire, his individual judgment are mere blunders in comparison to Nature—in the form of class or race—of which he is only a minute part. Spellbound by the big drum of nationalism, he jumps into the lap of his gigantic Buddha, Nature, and cuts his own throat.

tion, so today's tragedy of Europe has come from her unqualified surrender to "vitalism," the catchword for the pre-Greek and pre-classic urges.

Conformism in economics is as bad as conformism in any other field of life. Our faith compels us to resist unity on too transient a level. Since we believe in one God, we need not believe in one political panacea or one economic millennium. While the dictators proclaim a thousand years of this or that "ism,"[3] we, in virtue of our faith, seek the unity of mankind outside Capitalism or Communism. We thank God that Capitalists and Communists fought on one side in this war and thereby rose beyond class prejudice. Economic systems have to be restrained from becoming religions. The war against Hitler was a religious war; Hitler had explicitly denounced and renounced the unity of mankind. Religious wars are the only wars which are inevitable; economic wars are superfluous as, from the economic point of view, no war pays.

Man's liberty can be made to tower above contradictions in the material orders of our existence. The peace of the world depends on this proper distinction. If economics is God, then a third world war is at hand. But as we know from our Christian tradition that economics is not God, we may also try to believe this in our acts and words; then no blood will have to be shed.

And it is here that the schism enters everyone's personal life.

May not the Eastern Churches emerge from this ordeal with a deeper comprehension of their enemy Communism than any one of us has yet reached? The Orthodox bishops and laymen have learned and have stated two truths: one, that the fall of the heir of the pagan Caesars, of Czarism, was God-willed. Two, that the victory of the communist Soviets over Hitler was providential.

Both experiences ask for their faithful appreciation by the West. As to Truth One: by approving finally of the fall of the Czars, the Greek Church has expiated Chalcedon, and her flirta-

[3] The pressure to which they respond is explained on pp. 203, 212.

tion with the pre-Christian world. Only now has she cut loose from her moorings in pagan antiquity.

With regard to Truth Two: by her approving Stalin's victory over Hitler, the ship of this Church has moved far on the river of our own era. For the Soviets are a literal antithesis to the Christian clergy. As I have shown in detail in my comparison between "the keys of the kingdom" and the key of "the Five Year Plan,"[4] the Soviets are the jealous watchmen of a purely material "Zion," an anti-Sunday clergy so to speak. The Greek Church seems to assimilate the most painful lesson which any clergy could have to learn that the Sunday Church is to be checked and chastised by its own counterpart of a week-day fanaticism not because the gospel is deficient but because its ministers are.

Christians cannot help include this, their indubitable foe, Communism, into the world as God has now made it. For don't we know our own abuse of the gospel? We abhor every word Communism professes. However, since we also must hate so many of our own actions, we may understand the wisdom of our Maker: our many disastrous actions have hatched the disastrous phrases of Communism, despite our gospelling. Let us hope that despite their blaspheming, the Communists may enact some actions which are begotten by the truth of our preaching. In this unexpected manner, the schism ends; the most retarded branch of the Church is flung far ahead.

Church History

This prompts a general conclusion, a conclusion by which the historian of the Church distinctly is divorced from the scientific historian of the world. The Church is a teleological institution; it stems from the end of time as much as its founder. It can be understood only in terms of its fruits not of its causes. For

[4] *Out of Revolution,* pp. 113 ff.

a century or more, Church historians have practiced the method of reductionism. They have virtually explained Christianity away in terms of all sorts of sources, motives, types, loans, influences, precedents, until nothing properly Christian was left. The reductionists have been too busy chasing causes to realize that the effects contain the meaning, just as a newborn child has its meaning from tomorrow, not from yesterday.

The reductionists had a wonderful way of eliminating the central Christian thesis: by their fruits, ye shall know them. They debated the question whether the end sanctified the means or not. This idiotic question has occupied the academic world although every child knows that this is not the true question at all. Our ends certainly do not sanctify our means. But the reason is that our ends never sanctify anything. Our ends certainly are not good enough. If, however, we fulfill the ends imposed on us, sexual intercourse, for instance, a means which has irked Bernard Shaw all his life as disgusting, becomes sanctified. Does anybody deny this? But marriage is not the fulfillment of "my" end. The crucifixion is a scandal to any "healthy" instinct. If salvation had been Jesus' "end," this means to salvation would have been obscene. But by their fruits, ye shall know them, and Jesus was sent into the world to do his Father's "end." The whole Protestant-Jesuit debate about means and ends falls dead to the ground in the face of events in which we do not pretend to follow our own ends. Did the United States follow their own ends in the two World Wars? I doubt it very much. The means of war were sanctified by this very fact that the end was not American-made.

History in the religious sense has significance only when looked at from the end toward the beginning. By their fruits ye shall know them—not by their motives.[5] God alone knows our motives. We have seen that the fruits, dividends, realizations of later stages explain the importance of the founding and beginning of so strange a creature as the Church. Regarded with the eyes of

[5] See above p. 149 for a historical example.

reductionist history, the Church always is a failure, always miserable, bankrupt, about to collapse. Regarded from the end, she always is miraculous, indispensable, providential, revealing.

Fructus laboris nomen est, the fruit of her labor is her name, was said of the first witness of the Church.[6] Should even the name "Church" have something to do with our way of reading her history from the end? What then is her name? We seem to attach no longer much significance to this Greek word "kyriake" which became "Church." However, Church not simply meant kyriake, "the Lord's . . ." but it exclusively meant "the coming Lord's . . ." In "the Lord's own," in the Church, he who shall be who he shall be, was worshipped as the Lord. For ever shall the ways in which he becomes known tomorrow be new ways. This is his difference from the idols of causation. Julia Ward Howe's "Mine eyes have seen the glory of *the coming of the Lord,"* is an orthodox song of the living Church. It may come as a surprise to many that the Church received her name as the unity of those who believed in the coming of the Lord. In the New Testament, the word occurs twice only, not for Church as a building or a corporation but for the two events in time in which the faithful became especially parts of the coming Lord, the Lord's supper and the Lord's day. Both events anticipated "the Day of the Lord" of which Peter speaks in his second letter where he says that fifty thousand Sundays with God are like One Day of the Lord. Therefore, Church history denies its theme unless it reads from the end of time and judges the roots by their fruits. For we never are Christians by what we have seen unless we have seen the coming of The Lord.

[6] *Ennodius carmina* I, 14, hymn for St. Stephen.

VII

THE PENETRATION OF THE CROSS

"If they are the planting of the father, they will unfold as living outgrowths of the cross of the son."

Ignatius (c. A.D. 100), *Letter to the Trallians*, ch. 11.

The Cross as Reality—Buddha—Laotse—Abraham—Jesus—The "Social Sciences" as an "Old Testament"

Nine years before the present war reminded us how deeply the meaning of the Cross is embedded in human experience, Winston Churchill wrote, "After all, a man's Life must be nailed to a cross either of Thought or Action."[1] The story of Christianity is the penetration of the Cross into more and more fields of human existence. Its every advance into another sphere of our minds or bodies marks, as we have seen, a new epoch in history. Something of the extent to which this penetration has taken place can be seen in the way the word "crucial" has invaded our scientific, artistic, political and social vocabularies.

Since the crucifixion the Cross has accordingly come to mean more and more things, and to be expressed in different ways as new streams of Christian language break forth. But as Chapter five suggested, the old words have been so abused and exhausted that Christianity can renew itself today only by nameless, unlabelled forms of common service. It is in keeping with this need that we should attempt to translate the Cross itself into non-ecclesiastical, post-theological language which may help us to re-

[1] *A Roving Commission*, New York, 1930, p. 113.

spond freshly and directly, freed from the pall of accumulated inhibitions.

The Cross as Reality

Reality itself—not the abstract reality of physics, but the full-bodied reality of human life—is cruciform. Our existence is a perpetual suffering and wrestling with conflicting forces, paradoxes, contradictions within and without. By them we are stretched and torn in opposite directions, but through them comes renewal. And these opposing directions are summed up by four which define the great space and time axes of all men's life on earth, forming a Cross of Reality.[1]

Under the spell of mathematical and physical concepts, we are accustomed to think of time and space as homogeneous or uniformly the same at every point. Time, for example, though conventionally divided into past, present and future, is usually represented diagrammatically by a straight line, on which there is obviously no real basis whatever for distinguishing past and future. And this seems to be actually the case with inorganic nature: it knows no future but only perfect and imperfect tenses, only processes that have ended or processes still going on at any given moment.

We have shaken off the prevalent superstition of our time that time and space can be lumped together as the two general frames of reference for all experience. People will talk glibly of "space" and "time" as though we experienced both in the same manner. But every reader can experience that this is untrue. Space comes to him as a whole. Whatever his eyes comprehend, they compre-

[1] This is not symbolistic fantasy or arbitrary schematizing, but something that has grown through two thousand years. The Jesuit writer, Hans Urs von Balthasar (*Die Apokalypse der Deutschen Seele*, Salzburg and Leipzig, 1939, III, 434 ff.), cites the authority of Origen and Augustine, in their commentaries on Ephesians 3:18 for his kindred interpretation of human existence, and even goes so far as to say, "In the philosophical object of knowledge the figure of the cross is engraved like an indelible watermark."

hend as one universe of space. All things inside the universe are subdivisions made by us after the whole of space first is given.

Now test your time experience. You realize nothing but moments, seconds. As Homer said, the present is as inconvenient to sit on as the blade of a razor. Yet, we speak of the "present" Constitution although it goes back to 1787. And we speak of "our" era, of the steady progress of science, of the spirit of Florence through the ages. What does this mean? Time is not given like space, as a universe. It is given us individually as a phantom moment or as innumerable phantom moments. But together we create times: any body of time exists only *because we say so.* The thing, the molecule, the atom, the electron, these are subdivisions of space because we say so; they are history-made parts of One space. But the hour and the year and the centuries, they are history-made units built by our faith, out of innumerable moments. When we deal with space, we descend from the universe. When we deal with time, we ascend to bodies of time by saying so. And we are unable to say so unless we, in a common effort, throw out some particles of time as "past," and determine others as future. It is here that Christianity comes in, as discovering the true quality of the times as acts of human faith by our saying so together. Jesus became the future although he had already died once. And now, man could move in time, past, future, present, with real freedom. He became the creator of all the bodies of time, small and large, in the light of the one body which comprised all inspired beings, all who had created times ever, all men.

If this is so, all men are men because they face backward and forward at the same time. We are crucified by this fact. *Nobody lives in one time.* At any moment the community re-determines its own past as well as its future. The creation of the Church led to a perpetual renewal of our historical past. The "Renaissance" is only one act in this drama of our era by which all the times are reenacted when they are needed. Real Man lives between a declared future and a reborn past.

Likewise space is differentiated by life into an internal and an external world. This is most obvious in the way in which an animal is separated from its environment by its skin, or a cell by its walls; but it is equally true of every kind of social group that the members feel themselves forming an inner circle set over against a more or less hostile outer world, and the skin which divides them from "outsiders" is none the less real for being intangible.

So it is that man's life, social as well as individual, is lived at a crossroads between four "fronts": *backward* toward the past, *forward* into the future, *inward* among ourselves, our feelings, wishes and dreams, and *outward* against what we must fight or exploit or come to terms with or ignore.[2] It is obviously fatal to fail on any front—to lose the past, to miss the future, to lack inner peace or outer efficiency. Would we run forward only, all the acquired qualities of character and civilization would vanish. If we look backward exclusively, we cease to have a future. And so on.

Yet it is equally obvious that no individual can move adequately in all four directions at once. Therefore life is perpetual decision: when to continue the past and when to change, and where to draw the line between the inner circle we speak to and the outer objects we merely speak of and try to manipulate. Hence both mental and social health depends on preserving a delicate mobile balance between forward and backward, inward and outward, trends. Integration, living a complete and full life, is accordingly

[2] The Cross of Reality formed by the four fronts is so self-evident, once it is grasped, that it is apt to seem trivial at first. But our "natural" minds deny this trivial truth. They do not admit that we respect the past. They claim that the past "causes" the present and the future. They do not admit that all thought is an inner conversation of a fellowship, and all "nature" external and outside this fellowship. It follows that the Cross is not trivial. It contradicts the abstract mentality of the "onlooker." The importance of the Cross is measured by the fertility of its applications and by the disastrousness of forgetting it. For a suggestion of the fertility of the idea of the four fronts, see the author's *Soziologie,* 1925, and A. Meyer, *Bios,* I, 1934.

not some smooth "adjustment" we can hope to achieve once for all and then coast along with, as popular psychology imagines; it is rather a constant achievement in the teeth of forces which tear us apart on the Cross of Reality.

Society compensates for our individual inadequacies by division of labor. For example, teaching, ceremony and ritual preserve our continuity with the past, and teachers, priests and lawyers serve on this front for all of us. We build up social unanimity by playing, singing, talking together, sharing our moods and aspirations, and on this inner front poets, artists, and musicians are typical representatives. We win our living and protect our lives by learning to control natural forces and manipulating them for our ends in farming, industry and war; scientists, engineers and soldiers typify the millions who fight for us on the outer front. Lastly, religious and political leaders, prophets and statesmen are responsible for initiating change and drawing society into its future.

Since the four fronts differ in quality and direction they are *ultimate and irreducible dimensions of human existence,* but the mind with its imperious urgé to relate and unify everything is tempted to over-simplify life and deny the Cross of Reality by reducing the four to one. This is the main source of viciously one-sided fallacies about man and society—sentimentalism and mysticism which engulf everything in the inner life of feeling, utopian radicalism which would bring in the Kingdom of God by violence, reactionary romanticism which dwells wholly in the feudal past, cynical rationalism which reduces man to a mere object of natural science.

As a less extreme example, Josiah Royce rediscovered the tremendous importance of loyalty in human life, but in writing *The Philosophy of Loyalty* he could not resist the temptation to explain everything in terms of this one power which essentially binds us to the past. Loyalty is an expression of historical continuity; it can never justify a decisive break. But for Royce it had to become a chameleon which also means "love." The subjugation of love to loyalty may be a typical Old and New England attitude, but to say that a man leaves father and mother and cleaves to the wife of his choice out of loyalty simply does not make sense.

Our own civilization, dominated for several centuries by natural science and its applications, suffers most of all from obsession with the outward front. The essence of man's attitude on this front is objectivity: whatever we treat as something merely to classify, experiment with, describe, control, is thereby externalized, treated as if it had no solidarity with us, estranged from our living system. The scientist disciplines himself to keep his emotions, loyalties, loves and hates out of the picture. It is quite proper for him to do so in studying physical things, but when he treats human life in this way he is apt to forget that he represents only one-fourth of our full reality. To mistake that quarter for the whole, and so to reduce man to a guinea pig or a mouse running a maze, is to multilate human nature. The naturalist's picture of man may be useful, but when mistaken for the complete truth it cuts our roots in the past, keeps us emotionally immature for want of normal expression, and deadens our scent for the trail into the future, our sense of what is vitally important. The Cross of Reality shows us that the scientific attitude is only one out of four equally valid contacts with reality, and that it depends upon the existence of the others for its own meaning. No man, because of this Cross, can be a member of one time or one group only. His groupings represent all the times which he must live. It is the essence of man that he belongs to more than one group; ever since the Stone Age, this has been true of every human being. No wonder, therefore, that man thinks because he has to shift and is shifted. Man does not think because he "is." We think because change is ahead. Cogitation is not the primary fact which Descartes thought it to be. We dread change; therefore we think. Daily, we must die to one temporal form; therefore we think. Not *cogito ergo sum,* but *mutabor ergo cogito,* is everybody's starting point.

The uncritical doctrine of our vulgar psychology is that human thinking is due to prior causes; but actually it is provoked by ends. Our end being death, we think so that we may survive.

At the same time, since nobody can be at all fronts of his cross at once and all the days of his life, each act of thinking proceeds in solidarity with all those who act in our stead at all the other fronts while we are engaged at one. How could we enjoy a restful sleep without civil peace? The Gestapo in many countries changes man back to the deer whose sleep is perfunctory and scanty. Our thoughts are untrue if they do not include those who must wake when we are asleep. For this reason, mere professional thoughts do not suffice for a whole community. Ministers, lawyers, doctors, among themselves are apt to forget the full truth because the soldiers, the poor, the workers, may be omitted from their councils.

Similarly the husband cannot be the perfect husband, the daughter cannot be the daughter, the son cannot become the son, if there are not the corresponding roles represented by their partners.

That all our special skills are due to the division of labor is, of course, widely known. All we ask is to deepen the notion. The division should be freed from its limitation—"of labor." Not labor alone divides us and distributes us. The greater fact is that the individual himself is divided because neither one space nor one time contains us. We are conscious because we are contained in at least two times—past and future, and at least two spaces—an inner and an outer. The division by labor in our factories concerns only one fraction of the man who is more fundamentally torn than by his specialisation.

It is every modern man's daily experience that we enter any house or town today in the faith that they are not our abiding or ultimate home. Industry would be unsupportable without this freedom of movement; even Bolshevik industry had to allow the people to move by the millions from town to town, and to crowd the big cities. All our spaces have become fleeting. Perhaps it was for this reason that the unity of our time has been stolidly maintained: we have been told that we are all contemporaries; and the fact that a man belongs to many times has been suppressed and usually overlooked. We have been moulded into contemporaries of the latest news; fifteen million people were said to listen to Raymond Gram Swing during 1941.

But the Cross of Reality may remind us that we can never surrender to complete contemporaneity. We are just as much—and I have had to coin the new word for this fact—distemporaries of the people we meet as we are their contemporaries. Of course when we meet nice people, we wish to become as much as possible their contemporaries. But this is an act of friendship to be accomplished and it is not a natural or presumable fact. We ourselves represent more than one time within ourselves; so, how could we be wholly prisoners of one time? We often have to live with people who think that we are fossils or who themselves died long ago and are the only ones who have not noticed it. To the rationalist, I am antiquated because I battle for Christianity, something he knows to be a "residue." And to me, perhaps, pragmatism or "The Nation" may belong to the Stone Age of superstition, a revival of good old Confucius.

The disconcerting truth is that at any hour of our lives we are both older and younger than others in the community. And with everything which we think and say, we choose a specific time: This may be a filial, and this a founder's idea, this may be wise and this childish; always it will belong to a peculiar time. These are a few examples only of the "fullness of time" to which we must remain open, distemporaries that we are. The Cross of Reality allows us to diagnose the complete soul.

No front is sufficient alone, but each is essential.[3] Death lurks

[3] My late friend Richard Cabot, in his book, *What Men Live By,* first published in 1912, came very near this Cross of Reality, for the individual. The Mayo Clinic now experiments with his system of coordinates, as a diagnostical and practical help. A more complete introduction of the Cross of Reality as our social means of organizing time and space is my *Soziologie,* Berlin, 1925.

in wait for us on every front, if we fail. In society, death takes the form of decadence, revolution, anarchy or war, according to whether we are inadequate on the forward, backward, inward or outward sector. Decadence, for instance, means being unable to reach the future, in body, mind or soul. It is not merely a biological failure but a weakness of the whole man. When it appears in our bodies, we cease to have children. When it taints our souls, we lack the stamina to inspire the next generation with aims which would carry them beyond themselves—a lack tragically prevalent in the 1920's. The decadence of an older generation condemns the young to barbarism. The only energy that can fight this evil is faith. Faith, properly speaking, is always belief in some future, a world to come.

For the past eight hundred years, the two space fronts and the two time fronts have been parcelled out in a standing division of labor between philosophy and theology, or science and religion. The two sides have generally ignored or fought each other; at best they have divided up reality between them in a pedantic compromise. From Thales to Hegel all philosophy began its thinking with the world of space or the knowing mind and a corresponding logic of timeless abstractions, and time appeared consequently in foreshortened perspective, being considered primarily from a spatial point of view. The sciences, being the offspring of philosophy, followed suit—the tendency of the scientific intellect to spatialize everything, even time, is a commonplace since Bergson. Theology, on the other hand, never started with space nor did it admit the equal dignity of space problems. It was interested in time, in history; it dealt with the creation of Adam, the birth of Jesus, the death of the Lord, the founding of the Church, the Last Judgment—all topics that a philosopher need never even mention.

The division of labor between philosophy and theology has been the expression of a working compromise under which Christendom made room for the revival of Greek philosophy, with the attendant arts and sciences. But today the compromise has ceased to work; amid the stress and confusion of revolutionary change, the old clear lines refuse to be drawn, yet the Western mind is paralyzed by the inherited split between two modes of thought that should be supplementary. If conceiving Reality as a Cross enables us to overcome the division and fuse space-thinkers and time-speakers into one new profession, it will accomplish the penetration of the Cross into the last stronghold of paganism within our own traditions.

We shall gain strength for this step if we make another at the same time and invite the great civilizations of the Orient, China and India, under the Cross too. For the Cross is not an exclusive symbol of the egoism of one group; it is the inclusive symbol of the reunification of man, and every spark of life is welcome unless it refuses to die in time. Even the primitive cultures must be included eventually.

Today Orient and Occident are shaken by a cataclysm which shows the insufficiency of both in isolation. A new penetration of the Cross is required which shall draw together the hearts of men in East and West by showing that each has some essential ingredient of life which the other needs. From the purity of Eastern eyes and ears we may learn to cure the destructiveness of our sciences and the feverish expressionism of our arts, while the religious and political stagnation of China and India may be overcome if they are shot through with the Christian power of death and resurrection.

As a contribution to this end, I wish to show how Orient and Occident both have given us a pair of re-founders or re-directors of human nature—Buddha and Laotse, Abraham and Jesus—who together have created man's full freedom on all fronts of the Cross of Reality. Unlike the animals, man by his gift of speech is able to enlarge his grasp of reality in all four directions—his loyalty to past creation, his solidarity with other men, his power over nature, his love and faith in the future—yet, as we have seen, he is prone to get stuck on one front to the prejudice of the other three. The great re-directors have overcome this tendency to fixation by living each direction of the Cross to a paradoxical extreme which emancipates us from the characteristic obsessions of that front. By emptying each direction of its accidental content, they enable us to re-enter the other fronts, and thereby assure the perpetual flexibility and movement of life.

It is significant that each of these men arose in protest against a culture which was a model of its kind. They are misunderstood if we take them for men who improved a given society by remedying this or that imperfection. They freed us rather from the tyranny of perfection, showing that even the social wisdom of Confucian China, the philosophic profundity of Vedas and Vedanta, the massive stability of Babylon or Egypt, or the glories of Greece and Rome, are not enough.

At this point, the reader may remember our second chapter in which America's invasion by the East was discussed. Pragmatism reintroduced Confucius' gospel of total social integration into this country when the frontier disappeared. And Darwinism broke away from the Platonic world view and steeped us in a vision of total and universal struggle.

It is, then, of practical significance to look for the antidotes created in the East against Confucius and Veda. This, however, does not mean that we shall discuss here any practical applications of these antidotes. The really practical attitude is, as in the case of a medical diagnosis, to suspend action and to pause. The practical attitude is to indulge in meditation. In no other way, will the greatness of Buddha and Laotse, of Abraham and Jesus be realized. Greatness does not yield its secret to the curious mind who hopes to exploit a recipe. Greatness defies activism. Its demand on us is "perceive me." For, in our hurry, we are blind to it. The interaction between the four changers and emancipators of our race fills me with awe. That men separated by continents and centuries should have undertaken a complete conquest of the soul's freedom, and should have established themselves as guardians of this freedom once for ever—this commands attention.

I have sacrificed detail and completeness in the following brief pages to the intention of making conspicuous the unity behind the four men. What is said of every one of them is a minimum; it is that minimum which suffices for an appreciation of their interdependence and for the fact that Jesus came when the times were fulfilled. If Jesus came when Abraham, Laotse, Buddha, had established themselves, then, indeed, we might recognize the oneness and the interdependence of all mankind with a new degree of clarity and definiteness.

Buddha

Buddha lived in a culture that was peculiarly obsessed with the outward front, so much so that nature had invaded society itself: the caste system was only one step removed from cannibalism and the horrors of the jungle; it made social divisions almost as deep and fatal as animal ones. The Hindus had expressed the cosmic struggle in their religious myths and, later and more profoundly, in the philosophy that grew out of the Vedas. That philosophy envisaged nature as a realm of illusion or appearance, called Maya. Maya was composed of many worlds, many lumps of world succeeding each other endlessly; it was utterly lacking in unity in either space or time. Maya included all social relations and attachments too. Unity was to be found only by "seeing through" Maya until it vanished altogether and the mind attained the blissful knowledge of Brahma, the ultimate Being.

Buddha was not satisfied with mere description of nature as illusion; he set out to heal its strife. For this purpose he painted Maya in colors darker than ever: confusion and suffering reign everywhere; everything shoves, lusts, sweats, murders; man is in the fight himself, suffering and making suffer; murder alone makes life possible. Before the Buddha's unflinching gaze all human activity reveals the same pitilessness. Acts never before thought of in this light, like eating and breathing, are seen to be full of violence. Yet through the two central experiences of his life, the Great Renunciation and the Great Enlightenment, Buddha showed the way to mitigate the universal struggle. He taught that man could renounce his own partisanship in the cosmic mêlée by focussing his whole existence in his eye, his enlightenment, his mental concentration, to the point at which all desire is extinguished. In this way Buddha outdoes those who tend to monopolize life for the outward front, by pushing their very attitude to the ultimate extreme. That attitude, we have seen, consists in treating things or people as ob-jects, i.e. as outside of and opposed to our own living system, and therefore as merely there to be dissected, manipulated, exploited as we please. But if, as Buddha teaches, we empty ourselves *wholly* into the object we perceive, if we focus our consciousness in absolute objectivity, nothing remains of the greedy vital urges which prompt us to exploit. In Schopenhauer's expression, we have become all eye. When Western man faces the chaos pictured by recent science, and aggravated by its destructive applications, he cannot help accepting something of the Buddha's insight. If future scientists were trained like one gigantic Buddha, science might be brought to diminish rather than increase the world's strife. When a man withdraws from the struggle, he removes a cornerstone on which the whole structure of mutual aggression rests. The self-annihilation of one particle of the frightful will to live mitigates the pressure between all. Most of us have found that some degree of restraint, of asceticism, is a way of making life less terrible. Actions beget reactions. Do not react, and you lessen the conflict, undo the fighting.

To be sure Buddha's attitude was illogical: he had to live a long life in order to proclaim the negation of life. But the point is that he actually represented within life the power of negating its ubiquitous strife. Absolute negation for its own sake is meaningless, just as absolute zero is meaningless except in relation to heat, or absolute black except in relation to colors. But as mathematics attained a vast new freedom for its operations by treating zero as a number, so the zero situation created by Buddha simply doubles man's potentialities by allowing him to swing toward self-renunciation as well as toward self-assertion. We must continue to move along the outward beam of the Cross of Reality as soldiers, workers, exploiters of nature, but we also need to win our freedom from this trend; man the fighter needs also to discover non-fighting, non-resistance Nirvana.

Laotse

Nature is war; society is a colossal coordination. On the inward front, we ourselves are integrated into its innumerable functions with irresistible kindness and force. The meshing of services in a big city is breath-taking. Sewers and food stores, real estate agents, theatrical managers, electric power, hospitals, museums, railroads, and the skiing at Macy's, all form an organized world which is just the opposite of the chaos described by Buddha and Bertrand Russell.

Ancient China lived a social monism, being as absorbed with the inward front as India by the outward. The social system was one world outside of which nothing asked for recognition when man began to reflect on existence. Nature merely served as background for the Son of Heaven, Heaven itself being a social and imperial institution; even the winds and seasons and the demons in the fields were mainly thought of as lending the finishing touch to society. The Chinese had no reason and no chance to stand off and look at themselves objectively from the standpoint of another civilization—Montesquieu's wish to stare at France as though it were Madagascar would have been quite inconceivable to them. It was no accident that they despised war and militarism. Their life turned inward among themselves exclusively, and their trouble was not too much war but too much peace.

To the eternal Chinese within us, "service first" is instinctively true. We love to function smoothly. The first thing a socially established dignitary has is a rhythm of daily routine by which he realizes how well he fits into the humming world about him. And the first rule of any society is "Keep smiling," for associated life is based on unanimity of effort and emotion. As we settle into a community, it becomes so much a part of us and we of it that our smile is like a ray falling on us from a whole solar system of cheerful social harmony.

But we keep smiling at a price. The cost of incessant functioning is increased wear and tear from strain and friction. Nervous breakdown is apparently the only way modern man has of keeping from being dragged on and on to more and more telephone calls, appointments, acquaintances, committees, memberships, bills. Confucian China was likewise an intricate system of ceremonies and duties, and from them Laotse brought release by reducing to absurdity all the noise of industriousness and social importance.

As Buddha established a zero for the outer front, so did Laotse for the inner. The safety valve for society is to return from functioning to non-functioning, from importance to unimportance. Laotse showed this in his own life by retiring from public office and even writing his book anonymously—"Laotse" was not his actual name—and his school enshrined his total attitude in the legend that, as an old man, he simply vanished over a mountain and was never heard of again. "He aimed at self-effacement and namelessness," states the book *Shih-Chi*. "Men all seek the first. He alone sought the last. Men all seek fulfillment; he alone took the empty." [1] His anonymity and vanishing are two anti-social possibilities which man must practice to make society bearable. Laotse's most famous illustration of his Tao, or way of life, is the

[1] Fung, Yu-Lan, *A History of Chinese Philosophy*, Peiping, 1937, pp. 170 ff., 221 ff.

hub of a wheel: it is motionless, but without it nothing else could move; so Tao is an effortless center of non-activity on which all things turn. "Without sound, it stands alone." "The world is invariably possessed by him who does nothing." "The practice of Tao consists in subtracting, day by day."

We can learn much from Laotse. We are possessed by the idea of reputation, name, fame, records: *Who's Who* is our typical yardstick of worldly importance. Our economic system delights in advertised brands and insists on labelling all services to society. In our urge for artistic creation we are in danger of not ripening the fruits of creativity because we strive for them too feverishly. Thousands of college people—professors, their wives, boys and girls—are trying to solve their problems by writing books, but they have forgotten the equally important problem of creative silence. Respect for the question, when to be creative and when not, is so rare that most authors simply go on thoughtlessly producing book after book. We must cultivate the courage to stay silent for a while among the people with whom we live, so that when we do speak our voice will have become theirs.

It does not require dictatorship to make a society totalitarian in its impact on man. Our modern World Society is as totalitarian in its way as Confucian China was. Our stress on adjustment to environment, the avoidance of conflict, the pragmatic value of truth, our concern for practical success—all are reminiscent of China, but we still lack the Taoist ear. We may become the "hub" by listening in to the secret and potential harmony behind the obvious dissonances of a social process. L. P. Jacks in his delightful *Legends of Smokeover* had his high-strung psychologist listen to the fragments of a possible rhythm in the chaos of Smokeover and this man is flushed with enthusiasm when some symphonic solution evolves. Laotse's followers actually tried to "dance the universe." "About the whole cosmos there is a tense and secret festivity like preparations for a great dance."[2] The

[2] G. K. Chesterton, in his immortal essay on Mr. McCabe in *Heretics*.

correct term for Laotse would be "orchestration" since originally the term orchestra did not mean a group of musicians, but the unity of dancing and making music. And it would seem that the fine ear for cosmic orchestration was the corrective against the boredom of Confucius in China.

Tao, like Nirvana, offers a new dimension of freedom. It is not enough to seek success; it takes more than ambition to become the real man of the hour: one must have ambition and non-ambition as well. Daniel Webster had the inelastic single-track mind which thinks that only the straightest line leads to success: by declining the Vice Presidency, he lost his great chance to become President of the United States—the new President died in his first month of office. Theodore Roosevelt made the opposite choice, and won. André Maurois, in his *Disraeli,* has painted a delightful picture of Gladstone chopping trees in his times out of office. The arrow of one's life must swing freely both away from zero and towards it.

Abraham

As the eye and the hub inject into the spaces of the East a solvent, so Abraham and Jesus inject peace into the times of the West. Backward and forward, not inside and outward, Abraham and Jesus teach us to live. Since most of the readers are "space-bound" by their scientific upbringing, they may be surprised to find that the relation between the two redeemers of time is not the same as between Buddha and Laotse. Buddha is outside, or takes us outside. Laotse invites us into the center of the social space. Hence, it is really one front solely, to which we are called by these two. But Abraham as well as Jesus came into a Western World in which Chronos, that is "Time," was said to devour his own children incessantly as soon as they were born. Both, therefore, created an *historical* faith, a faith which would stand up under the pressures not of space but of time. Both gave man instead of a point to stand on in space, an hour to live in, through time. The "hour" of a man keeps time either from collapsing and drowning by the onrush of flux or from paralyzing him by the absence of dynamic movement. His "hour" must be preceded and succeeded by other "hours." This fundamental relation is expressed in our being fathers and sons. For Israel as well as for Jesus, the relation "Father-Son" became decisive. But the Church was built on the dialectical opposite of the solution given by Abraham. Let us analyze the solution of Abraham first.[1] Since nothing seems to be known so little as the faith of Abraham, I may use the same example by which a Jewish friend nearly thirty years ago refuted my own misunderstanding of Judaism.[2]

I had said that after all, the Greek King Agamemnon's sacrifice of his daughter Iphigenia was about the same as Abraham's willingness to sacrifice his son Isaac. Whereupon my friend came down on me with terrific energy.

Agamemnon, he replied, sacrificed his daughter for the sake of having his army conquer Troy. He did sacrifice his dearest for a man-made purpose. But Abraham, lest he sacrifice his own son, in the opinion of his own days, forwent all prospect of any victory or domination or kingship or establishment of perpetuity.

The reason for this is that in a Scottish or Macedonian or Sioux clan, the son reaches the true spirit via his ancestors. The treatment of any Crown Prince, or Prince of Wales, or of a Vice President in the United States, is one of suspended animation. They have no spirit of their own. They wait and expect to step into someone else's shoes. The strongest expression of this linear succession of the spirit from father to sons is the right of parents to declare war and to have their children fight this war, in faith to their father's spirit. The direct individual sacrifice of the first born male was a voluntary substitute for war. By sacrificing one's

[1] For more, see my essay "Hitler and Israel," *Journal of Religion*, April 1945.

[2] The occurrence is recorded in Miss D. Emmet's article, *Journal of Religion*, October 1945.

son one, so to speak, hoped to achieve the same end of bending the gods to one's own will, without the complications of a war. And as long as we have wars, obviously, we can understand Agamemnon. But Abraham is more difficult to grasp, for he emancipated his son's life. By doing so, he acknowledged God as the father of all men, even of his own son.

That sounds funny in the ears of modern man who promotes the fatherhood of God by a League of World Citizenship. Such societies institute an abstract principle. But how do the members of this society treat their own next of kin? Don't some of these members claim some rights over their parents, their wives, their husbands at least? If they do, they deny, in this one relation, the fatherhood of God. Our own children are as much God's children as Jesus. So, we must let them live their own lives and wait for God to come into their own lives and not be their gods ourselves.

Hence, Abraham instituted the new principle at the point where it then was hardest to fulfill. And, my friend continued, for this reason, Israel always has considered the act of not slaughtering Isaac as the great spiritual revolution. God's final purpose with man stood revealed as peace, not war. And such had been God's intent always. In the clash between human desire of victory and God's right over all men, God won out. For this reason, God ceased to be the God of Abraham; he now was called the God of Abraham, Isaac and Jacob. (2 Moses 3:6, 15, 16; 4:5; 33:1. Acts 3:13.) And for this reason, we must hope to abolish war one day.

Faith in the immediate communion of the spirit with each generation from beginning to end, was Abraham's sole merit, as the Bible so strongly asserts—otherwise he was just an ordinary man.[3] By his life he told men that a supreme loyalty exists, a loyalty to the One God who created heaven and earth, by which all earthly loyalties are measured. Josiah Royce described Abraham's position literally in his philosophy of "loyalty to loyalty"—loyalty

[3] See Eric S. Robertson, *The Bible's Prose Epic of Eve and Her Sons,* London, 1916.

that includes all men's loyalties which are not at war with each other. The men of Abraham's day worshipped, in divided loyalty, different parts of the earth and sky. The only way to lower the walls erected by divided loyalty was to go back beyond any historic past and thereby transcend the ties which make natural man worship the values embodied in the mother tongue and fatherland beyond everything else. So the opening sentence of the Bible says, in effect, that despite the way in which man has partitioned heaven and earth all things were originally created in unity.

As in the case of Buddha and Laotse, Abraham's biography is summed up in two central experiences, his exodus from Ur and his discovery that a father need not sacrifice his first-born son. By leaving his home country—a land of loyalties divided between many antagonistic deities—and waiting for God to fulfil His promise, he testified to his faith in the unity of creation. From that day to this, exile and waiting have been the perpetual function of Israel in human society; with neither country nor national civilization, the Jews have counted the years simply from the creation of the world and waited for the Messiah to restore this world to its original unity. Each generation, of course, has had to act differently in order to represent the same thing, but we must not let the differences blind us to the essential identity of meaning running through Abraham, Moses, the prophets, and the Jews of the dispersion, whose scattering over the face of the whole earth corresponded to the locally divided loyalties of the Gentiles.

By his waiting attitude the Jew made all existing loyalty relative. No *status quo* was divine, no monarch a god. Daniel and King Nebuchadnezzar agreed on this devaluation of royalty, but the courtiers wanted to deify their king; so Daniel went into the lions' den. The same thing happened today in Japan or Germany exactly as then. Israel is a dangerous interrogation point for any idolatry.

All pagan religion tries to make man strong against the powers which surround him, compelling them to do his will. Abraham introduced the reverse process. Whereas the Semites were accustomed to sacrifice the first-born to give new strength to the father,[4] Abraham's hand was stayed from slaying Isaac.[5] This experience throws into relief the true meaning of Abraham's abandoning the safety of Babylonian society: he was in God's hands, with or without sacrifice, and so was his son, whom he designated a living sacrifice for the whole of life, rather than a victim on a stone altar. So each generation in turn, instead of being killed to make the father strong, had to experience the same helplessness of the refugee in the hands of God.[6] This powerlessness is the essence of Israel's story. Israel is bound to remain weak so that God may be seen to be strong. Isaiah 53 is the final song of triumph of a whole people who do not sacrifice but *are* the sacrifice that binds back all the Gentiles to their true unity of origin.

The weakness of Israel was its only strength. It had to keep so disarmed, so small, so scattered, so leaderless, because it had literally to face the lions' den of innumerable loyalties that make people die for a particular cause, land, or language. Thereby it transcended the pagan meaning of religion, which expresses the separateness of a particular group, and invited all groups into a

[4] At the end of pagan times in the north of Europe, a king of Sweden sacrificed six out of seven sons to keep the royal power intact. When the seventh son was in danger of sharing his brothers' fate, the people rebelled, killed the old power-lusting king, and, under the young prince, were converted to Christianity. They gave up playing providence themselves and changed to faith in the Living God who, tomorrow, may either give power or withdraw it.

[5] Abraham invented Antisemitism. And the Jew baiters should come out openly with their hatred of Israel, for Abraham turned against Semites and "Orientals."

[6] Jacob, when he was to meet his deadly enemy, his brother Esau, was filled with fear. In the night he wrestled with an angel, and awoke lame. Lame and helpless he was, therefore, when he met Esau. In this helplessness he defied once more the magical powers which another man in his place would have used to arm himself.

messianic kingdom where swords would become ploughshares and the lion would lie down with the lamb. And heaven and earth would be one, and the serpent of group pride would have to admit it.

In Christendom, men first had to leave their native land for freedom of religious worship in the time of Calvin; he advised a person to emigrate for this reason. In 1552, a new world was envisaged by people who discovered the creative meaning of emigration. In the course of time, "loyalty to loyalty" became so much our common denominator that its specific representation by Israel was no longer necessary, and the French Revolution emancipated the Jews.[7] When France and America proclaimed the natural equality and natural rights of man, they said in effect that every child begins afresh like Adam, and all nations' return to nature thus became an antidote against the intrinsic paganism of divided loyalty. The Jews could be reconciled with nations which had ceased to be Gentiles.[8]

In our time, Hitler was a reactionary who insisted once more that the destiny of man was to become more and more divided; he literally nullified loyalty to loyalty, and hence compelled Israel to take up her ancient watch on Zion again. He deprived men of their right to purify their loyalties, to deepen their understanding of mother tongue and fatherland until human speech and earthly habitation were seen to be one for all men. But the helpless seed of Abraham is mightier than the idolatry of blood or soil. For blood and soil divide a man's loyalties as much as they unify them. I am my mother's and my father's son. If I bow to their vow of union as made when they became my parents, I keep the creative unity which their marriage has created and I become the first of a new race. But if in my curious quest of

[7] Cf. *Out of Revolution*, pp. 216–237.

[8] On the legal changes in the Law of Contracts which accompanied the emancipation of the Jews, see "Hitler and Israel," in *Journal of Religion*, April 1945. The French Revolution was a blending of Greek genius and Israelitic messianism.

my origin, I dissolve their union into a Mendelian game of hormones, the two strains of my blood disintegrate into paternal and maternal origins. Then, my father literally ceases to be my father and my mother my mother. For, only as inseparable, is this couple "my parents." As female and male, they do not command my respect at all; the creative act of their union is destroyed. Origins war against each other. Every man's blood is divided unless he respects the seal of unity his parents have placed upon their union. A blood unity which voids the words spoken at the wedding of one's parents, at the beginning of their creation of a new people, ends in jealousy and strife. Fear must rage and blood lust, once the sanction is removed from the parent-children relation. The loyalty of race is unable to sustain itself. It splits us apart into the children of one man here, one woman there.

Laotse added to the wheel of society the inside, the hub. Buddha added the outside to the external world, the eye which sees this world. Abraham discovered the fatherhood, the undivided unity before all the divided loyalties, the "before the before." He recognized God as the origin of all origins, as the springhead of all ancestral spirits, as the father who calls us to order and forbids us to dissolve the unions of men. And since he believed that man was the image of God, Abraham himself was called Father Abraham, and what it means to be a father, a patriarch, not a god, to one's child, we know through him.

The hatred of the Jews is a religious hatred. All Anti-Semitism is a pretext. The pagan or Gentile pride is hurt by Judaism because no temporary glory is allowed to shine with unrefracted splendor before the Star of David. Vice versa, the Jews look down on the pagan residues of Christianity with contempt. Peace between Jew and Gentile does not exist except under the Cross. The two do not even exist for each other intellectually. Japan is the best modern illustration of how important the contribution of Israel is. The United States cannot win this war in a deeper sense unless the mythology of Japan is destroyed. To this day,

Japanese children learn that the empire was founded in 661 B.C. The truth is that it is almost one thousand years younger. This is no minor lie. That which we all are tempted to do, to ennoble the past as though we had it as our own title to a coat-of-arms, has kept its hold over a whole people in the case of Japan. This lie makes peace between them and us impossible. Abraham asked for one single history of all mankind. And inasmuch as our American tradition asks and requires *just* this,[9] it is the right heir to Irael's immortal contribution. If and when all participate in Israel's discovery, the individual group of Jews may be emancipated from its peculiar task among the Gentiles. Later, the years from 1789 to 1940 will rate as the short time-span in which the task of Irael was taken over by all men of good will, and during which, for this reason, the old burden of representing Abraham to a hostile world of Gentiles could be abandoned by the Jews. With the general sharing in Abraham's faith, the specific Jewish situation may cease. An orthodox Jew exclaimed in 1933, "Hitler is the Messiah." He may be, indeed, the beginning of the end of the exile, of the mutual impenetrability of Jews and Gentiles.[10]

Jesus

Three directions of the Cross were thus impressed on the souls of our unquiet race. To them, the Son added the "hereafter," the attitude which would be needed after all filial rebellions, all innovations of the next and the next and the next generation should have been brought about. Jesus said: Granted that every generation live to themselves, in the spirit of their time; there still would be the arrogance and the disloyalty and the indifference of the last generation towards all the previous. By the simple inertia of new life spilling over and dispersing over the globe, the cycle

[9] On this fact, see the chapter, "The Americans," in *Out of Revolution*, pp. 672 ff.

[10] See my chapter on the "Emancipation of the Jews" in *Out of Revolution*, also G. Altmann, *Journal of Religion*, October 1944.

of life would lead from one blindness to the next. He stopped this ceaseless splitting into new beginnings. After all these "afters," all these juvenile "waves of the future," the mere beginner would still have to be converted into the son and heir of all times. In the disconnected "mentality" of our own suburb or our own generation, "conversion" plants the convergence of all generations. Anticipating the last possible generation and any generation's rebellions, Jesus turned back into his own time with a yardstick for all temporary movements. While the life-urge of the living always shouts: *"Ôte-toi que je m'y mette,"* "later is better," Jesus embedded all times, including his own, in one supertime, one eternal present. He made the hub, the eye, the father's and the son's attitude available in any place and at any time. And thereby the Cross of Reality was completed. We now gained full freedom towards all trends.

Jesus accepted the Cross of Reality; every man is torn between two times and two spaces. This "torn-to-pieces-hood" cannot be altered. But together we may look for a supertime, for the fellowship in which we can relieve each other's crucial split by solidarity. By the fellowship of all the generations of man, man can come home. The key to this supertime has to be reforged by the faith of every generation, and in our last chapter we shall try to unlock our own life's chambers with the appropriate key; but it is the simple application of the principle of unlocking the doors between the times as practiced by Jesus first.

As the center of history, Jesus can now be seen to unite Buddha, Laotse and Abraham around the Cross of Reality. Since the crux of Jesus' achievement, the creation of genuine future, has been discussed at length in Chapter three, I need only restate it briefly to fit the present context. The whole idea of the Christian era is but this: "Now is the time." "Today the prophecies are fulfilled before our eyes."[11] Jesus became the center of history by *being* the

[11] "This now remains to be said with all possible emphasis: the religious apprehension comes first not as an assertion but as a command." Lord Charnwood, *According to St. John*, Boston, 1925, p. 309.

human soul made visible, the Messiah whom the Jews expected only at the end of history. In this way he introduced the end of time as a directing force in the present. Whereas the Jews identified end and beginning in God and virtually ignored everything in between, Jesus created a historical process in which every year, every day, every present is equally immediate to God because it is equally a meeting point for all the imperfect past and perfecting future. In Jesus the beginnings of antiquity all come to an end and all the ends of modern man make their beginning; the promises of old, to all the nations, are now turned progressively into realizations.

The two central acts in Jesus' biography which made him the beginner of the new era were his death for being the Founder of the Messianic Kingdom and his resurrection as an inspired body of all who wanted to die and rise again with him daily. As long as he was alive he was subject to the old Law and had to carry out his duties as a descendant of Abraham. His death was therefore all he had to invest in the future, and his great discovery was that true future is opened up by the power that survives death. In revealing this power he created man's perfect plasticity on the forward front, his ability to begin anew each day like a new-born child. He redeemed mere birth by revealing it as the fruit of death.

* * *

Buddha, Laotse, Abraham and Jesus concerned us not as isolated individuals or men of genius, but as founders. To found means to lay a new basis for all; it is the step by which a man drops his solitude and frees the many from their fate of being many. Millions have shared and now share in the experience of these four men. They lifted their followers to the level of freedom and regeneration. From now on their respective attitudes are every man's liberties. He needs all four together to unshackle him from slavery to the fronts of time and space. The founders have mastered each direction of the Cross of Reality by living the pure eye, the silent voice, the humble heart, and the fire of new love. Nirvana, Tao, loyalty to loyalty, and rebirth are permanent standards for the full life of man.

The "Social Sciences" as an "Old Testament"

One inconvenience or deficiency in the eyes of the practical man has to be admitted in the work of all these four founders: The task to which they invite begins in every generation all over again. They did not think that the past could prescribe to unborn men how to live. They expected every newcomer into this world to turn against his environment. Well do I know that hereditary Israel, hereditary Buddhism, traditional Christianity, institutionalized Laotsism, do exist. They are, however, rudimentary unless they are taken up in the middle of life with a personal resolve and carried to a new realization. The "Christian Front," for instance, abused the word "Christian" for Gentiles; so did the "German Christian Party"; both were contradictions in terms.

Our four founders conquered the pressures of castes, institutions, ruling classes, money, cults and the frictions which, from the inertia of mere repetition, make the mere permanency of any form of life oppressive.

Confucian education, pragmatic socialism, ruling classes, money, Brahmins, have the opposite tendency. They aver their intent to stay and to become hereditary. At first glance, history demonstrates the desire of all these forms to become static and to be taken as final. On the other hand, Laotse proved especially successful against the boredom of Confucian education, Israel survived all tyrannies, Christianity and Buddha were successful against the moneyed interests; and this list could be expanded.

Hence the individual newcomer into society finds four arsenals for his personal decisions under the most terrifying social pressures of one sort or another. And a frank fusion of these arsenals is needed in our time, without, however, abandoning the order of the Cross. For it is under the Cross that the four arsenals make sense together.

Why is such a fusion desirable? Because the enemies of freedom, creativity, fellowship, and authority are all working today from the opposite angle as in the past. They no longer contradict the four founders but they outdo them! If Christendom, for instance, disclosed the unity of our era, the modern secular movement would go one better and proclaim a program for some thousand years. An English friend of mine after a journey to Egypt wrote to me: "We too must build for four thousand years." The demagogues shout: roots, stability. What is Judaic messianism compared to its secular rival: communism, with its promise to abolish all human suffering? And the times favor such overstatements. Roots, heredity, stability, security, are much in demand. "We need princes," Robert Frost has said. We need forests. We need soil conservation. We need a patient collaboration of many generations to come, for social conduct. Long-range living is at a premium. If Socrates spoke of the *polychronical* wisdom of many generations (Xenophon, *Mem.* I, 14) as the greatest wisdom, we who are lacking it are not able to gloss over such a remark.

If the crisis goes far beyond our individual spans of life, our four founders seem to offer little help. Whereas they speak to the individual, the irrigation of the land, the permanency of the whole soil of the earth, the longing for lasting roots seem to take precedence over the salvation of the individual. Indeed, the values of tradition and loyalty are so rare that we may all feel tempted to go ahead with plans for a mere traditionalism. There is, however, a serious "but" to this. Values like roots, traditions, loyalty must be enacted in freedom, or they become embodied in tyrants, dictators, superstitions, blueprints, medical high priests. These latter especially are on the verge of coming forward with artificial semination, castration, mercy- and cruelty-killing, and other veterinarian-like treatments.[1] The political specialists are playing with the transplantation of whole ethnical groups, elimination of minorities, etc.

For this reason, in our quest of "roots" our four deliverers must remain on top of this otherwise all-too-easily enslaved race of "*homo sapiens.*" They tell us to deal with the future in quite a different manner: not by mere will power, violence, planning for others, but by first bringing ourselves in the right germinal situation, and to follow it up by an apostolate. From germinal acts, not from action committees, authority results instead of tyranny, service instead of blueprints, fellowship instead of intellectual curiosity, creation instead of causation.

The living certainly have a task as difficult as the founders and it is as new and exciting as theirs in their own time. But their times were in exactly the same predicament as ours. And from the Cross of the four founders the human hive, then as today rushed by crisis and war, was penetrated by a timeless orientation, timeless newness, timeless originality, timeless personality.

Granted that the next centuries will clamor for all kinds of permanent solutions and stabilities. From this anguished cry of the multitudes, only more anguish and more upheaval must result if blueprints try to dominate and to preempt the future. Such paper work never commands the respect of future generations; it is quickly discarded for another and another and another scheme. It is not enough to plan for one hundred years because it is more important first to ask: under which conditions are human beings willing to toe the line for one hundred years? Nothing lasts into which the soul of man has not entered with a full act of complete faith. It is only by taking the four founders with us into our future that the soul will enter these future solutions and make them last. The four founders have changed the

[1] It is significant that the Nazis in a great number of cases made the veterinary the head of the university. He had less qualms.

foundations of human nature. They have enabled us to base our thoughts about ourselves, or our society or our history or our economy, on our crucial nature. In contrast, our modern four sciences of society—sociology, psychology, economics, history—start from a Stone Age picture of man. The four departments of economics, psychology, history, sociology, do not put freedom, authority acquired by sacrifice, creation, fellowship, in the center of their assumptions. To the contrary, these sciences presume that the future is not created but caused, the past not looked upon as an authority but as mere tyrannical cultural lag, the mind not experienced as a brotherly fellowship but as a blueprint, and the earth not experienced as waiting to be led to its perfection but as an objective obstacle to be crushed or exploited.

These four departments have not been changed, circumcised, revealed, or converted. They are precrucial. The pooling of energies from all four corners of the Cross is, it would seem, the condition for a concerted attack on this prehistoric attitude of these "sciences." They are prehistorical because they do not admit that in the center of time our own nature became conscious of itself and thereby was definitely transformed. They do not admit that the very existence of any science proves the existence of creation instead of causation, of fellowship instead of bureaucracy, of authority instead of tyranny, of service instead of exploitation. These sciences, then, have not become self-conscious themselves in their own center. For it is in the center of our lives that we cease to play with the world as a mere object, a mere tradition, a mere mental picture, a mere leviathan. In this central moment we transform facts back into acts and begin to live in the name of the same powers under which those acts can be enacted. We shake ourselves free from the nightmares of an intellect which thinks that loneliness, privacy, self-centredness, scepticism, are inherent to thought. We discover that neither we, in our preintellectual existence, nor any other man worthy of the name "man," ever has made any important decision in his life on the basis of such an intellectual process which was thought up for law courts and cases, but not for positive acts.

In the center of our lives we get hold of our real way of living. And we hear the four founders tell us to think up to the very best in our own actual experiences and to discard all our abstract principles. They say: Surrender to the greatness of a great soul who gives you freedom when he could do otherwise. Surrender to the call of destiny when indeed it would be convenient not to do so. Surrender to the freedom of a new start. Surrender to the love of the neighbor who has fallen among the thieves.

The four sciences—history, economics, psychology, sociology—stand for the opposite: They ask man to "live up" to the factual statements of the mind. Cause and effect, mind and body, environment and adjustment, action and reaction, profits and interests, they make the basis of their reality; but these are the forces which you and I may experience every day as ruinous and fatal for our own best way of life; those we are told to believe in as ultimates.

Innumerable individual scientists have protested against the prehistorical method of their departments.[2]

But all the leading men in these fields who have not forgotten their deepest insights were on the defensive against the all-pervading methods of looking for causes, power, tyranny, laws instead of authority, creation, fellowship, and service. As training grounds for new scientists, these areas were held together by a precrucial method. If you said that as believer you could not start from the hypothesis of a "natural" mind and its reasoning, you were deprived of your rank as a "pure" scientist. I myself had to play this role of the volunteer for "impure," and that means "crucial," thinking through my whole academic career, abroad as well as in the United States. The humorous climax was reached at Harvard University. There I was found competent to teach in six different departments before graduate students. How-

[2] A splendid example of such a protest is A. L. Kroeber, *The Superorganic*, Hanover, N. H., 1927.

ever, when my "unscientific" principles became known, a biologist, a physical chemist, and a journalist, banded together, made such a row that I was "relegated" to the Harvard Divinity School. The poor people of this institution were deeply shocked because they tried everything in their power to prove to the other departments that the Divinity School was "scientific" according to the prehistorical standards prevailing in the social sciences.

I do not criticize this reaction. I well understand that the academic world is horrified by the idea of a "Christian" science. Who could blame them? But to a community which thinks crucially about man and which is based on the creation of the four founders, not the same objection could be made by our four social sciences. The Cross erected unknowingly but securely by the four is neither denominational nor ecclesiastical. It is objectified as much as granite or coal; it is created Reality. The synthesis of the Cross of Reality from East and West should be powerful enough to enjoin on these sciences a change of method. Why is the family the bulwark of Israel? Because here the patriarch did not sacrifice his son for his own purposes. Hence the father gained authority instead of tyranny. Why is conversion the bulwark of Christianity? Because here the son laid down the ambitions, the talents, the genius, the leadership of his own generative inspiration for the perpetuation of peace among men. Hence the poorest sinner now may easily forego his private whims, too, for the peace of the world. Why is asceticism the core of Buddhism? Because the powerful withdrew from the exercise of his power. Hence those who lust for power can be led by the powerful beyond power. Why is the feather-weight of the incognito dancer the secret of Laotsism? Because he left no trace, no name, no weight behind him, only the joyous feeling of some rhythm. Hence this joyous rhythm could become infectious.

But in the light of these experienced lives, the known social facts now can all be deciphered by a final standard. A social order may be pronounced *sick* according to the amount of tyranny instead of authority, or causation instead of creativity; or it may be predicated *healthy* because of its degree of fellowship, of rhythm and symphony instead of blueprint bureaucracy, or of its quality of serviceable compassion instead of power. From the Cross, light shines into the caves of society. All "value" judgments, without which no talk about social processes is possible, must be based on the frank admission that we already know, from the Cross of created human nature, what the full freedom, the full creativity, the whole-hearted fellowship, and the perfect service of mankind ought to be. The immense material provided by the research of the social sciences is like the Old Testament of the World which waits to be read with the eyes of Buddha, to be listened to with the faith of the prophets, to be harmonized with the ease of Laotse and to be incarnated with the love of Christ.[3]

We have spoken of the penetration of the Cross in this chapter. It is the jumble of the innumerable facts of the social world which wait to be sorted, to be organized like Chladni's sonorous figures when the bow of a violin is drawn along the edge of a glass and the grains of sand on the glass move to some perfect geometrical form. At one time, in history, the heart was circumcised, the eye opened, the ear "orchestrated," the creature made creator. And on this time-created crucial standard our sanity and the sanity of the mind, including the mind's organized sciences, depend.

Students who are not shot through with the experience of this standard, in their own education, community, service, spirit, cannot be expected to understand the world of man.

[3] To the relation between the social sciences and the full truth, the old adage may be applied: *Novum testamentum in vetere latet; vetus testamentum in novo patet.* (The New Covenant is hidden in the Old; the Old's meaning is disclosed by the New.)

VIII

THE RHYTHM OF PEACE OR OUR "TODAY"

The Enemy of the Holiday—The Coming Sunday—Short-Term Economy—Warriors and Thinkers—The Camping Mind—The Rhythm of the New World

The Enemy of the Holiday

We have lost the faculty of founding rhythms of community life, by the factory system. The efforts to settle rural areas, of colonizing Alaska—a country which could take in ten million people—failed in pre-war days. The Ohio Corn Belt witnessed an experiment in resettlement which ended in an average turnover per farm every three years. The short periods of the factory existence have come back with increased violence through the war boom. They are good for business but bad for people. Glorified migratory workers—most of us may expect our grandchildren to become just that.

If the land is not to be lost to hordes from outside, we in all the Western World shall have to recover the power to build communities. It is quite worthless to map out programs of rehabilitation or resettlement since not one of the individuals thus resettled or rehabilitated has the stamina to partake in the revival of the community. First of all, before any planners can carry out any plan, we shall have to create opportunities in which men recover their power to found or re-found communities. This power is lost. The modern mind has lost the recipe.

The recipe is eternal. The power of building a city is taken away from those who have "un-learned" how to celebrate a holiday together. On a holiday, we share one time and one space although we are divided by self-interest, by age, by wealth, by occupation, by climate, by language, by race, by history; we carry on as though we were one and the same man, regardless of birth, unafraid of death, unabashed by sex, unperturbed by fear.

We shall rediscover our crucial situation if we learn to oppose leisure to holiday clearly. Holiday itself has decayed to leisure more or less; therefore it is by no means simple to see their irrepressible conflict.

In 1929, Eduard C. Lindeman, leading American educator, rose before an international audience of four hundred people at Trinity College, Cambridge, and spoke "the winged words": "We are here as a conference of the whole world for the education of the adult men and women. Now, we in the United States have everything, the time, the goods, the money, the good will of the people. Will you now be good enough to tell us what to do with our leisure?"

A little over a month later the lightning of the Depression struck. And four years later, the recovery began with a "Bank Holiday." A strange civilization which spoke of "leisure" in fat years, and of "holidays" in misfortune. But perhaps even these two extreme usages of leisure and holiday were not devoid of meaning.

Leisure is, indeed, a "too much" or a surplus of individual time while holidays are rooted in a tragedy of the whole community. On holidays, a community triumphs over tragedy; a man at leisure idles away his time.

However lacking in style the Bank Holiday of 1933 was, it had in common with any holiday that it restored confidence after a period of suffering. And however optimistic Lindeman's view of life was, it had in common with the individual's pursuit of happiness that there seemed to be an abundance of time for such purpose vested in the individual.

Let us analyze leisure. Leisure is relaxation by doing things which need not be done. It is doing that which does not matter or doing nothing because this, too, does not matter. I am not under compulsion when at leisure and for this very reason, I am not quite my best or most outstanding self. I may collect stamps or ride horses or swim; but it will spoil my leisure if I turn into a professional stamp collector or swimmer. I do ride but I am annoyed because my riding club tries to make me participate in horse shows. Hobbies should be hobbies; they are spoiled by being taken too seriously. Leisure is less serious than "real" life. Leisure may not be unreal but it is nothing ultimate. In this we hold the key to its understanding. It is a tendency or movement away from the center of existence into some outlying district. Our experiences of leisure may take innumerable forms, but since they all depart from our center of pressure they can move into a restricted number of directions and combinations only. The man at leisure, trying to get away from himself, may go before himself into the past, after himself into the future; he may penetrate into the inner core or look around in the external world. In these four directions, the elements of leisure are found scattered. For instance, we try to get before our birth, in all degrees. The child listens to grandmother's tales, the adolescent to history. In the man, pedigree becomes a potent agency. And this ancestral pride will not rest before the pioneer has been linked up with some medieval castle by hook or crook. A famous American architect tried to convince me that he was the descendant of an English shepherd, and that this English shepherd mysteriously was the seventh son of a German nobleman on the continent whose pedigree went back to the eleventh century. This funny break—in this case, in the sixteenth century—occurs in nearly all the made-up pedigrees. Now, this tendency is the idea of "background," which flourishes in all suburbs, turned into an obsession and running wild. I have seen it taking the form of a remolded silver spoon which came over on the Mayflower as an heirloom. And the Icelandic ruins discovered in the midst of America are meant to ennoble this whole continent by extending its discovery by the white man backward.

A pseudo-history like Japanese Shinto or Nazi myth may be the final result of this eccentricity.

On the other end of relaxations, we play with the future. Here are many of our charities, donations, Sunday school teachings, joining of revolutionary parties and Jehovah's Witnesses. On all these ways, we hope to play some part in the future. We all wish to have offspring of our ideas. We dream of utopias and toy with them.

A third type of hobby penetrates into the outer world, in a mental Don Juan attitude of irresponsible conquest. Travel and sight-seeing is one form of this urge which overwhelms many. The globe-trotter seems different enough from the seducer. But the secrets of something outside of us, separate in nature, stir our curiosity in both cases. I have seen families where this zest for external exploration suddenly changed into a craving for the opposite, intimate cultivation of music. The same people who had given their all for a trip to Europe now would shed tears over the late quartettes of Beethoven and despise anybody who still took pleasure in external sports. This mystic trend towards the emotional life of the inner man is most marked today in the cult of good music.

Every one of us has made use and will make use of these amenities on one or the other eccentric front; at one time or another, and as long as we turn to them freely, they are excellent means of restoring our equilibrium. They are compensations for the lopsidedness of our vocational activities.

However, in many cases, the leisure of modern man is spent in a kind of constant dutiful shift from backward to forward to inward to outward entertainment; like a man on his sickbed, many souls roll from one direction to the other since they do not understand the rhythm and flee the center of their lives. They do not dare to reconcile opposing urges and to stick to man's true place in the middle of the Cross. This truth, by the way, is the great lesson taught us by Nietzsche's madness. The man Friedrich Nietzsche hung in the middle of the Cross as we have described it, a mental Cross. And he broke down because he knew of no fellowship. The place on the Cross is unbearable without fellowship.

The Coming Sunday

This place in the middle of the Cross is our common wealth and we all are invited to celebrate our holidays in it. Here the human soul that celebrates a holiday becomes certain of her true nature. This precisely is the meaning of a holiday as contrasted with leisure. During leisure we are absorbed in pastimes. On a holiday, we can look with "condescension," the same condescension which the commuter experienced,[1] on our conflicts because we have triumphed over them, and we find in the victory over tragic conflict the deepest meaning of our destiny. Leisure is secular because it divides us; we are dragged eccentrically in this or that direction. On her holidays, the soul becomes whole. She accepts her many weekday conflicts or trends because she no longer has to fear them as curses but may accept them as her wealth. She may do so because she proves to herself, on the holiday, her ultimate freedom from every one of them, by communion, by fellowship. Holidays are the mortar of society.

Here, a serious difficulty arises. Sundays and weekends have turned into mere leisure. It is hardly possible to recast their holiday character without first freeing them from any possible misunderstanding as though they were leisure. For instance, a holiday may well include work or services if only to show that the holiday is not simply leisure, nor suburban segregation from business. The holiday must tower as clearly above the suburb as above the factory district.

In his book, *The Threat of Leisure,*[2] the President of Colgate University, G. B. Cutten, listed two hundred and seven books and articles on leisure. Not one of these two hundred and seven at-

[1] See p. 22.

[2] New Haven, 1926, 2 ed. 1929, p. 10.

tempts made a distinction between leisure and holiday. Cutten himself was satisfied to say, "The Puritans were idle Sundays, Thanksgiving Day, and Fast Day" (p. 10), certainly a devastating description of the times in which the congregation constituted themselves as the living body of Christ, in their own estimation and in the clear architecture of their churches. If President Cutten ever entered Dorchester, Massachusetts, and experienced the architecture of the First Congregational Church there—the church of the Adams family by the way—he would have learned that people definitely fulfilled a duty, their highest duty, on Sunday, in founding the perfect body of which the mighty republic of the United States is a poor week-day edition. Then, the word that the Puritans were "idle" on Sundays simply would not have come out of his inkstand. But the reason for this loss of memory is quite plain. If religion is suburban and private, then of course it is impossible to list it as a general way of life. Private religion is no religion; it is its stump. But any community must have religion, must have the power which binds it together for better for worse, and therefore it must create holidays or cease to be a community. Fortunately, the unity of faith in this country is truly elating. The deep sorrow at President Roosevelt's death, and the solemn rejoicing on our V-Days, were expressions of a profound health of the American spirit. I felt great pride and gratitude for being allowed to share in them. We did not have to invent holidays of the hollow type created by the Fascists. With the experiences from April to August, 1945, we may very well live down both Mr. Cutten's idea of "idling" on Sundays and the millennial holidays of the neopagans. But even if we meet the modern mentality on its own ground of complete scepticism, we could still prove to them that the Puritans were not "idle" on Sundays. The President of Dartmouth College, whose M.A. I have the honor to hold, Dr. Ernest Martin Hopkins, once said to me: "It is astonishing how much horseshedding went on in the old days before and after Church. Horseshedding was the talk on the affairs of the town while the horses were tied in the shed." Horseshedding created the political atmosphere for the annual town meeting. Without horseshedding every Sunday, democracy becomes impractical. From this, we may conclude: The Puritans were terribly busy and went to great expense and labor for being idle *together*. The *gathering* of the idle was primary. But in a leisure class or in your or my leisure, the idleness is primary; the being at leisure with others is accidental and arbitrary, and therefore the communion does not reach into the depth of the leisure. Leisure isolates the soul. The headliner: "Everybody joins the leisure class," would exile the soul from suburbs and factories for ever.

Since both these environments chop our lives into small-time loans, one way of restoring the holiday again is to counteract short-range living by long-range living. The gruesome Fascist invention of artificial holidays, and the leisure-class fallacy that on holidays people are "idle," are equally cheap. They are subhuman. Any attempt to get back to normalcy may have to set up a far-reaching goal. In the light of such ultimate goal, even small steps which we may take immediately will be classified correctly. After World War I, the United States discussed leisure. After World War II, the whole world will crave holidays. For this reason, I advocate as final goal a seven-year or nine-year "week." A person should strive to spend the first year in each seven- or nine-year period of his adult life in the kind of fellowship I have been describing in the second chapter, a fellowship of reckless frankness, campaigning, and devotion. This would be in accord with the Christian meaning of Sunday.[3]

Christianity always begins with a new form of Sunday when it rises from the dead. The yoking of future and past is the history of the Church, and the Christian week does this by placing Sunday, on which we anticipate the future Kingdom of God, ahead of the week-days which carry on the patterns of organized work inherited from the past. That is the sublime reason why Sunday is

[3] See my contributions to *Credo Ecclesiam*, ed. by H. Ehrenberg, Guetersloh, 1930.

the first day of the week, instead of the last. In this way, the inspiration of Sunday slowly melts the frozen forms of week-day routine. A similarly progressive redemption of modern life, therefore, may come from our living together, for a Sunday year, in a fellowship which anticipates the Sabbath of mankind. It will be a Sunday of Pentecost, of many languages: on Pentecost, the Spirit began to rule the Apostles so that each in his turn praised the great acts of God. If on the coming Sunday of the Church of Hope we allow the worker, the farmer, the student to praise God in the idiom of his toil, stripped of the dead language of the suburb, our work will then praise God again.

When a friend read this, he exclaimed: "Utterly fantastic." Whereupon I merely listed all the evidence in favor of my thesis: The professor's sabbatical year, the lengthening of worthwhile conferences beyond mere weekends, the remarkable instinct that a good meeting should not contain people of the same type only. Then, there is the unrest in the professions. Fifty years ago, a doctor or minister or lawyer would practice fifty years with little or no time off. Now they break down after a decade, and they experiment with their daily routine nearly incessantly. Telephone, car, plane, mail, have enabled them to do as much, in mere quantity, within ten years as formerly in a lifetime. No wonder that they have to cease to exist every decade. They must retire every ten years as though it was to the grave, and start a new life simply because they have crammed a whole life into a much shorter time span. Is the vogue enjoyed by the "Nervous Breakdown" not the most eloquent argument for a seven-year week?

I also might have showed him a letter from the Mexican Minister of Labor to us of Camp William James, in which he wrote: The sabbatical year is nice for the man in research or for the artist. But it has been the fallacy of the liberal mind to expect the masses to find their holiday too in the excitement of science and art. This can never be. The many will always be passive in the line of these creativities. But the miner and the farmer and the housewife and the white-collar employee, too, must realize the creative life. Only, they should not be asked to imitate the scholar or painter, whose meaning, after all, is found in the fact that millions are benefited by his thought. The agencies of adult education misdirect the free times of the masses unless they allow every man who emerges from his mass existence, *to fight the devil.* The artist and the scholar do fight the devil. No Sunday for man unless he is allowed to fight the devil and to triumph over him. For the majority, this is done in good comradeship. Help us, the Mexican went on, to find ways in which the insipid existence of wage-earning men or peons can be enlarged and let many experience a good fight in the wastelands of our civilization, as the zenith of their life. The fight against the devil was asked here as one holiday at least within an insipid life.

Corresponding to art and science, there is a creativity in social and political action. Real campaigns of fellows banding together at the risk of their whole man, in the camping attitude of the soul on the highway, should be thought out by scientists and artists who really care for social equality. But instead, they promote guidance through the gallery of modern art where the nudes take the poor unprepared souls aback. Art cannot be appreciated outside a long-range desire. These people should at least first take a bath or undergo some other purifying ritual before coming face to face with the most hidden stirrings of their own emotions. It is a walkover now to impart art: "I can tell you all about Rembrandt in ten minutes."[4] But it is a pushover for the poor soul whose body is made to run through the exhibition. There is no build-up of expectation. Similarly, evening classes give more and more information about the research of scientists. And again, the best of the story, the faith which led the scientist through a long darkness, is withheld from the class.

This only means that we do not believe in essential equality of all men with regard to their right to elation or to a holiday. Our museums and our classrooms fit too much into everyday routines.

[4] Verbatim; overheard from an expert's mouth.

The herb against this evil has been grown for a long time. In the lives of men and women of the last century, we find great crises marked out by them as opportunities of revamping their whole life. "Stages on Life's Road" have been lived as great acts of a drama. We in our own lives were led through such decades several times, and each had its own fellowship, its own inspired mores. We did not plan them, but we had to recognize them as essential. Therefore, I know that this is a way of life and I also can point to scores of biographies in which life was reborn by new great acts of faith several times. And each time the new beginning was lived as the creation of an unconditional new fellowship among kindred souls. At least, this personal argument may reassure the reader that I know what I am talking about; it is my own life story. But this does not suffice to carry conviction. It could be an accident or an exception. However, a parallel line of thought is suggested by a stirring in the organized bodies of religion all over the world today.

This line of thought starts with the observation that all religions and even more all pseudo-religions aspire to rhythmical activities. Dance is sanctified; religious dance is recommended; and dancing is rhythm on a short wave. Then, we have liturgical movements to revive the rhythm of the individual service and of the whole year of the Church as well. Sermons grow into continuous chains over months and even years.

Summer schools and retreats are established. Is there a common denominator in all this? What is new in this, what old?

The first yet nearly-forgotten fact is that all religions have enshrined their truths in calendars. And calendars are rhythmical forms of memory and cycles of worship. The liturgical rhythm is expressed in the terms Sunday and weekday, Christmas and Easter, Pentecost and Advent. Philosophical systems are not rhythmical. Religion is. Why?

The reader need not fear that he must go into this annual cycle in any detail. Only the agreement of all worship, of any Church services, needs to be stressed: they try to lift man up to a level on which he may not live blindly but rhythmically. Education, inspiration, the good life, express themselves in rhythmical order. And man has known since Noe and Pharaoh that rhythm is the mutual begetting of opposites: weeping and joy, winter and summer, victory and defeat, birth and death, make up the rhythm, if and when we tackle them as opposite numbers and do not leave them to accident. One Sunday in seven days, one vacation a year, mark us out as educated people.

Whichever way we look at it, we shall find that the fires which warm the hearts of men light up rhythmically; if not, they destroy us. The lack of rhythm is bad. Our speed-up program for the duration sinned against the law of vacation. This period of incubation is essential to the educational process. Education without one-quarter of vacation-time is arhythmical and therefore sterile.

The full life has a beat.

So far, this sounds like pure commonplace and "natural." And indeed, the modern mind has been quick to perceive that the calendar of religion is not more rhythmical than the seasons of the sun and the stars. From this they concluded that the whole calendar was a purely astronomical business of science. And our chambers of commerce have doctored around our Sundays and Easter chronology for a long time on the assumption that the rhythm should be made completely "natural" or mechanical.[5]

Also, our teachers have told us that "originally" man celebrated equinox, solstice, harvest and sowing time, and that the calendar of later religions was created as a more or less superfluous disguise of this "real" and fundamental calendar of the seasons. This teaching begot in many of us a desire to return to nature's rhythm, and to celebrate nature's sacraments like sunrise and sunset, moon nights, and spring. We have done this sentimentally, poetically, and romantically, for the last two hundred years.

You and I know that our time rhythm is unhinged from the

[5] Cf. *Out of Revolution*, pp. 113 ff.

solar revolutions. Whales and horses may take their law of mating from the seasons. The human is made miserable because his appetites are unpredictable. Sex, politics, studies, work, and especially our worries and anxieties, make us exiles from the annual cycle. Man as the exile from nature's cycles, perpetually creates new rhythms.

Now, if man is not contained in the 365 days of the year, is not the liturgical movement a humbug? Or at least a sentimental and romantic cult of an annual process which is no better than Jean Jacques Rousseau's cult of nature? If the Church actually confined our life to annual cycles, she would be stony indeed. Fortunately, this is not the meaning of the calendar of a Church. The natural cycle is not accepted but defied by the liturgical year. The former is a calendar of 365 days. The latter expresses within the scope of 365 days the true infinity of all time from the beginning of the world to its end. For the reasoning mind, time consists of separate units, days or years. For our faith, one year's course inducts into the whole linear expanse of all history. The calendar of the Western World, with its Fourth of July, is independent from nature's mechanism. So much so, that from Christmas to Easter, a whole lifetime of thirty years is remembered, and from Pentecost to Advent, the whole experience of mankind through the Old Testament and our whole era is remembered. The holidays which you and I respect are composed of the memories of all the vicissitudes of man. So much then must be said in emphatic defense of the calendar: whereas in nature, any year is an end in itself, the calendar infiltrates into the passing seasons those long-range elements by which one day and one year become links in the chain of unending time. I myself have written the history of the last thousand years around the holidays and the calendars instituted during this epoch; and I am sure that this new method places the historian in the center of human history.[6]

[6] By this method, *Out of Revolution* could be written as the autobiography of Western man. See the theory of this in D. L. Miller, "The Calendar Theory of Freedom," *American Journal of Philosophy,* vol. 41, 1944, pp. 320 ff.

Short-Term Economy

However, when all this is said in defense of our annual routines and our holidays and Sundays, it is only fair to add that most people seem to have forgotten these facts. The onlooker's stare upon the revolving cycles seems to deprive him of inner participation. As soon as we think that these calendars can be kept alive without our underwriting them and sponsoring and living them, they wither. Those who go to church as a mere routine will not profit from any liturgical restoration. Something has to happen to them personally first; they must realize that new rhythm asks to be created, in their own or in the world's life. And of these real rhythms, the rhythm of the Church is a reminder and a challenge, but it never is the story itself. Christ is not crucified within the church on Good Friday unless he has been crucified on Calvary, in stark reality, first.

And this relation of original and reflected living is the reason why we must realize the larger rhythm of our own decades in stark realism before we can join the Church successfully. The full length of our group experiences and the full expanse of mankind's struggles for appropriate rhythms is compressed in the liturgy; but we shall decipher this cryptic book by some analogous experiences in our own life.

It is the only way by which we shall defend the Church against the abominable misunderstanding of many of my most well-meaning friends. These people say that the services of the Church are a beautiful myth, but a myth nevertheless. How is such a misunderstanding possible? And mind you, these men and women are the most conscientious. Well, they stare at the annual cycle as at a spectacle of nature, and not as a process by which we bind the years of mere nature into our era. The years of the Church are debased and degraded into a matter of fact. But the Church was founded for the real progress of our whole lifetime and of mankind's whole history. Her services were intended as the self-sacrifice of the congregation for the continuity of mankind and as our demand to enter this whole process and to shed our purely mechanical, purely blind cycles. The calendar of the Church became a myth when people began to listen to somebody else's sermon instead of offering themselves to a perennial way of life on Sundays.

The dear conscientious "myth-rakers," what is amiss with them? Their nervous system has been crushed by their daily petty schedules. They have been deprived of the wide breath of history in their own back yard. It would be too much to ask them to encompass their whole life at one glance. They change their environments too often for that. The anchor of their soul will bite shorter periods only, of a decade or of five years. The fraction of time which needs to be cultivated lies between the whole of life and any one year in it. Words have lost their meaning and have become "myth" because a new "optimum" for personal experiences waits to be taken up, a time-optimum, of which the last centuries did not conceive.

Because the new time-optimum has not been provided, psychoanalysis has taken the place of this. Psychoanalysis is the obvious reaction to this deeper lack of rhythm which factory and suburb imposed on us. The knots of personal time are untied by the analyst in an individualistic fashion. But even the doctors themselves are becoming aware of the deficiency of their method. The fellowship of a normal group, not the hothouse of sick individual consciences, is the answer to our hunger for rhythm.

For the sceptic who still exclaims, *"Fantastic!"* a simple equation in time may be interesting. Our pay-day humanity lives from pay-day to pay-day. The year of the community is their longest unit. This makes us into a mob because man is man solely by his uniting seventy and hundred and six thousand years. Formerly, the economic interest of a family was lasting, hereditary, and it bound them to some property for a century. The year of their congregations was short because their economies were long lived, a lasting inheritance of fields, orchards, house and barn.

Now, one year has become the longest economic unit which a

working man can encompass. Why are we so incredulous about creating the rhythmical counterpart to this change in the economic time unit? Economy, which was very long, beyond our own lifetime, has become brief; that which has been short, the soul's calendar, should be lengthened in correspondence to the shortening of the economic cycle. Man must experience long-range living now, by a special effort; his every-day experience has no vestiges of it.[1]

The sceptic may still shrug his shoulders. Will he answer the question, What happens when we do not respond to this need? The answer is written in blood and ruins: when everybody does his work in the mass, at the split seconds of scientific management, the super-compensation is the millennium, a thousand years of Third Reich, or some other inflated eternity. The balance between workday and Sunday is an eternal demand of the human soul. Is the work minute, then the slogans become hallucinations of many centuries. Why was Europe shrieking with repristinations of the ninth, the tenth, the eleventh centuries of our era as the standard for national frontiers? These nightmares of Greater Bulgaria, Greater Albania, Greater Germany, were antidotes to the insipid existence of the moment in the sudden rise of the factory system. The human periods of five, seven, ten years are the real new order which is needed. But of our failure to provide these short and yet livable periods, demagogues have taken advantage. In 1932 a diplomat accredited to Mussolini's government said to me laughingly: "They call themselves the ancient Romans, but they do build the highways which are needed." This cynical remark reveals the relation between the long-range ideology and short-range living. The demagogues sell their years by the thousands to an affamished public of migratory workers.

[1] Douglas Horton has drawn my attention to the role of the Hindoo Asramas, for our purpose. "A new conception of marriage, a new vision of the family, a new experiment in sociology came into existence, a new demand for the middle aged." P. Chenchiah, in *Asramas, Past and Present*, Kilpauk, Madras, 1941, p. 120.

If industry would have established group tenancy of tested workers over periods from five to fifteen years, Germany might have escaped Hitlerism. Because the connection was obvious, my work between 1918 and 1933 was devoted to such "de-concentration" of industry.[2] Men and women would have faced the stages on life's road as God created these periods, *i.e.* as rhythmical periods which bind us for a time, consistent with our nature, into a consecrated fellowship. Our nature demands to be fulfilled in equal distance from the split second and the millennium, and in this distance from both extremes we shall find our time-optimum.

Teams of between twelve and fifty people could coalesce in such temporary groups. These groups will not last forever, as our society changes too often in its ways of production. But they would be more than mere agglomerations of migratory workers. These work platoons or teams, if started on the right foot, could finish a common job, could hold on to a communal life until another group matured on whom the task could devolve, and could experience the stages of realization from the first fierce advance to the later stages of tough going and final survival. Compared to the commuting masses who are checked by the stop watch, these teams would work differently, at their own hours, under their own administration. For such farming out to personalized groups, our big corporations have innumerable opportunities. But first, people must come to know that we shall have neither towns nor citizens, but job hunters only, without this step. That is to say, this next step in industry will not come without a public spirit seeing this economic measure in its wider implications.

In the long run, the abolition of slavery paid in dollars. But long before it had to be realized that even though it paid, slavery was untenable. All economics are subservient. I can prove that modern ways of industry do not pay because the machinery is far too

[2] In 1935 the Lowell Institute in Boston asked me to deliver the Lowell Lectures on this theme. See now Philip Mairet in *Prospect for Christianity,* London, 1945.

bureaucratic. Farming out pays. But nothing is anchored in the depth of history which is not first decided *regardless of cost.* The decisive, compelling character of our crisis lies in the fact that the masses have no chance of living crucially. Neither can they show loyalty to their own past (Roman Empires were made their *ersatz* for such loyalty to their personal past) nor may they prove faith in their personal future (thousand years of Hitler's were *ersatz* for this faith). Modern industry has deprived too many people of their right to crucial living, of a wholesome suspense of growing from one phase of life into the next. Both our birth into a new quality of life, by founding a new community or fellowship or group, and our conservatism of seeing the thing through, are needed. This dual relation is the character of any living group.

Western industrial society did not produce this week, year, or this holiday in time. And so, the World Wars came instead. The wars did create for millions a campaign in which they could leave their insipid existence and have these very experiences. Destiny will haunt us until we allow ourselves to be remade by this war experience. It can teach us what a holiday is. For any war, and this is its honor, releases us after its high pressure for the mighty moment when peace or armistice is announced.

When the soldiers return, they may desire rest and leisure as individuals. But the community needs for its own health a holiday. On this holiday, the tragedy of losses in battles is not forgotten as when we are trying to take our minds off something disagreeable. The power of a holiday consists in the ascendancy over tragedy. No holiday without pain remembered and suffering sanctified. From this bravery a higher certainty of our true calling is acquired. Any army which comes home furnishes the community with the "natural" experience of a holiday. In it, our life is restored to the full stature of its strength because in pain, in disgrace, in desperation, the holiday is rooted; but its fruits are the rebirth of the community. For, when we discern the things which only pain reveals, we see behind into the things hidden from the eye, we see the connection of death with birth, of darkness with light, of heaven with earth. God created heaven and earth in the beginning. This fact does not suffice. It must be lived. The holiday is the occasion on which the sun of this truth rises again over the whole community.

The mercifully tendered opportunity to relearn the true character of holiday, almost ruined by leisure, needs not go to waste. We may derive a law from its emergence in a world war. Any time must tackle its central conflict, bring it into some rhythm, and finally ennoble it by a holiday. As long as the greatest conflict of a period is not faced, all its minor conflicts will re-open, under its pressure. Husband and wife in sex, capital and labor in production, youth and old age in culture, are minor conflicts, successfully reconciled in former periods, but now all breaking up again under the pressure of our central conflict for which we have no holiday yet.

What is this greatest conflict? The greatest conflict of our day seems to me to be wider even than factory and suburb. The extremes are reached when the warrior and the thinker of our days are confronted in their tendencies. What can Einstein and a Ranger say to each other? The cleavage between their official philosophies has been taken for granted. We have left peace-time thinking and war-time action completely unreconciled. Thinker and warrior have no common history. If we could create it, the community spirit would be reborn.

Thought has been academic, warfare has been brutal, these last decades. But quite another approach is open to us. Why not recognize the thinker and the soldier of any society in their relation, one manning the first, the other manning the last station on the road of the inspiration through a community? Why not consider the thinker the gateway through which an inspiration enters the city for the first time, and the soldier the wall in which the spirit has become incarnate so that living souls will defend the city as its best wall?

It will be our last task, on the following pages, to enlarge on the fellowship of peace lest it exclude the boys who return from the war. The experiences of soldiering belong on the future Cross of Reality. Purely civilian mentality cannot satisfy those who crave for the graver Cross of the whole reality around and in us. We need the whole potential of human nature.

Then we would be able to celebrate holidays regularly and not in that exceptional moment of the army's homecoming only. Then the devil who saps our power to found communities would be hunted down.

Warriors and Thinkers

A young man of my acquaintance tried to become an ambulance driver in Egypt because he considered himself a Christian Pacifist. This plan failed; he was drafted. Whereupon he found that he was not a real Pacifist. But now he went to the other extreme; he left the Episcopal Church. Not being able to live up to his own allegedly Christian standards, he decided to become a "pagan" all round, without trimming. It must have broken his heart, this absurd decision, because the daily service of prayer and praise used to fill him with joy.

Everybody knows that thousands of good boys are in a similar predicament, though perhaps not such an extreme one. Why not help them? But I find that most people are embarrassed. I see no reason for embarrassment.

Certainly, if our young soldiers now consider themselves as "fallen men," and confuse this fact with paganism, it is not their own fault. The civilian tradition of thought during the last decades did little to encompass the character of the warrior. And so, noble energy goes to waste in many souls.

The place of the warrior as against the thinker, the scientist, has to be illuminated and to be redefined. Since the millions are soldiers now, this mighty republic will lose its identity with its scientific and rational past if the connection between warfare and science is not found. The era of science must allot a reasonable place to the militant fighter. How can War and Peace be lived by one homogeneous and catholic people of thinkers and fighters? Instead of our cutting them into two frustrated halves of brutes and brains, how can the human soul triumph over the separation of thinkers and soldiers?

Is it true that "the only answer seems to be to have a completely separated body of people to do the thinking and planning of which the average 'warrior' seems incapable"? This sentence is from a naval officer's letter, after thirteen months of service on a destroyer in the Pacific. And he goes on to say: "Somehow I don't seem to be able to reconcile the ideas of responsibility to the immediate job at hand and rather complete irresponsibility to the greater task of creating a new and somehow better world. . . . My greatest need at present is to talk seriously with someone outside the service who is concerned more with the future than with the present contingency of shooting down an enemy unit associated with a machine which must be utterly destroyed, then forgotten while one concentrates on the means for eliminating the next unit."

And his letter continues: "The thing that has struck me as most dominant in the 'soldier' is the idea of 'forgetfulness.' This characteristic is most evident in our men . . ." (There follows description of battle scenes.)

"I know you can help me to be a better 'soldier.' If you don't maintain some sort of an ideological structure for us to gather up when we return I don't know what will happen—but I feel certain that you won't let us down."

Accordingly, I shall try to redefine the interaction of warriors and thinkers. For this purpose, the current identification of war with paganism and of peace with modernity will have to be abandoned.

And this fact may be most easily understood by a quotation from the Old Testament. Of course, the whole Old Testament says the same everywhere, as a whole, in the five books of Moses, in the first three verses of Genesis or in the Prophets. However, the Bible speaks our own language, I think, in the last two verses of the last book of the last group of writings. They are ascribed to the prophet Malachi, and he seems to have been as sociology-bitten as we are. For he expressed the secret of the Father-God, Spirit-Father, Father-Son mystery, in sociological terms. "Each time," the prophet said, "when the hearts of the fathers and the hearts of the children are not turned to each other, the land is cursed."

Progress has been so rapid in industry that the land is cursed today. The hearts of the parents and the hearts of the children in many lands do not entertain the same hopes and fears. Five years ago, a minister in New York City established a common living center for graduates from one of the great universities. And when they gathered in 1939, before the war, these young business men and lawyers, the wave of the future had engulfed them. They all were for a mild form of regimentation. They would not like to call it Fascism; however, the choice of their horizon practically was restricted to the two possibilities of Communism or some mild brand of American Fascism and corporate state. They certainly had very few religious or political convictions in common with the generation of their parents. Perhaps, they had not very definite convictions themselves. But instinctively they expected regimentation and were ready to be regimented. They did not fall in a rage when a German friend, by government regulations, was prevented from marrying the girl of his heart who had fled from Germany to England for love of him but could not enter the States for love of him. (They by now have waited more than six years and I still find that young people do not see any reason for excitement over this fact which, in 1850, would have been unthinkable.) But their own soul was of no great concern to them, either. The youngest college classes have gone even further in their apathy about their own importance.

Now, this situation of one generation is a sturdy fact just as the fact that we have two legs; each generation differs. And neither race nor creed nor class has as much influence on history or politics as this mutual seclusion of one generation and all others. "Every generation is a secret society, and has incommunicable enthusiasms, tastes and interests which are a mystery both to its predecessors and to posterity." [1]

This generation expects jobs. The previous one had a social worker's tender conscience. Before the children of men rushed for gold. Before again, they were Mormons, Oneida Socialists, Owenites, Millerites.

These are facts as stubborn as that some people are born black and others white. Aye, since the mystery of each generation is less known, it is even more stubborn a fact than black and white. As a temporal form of existence, the spirit of each generation is mere material, for exploitation. It is a pre-religious, pre-Christian, and pre-historical reality. Man occurs in the guise of his generation's spirit.

Before any man can enter history or turn his heart to his children or to his parents, his predilections have to be met, and only then will he listen or have anything lasting to say in history. For, in themselves the spirits of the times will not permanently interest the world. For, the spirits of the times are themselves mere phases of this world's cycles.

This would be different if one generation could be alone on earth. They indeed would be free to forget about their parents and their children. They would need no religion, and they certainly would never believe in a revelation which talks of Father and Son as equally responsible for the spirit. Obviously, such a nomenclature connotes some process which runs counter to the spirit of any one generation. The terms are clear. In the Divinity, Father and Son unfold the quality of being, by spreading it through two generations. And the Spirit, lest he be confused with

[1] John Jay Chapman, *Memories and Milestones,* New York, 1915, p. 184.

the wit of the moment, is explicitly said to descend from the interaction of two generations, the Father and the Son.

The analogy for man should be obvious. He can't be the image of God if he serves the spirit of his own time.

Neither the social workers nor the semi-fascists have a history in the future. For the morality of one particular generation does not survive the mores of that generation. Mores, thank God, are transient and when they are good mores, they do not petrify like vices.

But the merely generative mind, genius, worships its own products; the pagan mind equates the life span of his own creative faculties with the life span of the energy which allows him to think. It is the pagan's obsession to admire his own philosophy and to believe that his mind is generated within his own nature, at his birth. We hear people boast of their birthright and native nature, and condemn others for their different one.

But this equation of one generation's spirit and the spirit does not work. It is true that a man's physical life span is measured from birth to death. (The Church never did this but counted from baptism to funeral.) From this simile, man concludes that his mind is his lifetime companion, progressing also from birth to death.

However, while this life stretches from the cradle to the grave the life span of an inspiration reaches from the middle of one man's life to the middle of the life in the next generation. Thus the difference between our physical and mental existence is expressed in the difference of their periods or rhythms. As carriers of physical life, we feel our life to be an unbroken sequence. As carriers of valid thinking, as scientists, rulers, writers, parents, experts, officers, we can't have peace if we try to imprison this thinking process within us or if we think of it as synchronized with our own physical life-span.

These ways of thought invade our physical existence in the middle of life, mould us, put us into our class, vocation, or office.

And by our functioning in them and under "the rules of the game," we start younger men on the road to succeeding us in our social role. Shaped life attracts younger, more shapeless life always, because in nature all shapeliness commands reiteration. (The psychoanalysts call this the "compulsion to repeat," but it is the great economic law of the universe.) The young always try to inherit everything which there is to inherit from the past.

For instance, every boy or girl in this country learns the three R's. Now, perhaps they would have better minds if they learned the Greek letters and language instead, but they have no choice. This English is their heritage. Long before they could choose, their elders have moulded their minds and made them into English speakers, English readers, English writers, and accountants. The young depend on the choices made for them by their elders. An heir is not somebody who can chose what he shall inherit; if he could make his choice, he would be self-made. But, in so far as his inheritance is determined, he is an heir, and under the laws of heredity. And to his heredity a man may say either yes or no, but he is caught in this one alternative which is not creative. He does, however, determine the background of the next generation.

Hence, one's generation's background is due to the previous generation's foreground. My father's values determined my education. And by no action of mine can I cancel out the fact that his education preceded my own judgments. I am more the product of his intent or his omissions than his own life was. I am his heir. Only my own son or students may fully reflect my own choices.

Society is based upon a principle of dovetailing which is unknown in the animal kingdom. To ourselves and to the education of ourselves, one insight comes too late. We can only close the door of the barn after the horse is stolen. A man who would try to make himself would be bruised and scarred all over his body and soul. He would be hard-boiled. And in biology, hard-boiledness is equal to failure. Life needs plasticity. Therefore, our thoughts intervene between our bruises and the newborn baby's plasticity. The most important effects have already affected us when we come to think of them. Of course, when they have done their work, we may reconsider and doubt them, and act differently. But since we ourselves are already determined, our new conclusions stand a fairer chance of bearing fruit in others than in ourselves.

This constitutes the great human secret. Mendel's mutation takes place in the conception and birth of the individual. Our historical mutability, on the other hand, is effective as a mental relation between two people, two generations, two times. Those qualities or energies which link at least two, and weld them into a cooperative being, "transpeciate" our species constantly into new men; naturally, these qualities can only be found when they are not looked for within the individual. In him we shall never discover how any social function unifies the speaker and the doer, the first and the second doer, and so on. These energies must be processes between two minds, two hearts, two people, at least; perhaps between many more. The obstinacy with which psychology has studied the mental processes within the individual is no proof that its method is fruitful. The dream of a self-taught, self-ruling man is a bad dream. The measure for teaching and ruling cannot be found from the abnormal compression of these processes into one individual. Historical man is taught by others, and rules others; and in these relations, he is compelled to realize himself. "He," never exists, but is always between two times, two ages, as son and father, layman and expert, the end of one era, and the beginning of another. In their despair, the mental monadists—who look for the mind inside the individual—call our time a period of transition. Sheer nonsense; the essence of time is transition. In so far as we act or speak, we can act or speak meaningfully only between two other generations preceding and succeeding us, because we always come too late to ourselves.

My self is not the container for my acts and ideas. My acts carry out the ideas implanted in myself. My ideas plant the acts in somebody else because he will be purer to receive them. Since this is so, our will is not a vehicle for making ourselves. Freedom of the will is not the subject matter for self-worship or self-reliance. Freedom is given us because of our functions as enders and beginners. Our function as children requires to be superseded by our function as parents. The child is certainly not father of the man; I think that this is the central fallacy of mental theory. The romanticism of Rousseau and Wordsworth destroyed the continuity between generations; and as a substitute condemned the poor children to carry a burden which rightly their elders should bear. The child prodigy of the nineteenth century is the ghastly result of this impatience with the individual. He was in a hurry to be his own father; as a reaction, he usually remained childish. *Freedom is given us for the race.* If we try to interpret freedom as given us for ourselves, we grossly exaggerate our abilities. If we deny freedom, we fall into the snares of racial servitude. Jesus remained under the Jewish law to the end of his first thirty years. It took him the time span of what is called one generation to outgrow the synagogue. His obedience consisted in his patient walk through life. The risen Christ may walk with all men. He could not belong to the ages if he had gone at nineteen into the desert and founded a sect then and there. In his walk through his generation, if we walk with him, we are all freed from our native limitations.

It is the whole content of Christianity that we are free, but that we arrive too late at our own freedom for fully wielding its liberating forces ourselves. Our own time is a station between the times which our freedom rejects and the times which our patience prepares. The meaning of liberty is our power of creating a new kind of man. This power is capable of closing the breach between the mere fashions of each separate generation. Enslaved by the latest trend and current events, we rush to the worship of the gods of our days. And these gods of the day follow each other in a cycle similar to the business cycle. Every type of mentality automatically begets its undertaker in form of the opposite philosophy. And in the cycle of all possible philosophies the poor devils are caught blindly.

But we can wake up and see the cycle and break its spell and create peace beyond the warring spirits of the times. This power was the distinguishing feature of our era. Therefore when this power goes into eclipse, we are back to paganism, immediately. And in paganism, eternal war is the order of the day, and war only, between all the spirits of men. Accordingly, the Nazis who proclaimed "eternal war" and "annihilation" and "elimination" banked on the one generation of the "Youth Movement" which broke away from all peaceful relations with their parents. All the revolutionaries in Europe are "matters of one age" and play up their own spirit ruthlessly. The Nazis reveal that, if one generation may carry out its temporal spirit unhampered, war becomes the only principle of life.

But it is no good to retreat, in the face of this relapse into paganism, into the eternal city of peace. The eternalists would like to look down with superiority into the arena of human fighting. We have heard their protest of an eternal peace, and certainly the Pacifists are the indispensable antithesis to the ghastly warhoops of the temporal mind. But the antithesis is Pharisaic and incomplete.

They are right when they abhor war as the order of the world; it certainly is its disorder. The world was created for peace. But they are wrong when they do not add that the act of creating the world is a perpetual act. What we call the creation of the world is not an event of yesterday, but the event of all times, and goes on right under our noses. Every generation has the divine liberty of recreating the world.

The transient mind stares at war, finds it everywhere and proclaims it the form of life. The eternalist stares at peace and proclaims it the content of life. Both suffer from a fixation. Both are lacking in freedom. The soul knows that we move in a world at war to bring peace into it. In every hour of history the recreation of that peace, which was created into the world as its goal from the beginning, is the topic of our fight. Between the war party which places itself on the side of the world "as it is" only, and the peace party which places itself on the side of God only, our loves, hopes and beliefs force us to proclaim a "war and peace" party. The Cities of Men and the City of God form one crucial unity in a living person. The chaotic world at war, and the emerging new peace for this chaos which made the war, are the two aspects of a mankind in cooperation.

At this point, the greatness of the educational vogue of the last hundred years becomes clear. Liberalism as mere anarchy of beliefs or values does not impress me. But liberalism as willingness of parents to give their children a futuristic education strikes me as great. These parents were ready to let their children go further than they themselves could reach. The true Christian spirit of Liberalism lies in this willingness of whole generations to let the next generation go into a future from which the parents themselves were excluded.

Since the liberal anarchy of standards for the individual around us is so colossal, our fundamentalists easily overlook this very definite creed of the agnostic age. Between the generations, a bond of parents' love and children's faith was established which translated the parents' hopes into the children's lives. This should make us feel reverent.

However, although the parents made the sacrifice, the institutions of learning did not do the same. When the boys came to school and college, the older generation there declined to mould them into new men. The interpersonal energies which connect two ages were denied. Man had, they were told, his own mind to and for himself. And so the teachers and students on our campuses lived under the fiction that they were contemporaries and could feel and think the same things. Nobody was responsible for anybody else's thoughts; nobody was meant to be his brother's keeper. And the teachers left their lives outside the classroom deliberately. It was bad taste to teach with ardor.

At this moment, a young generation is in a new kind of war, a war which is not based on a settled society of the past, but on an industrial society of constant flux and change. This generation does not fight, as all former patriots did, for the father's laws and order because they know from their fathers themselves that change is of the essence. Change, so they have been taught, is their birthright. So, if they are to fight, the soldiers must fight for a future beyond the war, not for the past as it was before this crisis.

Our soldiers wait for opportunities, not simply of returning home, but of turning towards a new peace and of immigrating into the future. The morale of this army will depend largely on a change of heart in the articulating generations, the people who teach, write, speak, and occasionally think.

Our schools have tried to teach the boys and girls the values which we feel they should think about. That usually meant that they were asked to feel that which we thought. So they ceased to feel. Now, the discovery of the two-generation-way of the mind in action involves a tremendous change. The young first must be allowed to feel, to scent, to presage, to fight for themselves, to quench evil, to protect the world before we can speak to them theoretically. The old must think out lucidly that which the young have felt or can feel about the future. "We may conceive humanity as engaged in an internecine conflict between youth and age. Youth is not defined by years but by the creative impulse to make something. The aged are those who, before all things, desire not to make a mistake. Logic is the olive branch from the old to the young."[2]

In other words, the thinker (any man, old or young, who is asked a question, finds himself in this awkward role) should not ask the doer (the man who is about to act, perhaps on the basis of the thinker's answer) to share the detachment of the thinker.

[2] Alfred N. Whitehead, *The Aims of Education,* New York, 1929, p. 179.

This, however, is what our academic education does, and the detachment of the thinker-answerer is recommended as the only right emotional climate. "Don't get excited" is no wise counsel to young men. If they no longer can get excited the world decays, just as much as when the old men can't keep cool.

Therefore, the thinkers should try to think out clearly the same processes which work up the emotions of the soldier of life so deeply that he is willing to give his life for safeguarding order. The thinker's clarity should match the soldier's intensity, without ever forgetting that by his clarity he tries to rival the heat engendered in a human heart. Therefore, the thinker depends upon the flames of passion burning in the doer, and these high temperatures provoke and challenge his effort in lucidity and dispassionateness. These flames must burn without smoke.

The collaboration of soldiers and thinkers must be the central article of any society's constitution. Only then will the thinkers drop all pettiness and rediscover those truths which are vital.

This would be nothing but applied Christianity. It would carry the evangelical relation which has grown up between parents and children during the century of Liberalism to its logical conclusion. And the schools and colleges would now undergo the same conversion which the parents underwent when the *Autocrat of the Breakfast Table* was buried.

When the parents ceased to play God Almighty for the beliefs of their children, they did something of significance for the universal relation between thinkers and soldiers: they trusted the young.

Must not anybody who is asked a question about the road, and has to find an answer, speak cautiously, trying to make no mistake because the other fellow might march off wrongly upon the answer? The soul's delight is in doing this, here; the mind's genius is to think all in the proper system. As cautious as my answer to the stranger who asks for directions, so bold must be the action of the man who goes to war. Thought is born by circumspection. But a soul is born through the growing pains of suffering in action.

Before this war, our schools preached to the young to avoid conflict, to avoid pains, even the growing pains of that suffering which is the inexorable counterpart of acting according to your heart's command. When Aeschylus said that the counsel of Zeus prevailed, which ordained that the man who acted had to suffer, he said something as true as that "two and two is four." But this interplay of action and "passion," doing and paying the penalty for it, has been ridiculed by sociologists, psychologists and all the monadists. And so, they sterilized the young because the interplay between the generations was taken for granted. For thirty years, the Holy Ghost had abdicated in favor of the Spirit of the Times and the wit of the individual. The thinking of our college men became childish because the old and young tried to obliterate their difference in age, and played together as though they were one age. Compromise became the great slogan. Before they probed into the depth of their feelings or the profoundness of their thoughts, people hastened to compromise. And these compromises satisfied as much as did the Missouri Compromise; they did not create one common reality between different generations. Since nobody took the trouble to pour his real desire or his real vision into the compromise, no promise was fulfilled by it, and all hope was frustrated.

When a student of mine understood this, he wrote me one sentence which touched me to the quick. I had not foreseen this reaction; and I still stand in admiration before this lucid sentence: "Oh," he wrote—and this is a literal quotation—"I am a pagan; for I have no speech."

He had discovered paganism to be the lack of relation between the generations of mankind. And in the process he had made the much more important discovery that speech is not the by-product of individual action or individual thinking, but that we speak with power only when acts and thoughts meet. Our tongue, our power of the word to which the millions obediently march and serve and sacrifice, is not the "expression" of scientific ideas, or the war cry of blindly marching cohorts. The living speech of a community results from the polarization of acts and thoughts; like the spark which crosses the dark gap between the positive and negative pole of electricity, speech is a flaming arc connecting different generations. On the one hand, blind acts are speechless, and who does not know the dumbness of the mere busybody? But—and that is mostly forgotten—similarly, abstract ideas are speechless; in a sense, all science is nearly speechless; it is a whisper between experts. Only when *taught,* only when facing a new generation, does science recover speech. The blessing which results when thinkers and soldiers face each other is that public speaking is reborn. Speech blends the two processes of pure thought and pure action. The student who signed as a pagan did so because he found himself outside this electric arc; but whereas most of us remain unconscious of our exile, he discovered that we have, as children and parents, a spiritual office, in the never-ending chain of generations. *The links of a chain must overlap. The evolutionary scheme of the last century omitted this big question of overlapping,* of putting the rings of the chain together. Lest the chain remain unforged, children and parents cannot behave as though they were contemporaries. Both must go to the edge of life, in militancy against danger, for the reorientation of the species; one exposing their physical life as soldiers, the other exposing their social reputation as thinkers. (This is the reason why no progress in human thought is possible without the martyrs of thought or science.) A brave man is he who risks his *status quo* lest new life be stifled or higher life be destroyed. When we eat, when we breathe, we integrate lower life into richer life; our social acts obey the same law. The physical existence, in the soldier's case, and in the thinker's case, the moral existence, are the chips which we stake for the essence.

By now, the soldier will be seen as a spiritual agent, while we come to admit that thinking itself is risky action. The "spirit" is a comprehensive term for both action and thinking. When the spirit of France died, she lost Paris, her intellectual center, and Toulon, the center of her imperial strength, both. To the spirit, mind and body are both mere matériel.

If there is one spirit, thinkers and soldiers move in one common sense. And there is one spirit when the parent-thinker in us brings up his pearl of thought out of the same darkness in which the son is plunged by the feelings and passions of his youth. We should think up to our impulses and feelings, not as it is the fashion, drag our lives behind some abstraction, some "ism," of our mind's making. If a thinker rethinks the truth in the light of a doer's vital impulses and actions, the future way of life lies open again as it was proclaimed in the beginning of our era as the good news. New lives may be lived in freedom; the young may trust their vital instincts, no guilt from the past shall asperse them, for their elders will forge an armor of thought around their hearts' flames. The expert may retranslate this into theology. For my naval lieutenant, junior grade, the quotation of "original sin" at this point would add little. He is impatient to see the right relation restored: "I feel certain you won't let us down."

Thinking for soldiers, instead of ruminating for children, is a very new aspect of research and education. But this is the reform of our educational system which the three witnesses demand; the speechless college senior, the "forgetful" lieutenant, and the man who leaves the Church when he enters the army. Higher education in the future can only be planned for people who serve and fight life's battles, on whatever fighting front, who can see the flame of faith, the rays of thought, the reflexes in acts, all as incarnations of God's word.

Otherwise the bodies of the young might be slaughtered for the dated ideas of a senile science or the mature ideas of truth might be butchered by the rash instincts of brutes. In between lies the road of atonement between the body of young life and the mind of the old life. These two have to coexist and to interpenetrate.

In this, what else do we say than that which was known always? The coexistence of more than one generation at the same time, the deliverance from blind cycles and sequences, was called the achievement of the Holy Spirit. He was conceived as proceeding from the Father and the Son. We all know that a father's mind should enter into the impulses of his son. That is the reason why nobody may call himself a father, by mere physical procreation. Fatherhood is rethinking the world in the light of one's children. Why is God so inexhaustibly original? Because he rethinks the world for every generation of his children.

Beyond the level of brains or brutes, of scientists and warriors, the soul is born. The soul in the scientist ensouls him into a teacher; and the soul of the warrior transforms him into a soldier. All through this essay, we spoke not of "scientist" and "warrior," but of "soldier" and "thinker," because all the time we anticipated a mutual recognition between the representatives of war and the representatives of peace.

When the "warrior" learns to incarnate the spirit of his society, he is emancipated from any instinctive blindness. The soldier is a freed warrior. When the "free thinker" is drafted by the love of his neighbor, he is freed from the anarchy of his arbitrary thoughts and transformed into the teacher. The experience of such ensoulment will make us understand the power called soul, the power to change our mind.

In virtue of our soul, freedom and draft should change places. Free soldiers and drafted thinkers would recognize their identity. They are brothers. They can speak to each other. And this is the inspiration which was promised us as the Comforter through the Ages.

The Camping Mind

The soldier's great virtue is the direct attack, the hunch where to advance, the intuition on the basis of scanty information but so timely that the enemy is taken by surprise. But if the soldier had his way completely, he would soon run out of ammunition. The thinker's great virtue is his methodically covering the whole ground, organizing everything, systematizing everything. What it would mean if the thinker had his way, we may easily learn from the Belgian Minister of War; he reported to his people from Washington: "Every single request," he said, "has to be made out in 256 copies. If you know this, you'll be patient with me." The price of completeness is the loss of precious time. Systematic thinking incarnates Bureaucracy. Do we not all know that a woman's guess is more accurate than a man's certainty? Obviously, hunch and statistics must be reconciled.

Now, if it is true that external war should be made impossible, then we will have to incorporate some weapon against the 256 copies into our peace-time society. Or else this society will always come too late to any emergency, to any task. And the worst will have happened before the survey is completed. Therefore, the corollary to the abolition of war is the integration of the soldier's way of life into the mental life of the community.

Peace cannot be organized when the audacity of the warrior is not invited. And as the integration of the soldier's generative force into the community had not been achieved after pioneering was over, the two world wars were indispensable. Now the young know at least what we are talking about, as soldiers. They have realized the interplay of the generations; soldiers bridge the abyss between the founders of the nation and its future by an act of faith. The faith of the soldier may become an active force in peace-time, checking the reason of the old.

What would we gain? Would it not be very unpleasant to have these constant conflicts? Yes, it would be voluntary conflicts spread thin over innumerable occasions which should take the place of the huge explosion called a war. The world catastrophes would be replaced by an infinite number of controlled explosions. The parallel is the explosion motor in which we mix the fuel for a constructive result as compared to the vast and destructive explosions in a mine when the gases gather uncontrollably.

The greatest invention of our times, the explosion motor, has a lesson to tell. Our human catastrophes occur when the explosions occur blindly. We cannot have life without explosions; let us bring them under control by spreading them and by dispersing them and by putting them to some positive use.

The mixture of the explosive fuel in the realm of man would be composed of young man's faith and old man's reason. In war, the faith of the young is harnessed to the old man's reason or prejudices, anyway. But war is wasteful because the faith of the young does not rewrite the reason of the old. A peace-time exploitation of the new explosive fuel would reverse the relation of faith and reason in war.

It would try to make use of the two prodigious virtues of reason and faith, and it would try to eliminate the two vicious qualities of the two. What are their virtues and vices?

Reason is objective and gives us security. Faith is selective and has a sense of the important. These are the virtues. But reason deals with everything under the sun and plays with ideas regardless of urgency; it passes the buck. And faith is hectic and intermittent. These are their vices. If faith and reason operate in separation, the objective world of reason remains unimportant, and the important world of faith remains disconnected. And this means that wars will break out in shorter and shorter intervals. For wars are an expression of the "too late" of our thought, and the helpless "too early" of our intuitions. It has been said that life is an experiment in timing.[1] If this is true then life cannot be lived right when the generations are left to themselves, because one is too late and the other is too early, by their very nature. The *laissez faire, laissez aller* between the playboys and the bureaucrats leads to disaster. The condition for any victory over wars

[1] It was written on the door of Eduard Lindeman's room, during the World Conference of Adult Education, in Cambridge, England.

is a voluntary and perpetual spiritual duelling between thinkers and soldiers. The time lag of Reason cannot be cured unless it is put under pressure by the bold approach of youth; and, vice versa, a blind youth goes Hitler.

This rhythm above two and more generations ties in with the rhythm within any individual life as discussed in the previous section. We cannot be surprised by this analogy. In a mechanized world, rhythm has to be rediscovered everywhere as our free contribution and creative victory over the forces of blind living.

Our academic world has denied or overlooked the spiritual value of the energies invested in war. Thus it may be pertinent to give a new label to the new interaction of two and more generations. We have had the scholastic mind in the Church. And we have had the academic mind in the professions of the nations. Now the Great Society appeals to you and me to find forms for a third, unheard of, mentality. The Great Society which shall contain all the nations will receive no mental uplift by the threat of war. She cannot stay alive if the spirits of various times, inside of her, are not pitted against each other in all their energy. Lest we cease to compromise all our conflicts dispiritedly, we will have to go on destroying each other physically. A moral equivalent of war will not suffice. It may have to be a mental equivalent of war as well. For this adventure the ministry of neither the Church nor the State seems ready. So let us appeal to the "camper," to the man between two battles; the minds of such campers would be willing to change in order to avoid a bloody conflict. They would accept the clash of anvil and hammer, between old and young, and that means that these minds should be willing to die and to rise again. Instead of cramming all the facts that contradict the main theory in footnotes and appendices, such a mind would put the great question of the irresistible next conflict frankly in the center of the page.

I propose the name of the Camping Mind or the Drafted Mind for this mentality which should supersede the complacencies of the scholastic distinctions and the Platonic reflections on the world.

In Chapter two, we gave some practical anticipations of such camping mentality. In Chapter three, we saw whole sciences relapsing into vicious circles because the academic mind was helpless against cyclical thinking, by its own resources. Especially economics may serve us as an example of the choice which must be made between a relapse in mercantilism of the eighteenth century or a mental conversion to the real issue of our times. The choice will depend on whether we use the academic or establish the camping mind to do the thinking.

The camper's mentality can never be satisfied with the cyclical relapse, as he is born out of the knowledge of impending doom. This mind knows that it it is called forth exclusively as humanity's breathing spell between the last war and the next. Thought is breathing, inhalation, inspiration, a respite. Therefore, the economic shortcomings of the prewar crisis would not be tucked away as marginal notes to the otherwise classical theory but they would be placed in the center of the system. The camping mind would be transfixed by the question of unemployment as by arrows. It would make itself vulnerable by admitting that as long as these causes were not made central, economic theory was not yet scientific. By admitting its own shocking inadequacy, the science of economics would take the first step towards its own conversion. For although yet unable to answer its own questions, economics would acquire an insight into the proper degree of importance of its questions. The hierarchy of importance is unknown in the academic community; the unpaid laundry bills of Walt Whitman may be given as much importance as his "Ode for Lincoln." The good taste of the academic mind is the only barrier against such nonsense; yet it is true that the mind of mere peacetime thinking has no way of protecting itself against unimportant and superfluous questions. Everybody knows how new questionnaires are invented and new studies are manufactured from sheer curiosity or unemployment of the mind. The camping mind advocated by us as the institutional and mental result of our last catastrophes would insist on the *Unum Necessarium,* on the proper order of thought. It would distinguish between two states of a science: the one in which the great and important question is lifted up high above the secondary ones. And the later stage in which this grand central question finally is answered. Today, the secondary questions claim equal rank with the central question. Yet it is only on behalf of the central question that the public supports this specific science at all. And it takes a new resolve to shake off the parasites of secondary problems which beset the body of each science in unending multiplication.

We who, under the influence of science and techniques, are so accustomed to speak of the proper order of things must reeducate ourselves to the proper order of topics to think about. In politics, we all follow this order of the agenda. But academically our systems of thought defy this imposition. Now, don't misunderstand my demand. The cure of unemployment may make necessary innumerable detours of thinking and highly specialized investigations. All I claim is that nevertheless we already can know today that the economic significance of the returning soldier should create a turning-point in our economic thinking. We may try to fit him into our system by hook and crook. Then we would actually obdurate our minds to the mental revolution. This would leave economics as a science in the state of astronomy before Copernicus. The Ptolemaic System did digest new facts in the sky by hook and crook but it was far too clumsy and complicated. When Copernicus placed some real observations in the center of his thought, the new solar theory emerged. Similarly, our economic theory could remain in its timeless supineness to this catastrophe. But we have seen in the third chapter that if economics does this, it goes cyclical and already is back to 1770 because of this tendency to mull over all the aspects of the peace-time entrepreneur once more. Thus, for its own salvation, economic science now should place the returning soldier in the center of its thinking, lest it merely repeat itself. But this means quite some revolution. For the mind would thereby accept its datedness. It would admit that consciousness dawns as a free response to great suffering. It would accept the home-coming veteran as the crux of the matter instead of the gold or silver or the commodities or the capital goods. With the veteran the cornerstone of economic theory, Adam Smith, as well as mercantilism, would be superseded. This would be real progress because it would forbid the economist to fall in this thinking of us below the real role of each of us in the division of labor. The reader may recall that progress was "a less and less falling out or down or away from our truest nature" (Chapter three). Now the new economic theory would realize that man is not an entrepreneur or a wage earner solely but that he also is the founder and soldier of the same society in which he must be able to make a living. With the camping mind of the returning soldier made the cornerstone of our theory, ***the nature of the man*** whom economics contemplates would have changed. This man now reproduces society as well as he produces within society. He gives life to the social order and he makes a living. He must be used in this dual capacity by any economic system which deserves this name at all.

How can this "inthronization" of a new mentality be brought about? Certainly not by wishful thinking. A different daily practice is required. The soldiers must not return so hastily as to obliterate their scientific significance as the new cornerstone. They must become embodiments which tell us lastingly that they demand from the public consciousness to treat the peace as a time of grace between two wars. The actual presence of such servants of peace would dispel the laziness of science which would like to think of itself as timeless and which hates to admit that it is suspended on a "Today" between the last and the next catastrophe. What every soldier knows is not explicitly stated in our textbooks. This makes the new relation of soldier and teacher an urgent necessity. It is easier for whole nations to change their religion than for a body of science to change its fundamental ways of thinking. Lest we forget, lest we forget, the warrior and soldier must be asked to remain present to the mind of science institutionally.

Our peacemakers and planners must be supported by camps all over the globe, where youth, recruited from every town and village all over the globe, serves. This service must implement the global organization as the young must experience what the old are planning before the old can have any authority. Such camps, in which unselfish service represents the flames which knowledge and thought then may transform to light, would be a fitting synthesis of the two eras which are coming to an end. One was the era of the "Enlightenment" in which light was worshipped. The other was revolutionary and it worshipped fire, arson, fire bombs, demolition squads, revolutions, eliminations, concentration camps, etc.

Light in isolation, and fire in isolation had their say. But fire, light, and warmth are three equally necessary phases of the communal life. The fire of the service men and the light of reason, and the warmth spread from their interaction into the mechanized areas of production and consumption, this seems to me the full process of living.

The Rhythm of the New World

If the camping mind, the mind that does not gloss over differences in abstract idealism but dares to polarize them, receives recognition, after the war, the deepest conflict of the United States will be on the way toward solution. At the end of this book the reader is requested to look back upon Interim America as we found it in our first chapter and upon the peculiar American tradition ever since 1776.

This tradition implied an ambiguity. The ambiguity was the

term, The New World. Every European who came to this country used the term New World, with two meanings: geographical and spiritual. Geographically, America was new because it was discovered in the midst of our era. Spiritually, she did not share antiquity of the Middle Ages. She was new because she owed her settlement to an expansion of the Old World into the New. A new power geographically, and a new society spiritually, combined in the term, the New World! The newness was and is two things in one: an addition in space; an elevation in level or standard. The New World had a new quality as well as a new quantity.

From 1776 onward, the American consciousness liked to dwell on the new quality of its society; but the political reality still required her to expand in size and quantity, in the old frame of national sovereignty. Hence the blend of mental pacifism with a wonderful fighting physique. Hence, also, the dismay of the American thinking group whenever an armed conflict occurred. The new quality of life and the new lands in the West clashed. And especially one peculiar consequence was the long period of incubation before a war was heeded and digested. The resulting rhythm of America I have examined elsewhere at length. The American consciousness always was a half-generation behind the military event. The French-Canadian War, which drove the French out of America, conditioned Independence. The war also produced George Washington as the potential leader. But nobody in 1763 had an inkling of this necessary effect. The Mexican War forced a solution of the slave question on the States. But the country did not wish to see this. Fifteen years later the Civil War cashed in on the victories in Mexico.

Andrew Jackson and the frontier came forward by his victory at New Orleans, a victory won in great independence from the government. In 1829 he was President and revolutionized government by the spoils system.

In 1917, the United States entered the World War very much

against everything officially said before. And in 1932 the New Deal was elected to face the real economic disaster created by World War I.

Has all this anything to do with Christianity or with the Christian Future? Of course, it has. The state of our consciousness is a part of our conscience. The rift between the facts and the ideology made the mind lag behind the soul's ordeals and sacrifices. They produced the indescribable torn-to-pieces-hood of the American public spirit.

While to the American mind the world was already so new that man could afford to live without wars, to the American geography this was far from being the case. Each time a war was fought, it was done with the face turned away from it at first, with a bad conscience or with a loss of faith. A friend, an expert in government, wrote to me in January 1945 when the Greek and the Polish and many other questions weighed down the spirit: "During the last year, America has lost her simple faith." He was right. But I could give chapter and verse for the repetition of this loss of naive faith whenever a war took this country by surprise, as it always did.[1]

The artificial divorce between cause and effect, between event in outer reality and mental response, is the miraculous rhythm of America during the last 190 years. It was concealed from our history textbooks because the very first response and effect, the Declaration of Independence, usually was treated as though it did not follow necessarily from the French-Canadian War and the British Navy's victories.

The whole country of these United States today enters a new era because this rhythm is definitely interrupted. All the other wars created completely new spaces: and the mind slowly discov-

[1] For the reader's convenience, here is the list taken from *Out of Revolution*, on the lag of consciousness:

1756–63	1812–15	1846–	(1898—Spanish War. Theodore Roose-	1917
1776	1829	1861	velt a candidate in 1912: abortive)	1933

ered the political changes implied in these breath-taking advances.

This time we had a make-up examination. The same assignment was enacted twice. And, therefore, this is the first great American crisis in which the mind is up-to-date and the contemporary of the event, to a certain extent. We might face "The suicide of Europe," the veritable end of THE OLD WORLD with all that this end of the corollary to our NEW WORLD implies. Instead of merely dreaming of a League of Nations under a new name, we might become contemporaries of the real event.

But this cannot happen without deliberation. This deliberate effort would be a new process.

The Interim America of the Middle West could do its wonderful things in production and education without solving the ambiguity in the term "New World." The final position of America, after World War II, as the political heir of Europe, makes this ambiguity untenable. The background of our production in the factory and our education in the suburb now stands revealed as a world still at war, in anarchy, in revolution, or decay.

The catching-up of the mind with this background reality is a fact which promises a new approach to these enormous questions of Church and State, behind the economic and educational advances of the sciences and the arts. At this very moment, it is a question of life and death whether the mentality of the American Continent is allowed to slump back behind the experiences of the fighting men or not. If the soldiers are made to "go home" as quickly as possible, their souls, which are burdened with superhuman exertions and with memories of horror, are bound to rot. Then a new type of carpet-bagger will steal the peace. A member of Camp William James[1] after fighting with the infantry wrote me: "Those of us who have accepted death and come to life again many times will either have to find our moral equivalent for war or perish or degenerate."

[1] See pp. 27 ff.

Down to the New Deal, the intellect simply raced fifteen years behind the events. The events were the pacemakers; the speakers and the writers did not stick their necks out, in general, except when they could be best-sellers. And then, of course, it always was too late.

This has pampered the mind, and has made the young soft. They were led to believe that their impulses, their feeling responses to the world in which they served, were not precious. But they inject urgency and pressure into the discussions of a town meeting as well as of a group of educators. If the intellect would now understand the time lag of logic, and the value of intuition; if scientists of society would see that their logic is right at the price of coming too late, then the mind may expose itself voluntarily and in time to the intuition of the following generation. This whole process of the death and resurrection of the mind may now be faced, after the United States has gone to school for nearly two hundred years and experienced the difference in timing of the United States as a belligerent power, and of the American people as a peace-loving society.

The conflict between warriors and thinkers, then, is a conflict in the center of America's biography. The transformations of warriors into soldiers of the world, and of thinkers into teachers of The Great Society, is the logical consequence of American history. It is this, the first moment in which the term "New World" definitely comes to mean a new order of the globe. May it be tentative, incomplete, and so on, and so forth, it definitely is larger than the area of the United States. That the thoughts of the people of this country and the actions of war moved on a different time-wave was unavoidable. But this interim is now changed to a new order of things. We now can do something about bringing the mind up-to-date; and of exposing two generations, fathers and sons, to the real power of each other's time.

In the preface, the young soldiers were introduced to the men to whom this book is dedicated—the soldiers with their naive faith in the spirit of their time, to the men whose life work had been a retranslation of the Holy Spirit in new forms of utterance.

By now it should be clear that a new era dawns. In it the spirits of the times, of each generation, cannot be left to accident and the murderous goose chase of a meaningless pursuit of purely temporal or sensational new aims. The spirits of each generation must be made tributary to the power-line of the spirit through the ages, as its feeders and revitalizers, in a conscious act of reconciliation. The fear of the custodians of the Christian faith, that the spirit of the time is wrong, is as useless as the pride of the men of the world that the spirit of their time always is right. This spirit must be made to serve. God is the father of all spirits. And we have not understood him to the degree to which he demands our understanding before we have made the spirits of all times interacting and contemporary.

If we have the courage to do this, we may enjoy the rhythm of peace. For peace is not the sleep and the torpor of non-movement. Peace is not suspended animation. Peace is the victory over mere accident. Peace is the rhythm of a community which is still unfinished, still open to its true future.

INDEX

Names are not listed when used simply at random for the sake of sampling. The terms God, Cross, Science, Church, Time, Christianity, Future, Spirit, Incarnation, Resurrection, Jesus are scattered throughout the volume; the index lists only the vital places of their treatment.

Revised December, 1966

harper torchbooks

HUMANITIES AND SOCIAL SCIENCES

American Studies: General

THOMAS C. COCHRAN: The Inner Revolution. *Essays on the Social Sciences in History* TB/1140

EDWARD S. CORWIN: American Constitutional History. *Essays edited by Alpheus T. Mason and Gerald Garvey* △ TB/1136

CARL N. DEGLER, Ed.: Pivotal Interpretations of American History TB/1240, TB/1241

A. HUNTER DUPREE: Science in the Federal Government: *A History of Policies and Activities to 1940* TB/573

A. S. EISENSTADT, Ed.: The Craft of American History: *Recent Essays in American Historical Writing* Vol. I TB/1255; Vol. II TB/1256

CHARLOTTE P. GILMAN: Women and Economics: *A Study of the Economic Relation between Men and Women as a Factor in Social Evolution.* ‡ *Ed. with an Introduction by Carl N. Degler* TB/3073

OSCAR HANDLIN, Ed.: This Was America: *As Recorded by European Travelers in the Eighteenth, Nineteenth and Twentieth Centuries. Illus.* TB/1119

MARCUS LEE HANSEN: The Atlantic Migration: 1607-1860. *Edited by Arthur M. Schlesinger* TB/1052

MARCUS LEE HANSEN: The Immigrant in American History. TB/1120

JOHN HIGHAM, Ed.: The Reconstruction of American History △ TB/1068

ROBERT H. JACKSON: The Supreme Court in the American System of Government TB/1106

JOHN F. KENNEDY: A Nation of Immigrants. △ *Illus.* TB/1118

LEONARD W. LEVY, Ed.: American Constitutional Law: *Historical Essays* TB/1285

RALPH BARTON PERRY: Puritanism and Democracy TB/1138

ARNOLD ROSE: The Negro in America TB/3048

MAURICE R. STEIN: The Eclipse of Community. *An Interpretation of American Studies* TB/1128

W. LLOYD WARNER and Associates: Democracy in Jonesville: *A Study in Quality and Inequality* ¶ TB/1129

W. LLOYD WARNER: Social Class in America: *The Evaluation of Status* TB/1013

American Studies: Colonial

BERNARD BAILYN, Ed.: Apologia of Robert Keayne: *Self-Portrait of a Puritan Merchant* TB/1201

BERNARD BAILYN: The New England Merchants in the Seventeenth Century TB/1149

JOSEPH CHARLES: The Origins of the American Party System TB/1049

LAWRENCE HENRY GIPSON: The Coming of the Revolution: 1763-1775. † *Illus.* TB/3007

LEONARD W. LEVY: Freedom of Speech and Press in Early American History: *Legacy of Suppression* TB/1109

PERRY MILLER: Errand Into the Wilderness TB/1139

PERRY MILLER & T. H. JOHNSON, Eds.: The Puritans: *A Sourcebook of Their Writings* Vol. I TB/1093; Vol. II TB/1094

EDMUND S. MORGAN, Ed.: The Diary of Michael Wigglesworth, 1653-1657: *The Conscience of a Puritan* TB/1228

EDMUND S. MORGAN: The Puritan Family: *Religion and Domestic Relations in Seventeenth-Century New England* TB/1227

RICHARD B. MORRIS: Government and Labor in Early America TB/1244

KENNETH B. MURDOCK: Literature and Theology in Colonial New England TB/99

WALLACE NOTESTEIN: The English People on the Eve of Colonization: 1603-1630. † *Illus.* TB/3006

LOUIS B. WRIGHT: The Cultural Life of the American Colonies: 1607-1763. † *Illus.* TB/3005

American Studies: From the Revolution to 1860

JOHN R. ALDEN: The American Revolution: 1775-1783. † *Illus.* TB/3011

MAX BELOFF, Ed.: The Debate on the American Revolution, 1761-1783: *A Sourcebook* △ TB/1225

RAY A. BILLINGTON: The Far Western Frontier: 1830-1860. † *Illus.* TB/3012

W. R. BROCK: An American Crisis: *Congress and Reconstruction, 1865-67* ° △ TB/1283

EDMUND BURKE: On the American Revolution: *Selected Speeches and Letters.* ‡ *Edited by Elliott Robert Barkan* TB/3068

WHITNEY R. CROSS: The Burned-Over District: *The Social and Intellectual History of Enthusiastic Religion in Western New York, 1800-1850* △ TB/1242

GEORGE DANGERFIELD: The Awakening of American Nationalism: 1815-1828. † *Illus.* TB/3061

CLEMENT EATON: The Freedom-of-Thought Struggle in the Old South. *Revised and Enlarged. Illus.* TB/1150

CLEMENT EATON: The Growth of Southern Civilization: 1790-1860. † *Illus.* TB/3040

LOUIS FILLER: The Crusade Against Slavery: 1830-1860. † *Illus.* TB/3029

DIXON RYAN FOX: The Decline of Aristocracy in the Politics of New York: 1801-1840. ‡ *Edited by Robert V. Remini* TB/3064

FELIX GILBERT: The Beginnings of American Foreign Policy: *To the Farewell Address* TB/1200

FRANCIS GRIERSON: The Valley of Shadows: *The Coming of the Civil War in Lincoln's Midwest: A Contemporary Account* TB/1246

† The New American Nation Series, edited by Henry Steele Commager and Richard B. Morris.

‡ American Persectives series, edited by Bernard Wishy and William E. Leuchtenburg.

* The Rise of Modern Europe series, edited by William L. Langer.

¶ Researches in the Social, Cultural, and Behavioral Sciences, edited by Benjamin Nelson.

§ The Library of Religion and Culture, edited by Benjamin Nelson.

Σ Harper Modern Science Series, edited by James R. Newman.

° Not for sale in Canada.

△ Not for sale in the U. K.

FRANCIS J. GRUND: Aristocracy in America: *Social Class in the Formative Years of the New Nation* TB/1001

ALEXANDER HAMILTON: The Reports of Alexander Hamilton. ‡ *Edited by Jacob E. Cooke* TB/3060

THOMAS JEFFERSON: Notes on the State of Virginia. ‡ *Edited by Thomas P. Abernethy* TB/3052

JAMES MADISON: The Forging of American Federalism: *Selected Writings of James Madison. Edited by Saul K. Padover* TB/1226

BERNARD MAYO: Myths and Men: *Patrick Henry, George Washington, Thomas Jefferson* TB/1108

JOHN C. MILLER: Alexander Hamilton and the Growth of the New Nation TB/3057

RICHARD B. MORRIS, Ed.: The Era of the American Revolution TB/1180

R. B. NYE: The Cultural Life of the New Nation: 1776-1801. † *Illus.* TB/3026

FRANCIS S. PHILBRICK: The Rise of the West, 1754-1830. † *Illus.* TB/3067

TIMOTHY L. SMITH: Revivalism and Social Reform: *American Protestantism on the Eve of the Civil War* TB/1229

FRANK THISTLETHWAITE: America and the Atlantic Community: *Anglo-American Aspects, 1790-1850* TB/1107

ALBION W. TOURGÉE: A Fool's Errand. ‡ *Ed. by George Fredrickson* TB/3074

A. F. TYLER: Freedom's Ferment: *Phases of American Social History from the Revolution to the Outbreak of the Civil War. 31 illus.* TB/1074

GLYNDON G. VAN DEUSEN: The Jacksonian Era: 1828-1848. † *Illus.* TB/3028

LOUIS B. WRIGHT: Culture on the Moving Frontier TB/1053

American Studies: The Civil War to 1900

THOMAS C. COCHRAN & WILLIAM MILLER: The Age of Enterprise: *A Social History of Industrial America* TB/1054

W. A. DUNNING: Essays on the Civil War and Reconstruction. *Introduction by David Donald* TB/1181

W. A. DUNNING: Reconstruction, Political and Economic: 1865-1877 TB/1073

HAROLD U. FAULKNER: Politics, Reform and Expansion: 1890-1900. † *Illus.* TB/3020

HELEN HUNT JACKSON: A Century of Dishonor: *The Early Crusade for Indian Reform. ‡ Edited by Andrew F. Rolle* TB/3063

ALBERT D. KIRWAN: Revolt of the Rednecks: *Mississippi Politics, 1876-1925* TB/1199

ROBERT GREEN MC CLOSKEY: American Conservatism in the Age of Enterprise: 1865-1910 TB/1137

ARTHUR MANN: Yankee Reformers in the Urban Age: *Social Reform in Boston, 1880-1900* TB/1247

WHITELAW REID: After the War: *A Tour of the Southern States, 1865-1866. ‡ Edited by C. Vann Woodward* TB/3066

CHARLES H. SHINN: Mining Camps: *A Study in American Frontier Government. ‡ Edited by Rodman W. Paul* TB/3062

VERNON LANE WHARTON: The Negro in Mississippi: 1865-1890 TB/1178

American Studies: 1900 to the Present

RAY STANNARD BAKER: Following the Color Line: *American Negro Citizenship in Progressive Era. ‡ Illus. Edited by Dewey W. Grantham, Jr.* TB/3053

RANDOLPH S. BOURNE: War and the Intellectuals: *Collected Essays, 1915-1919. ‡ Edited by Carl Resek* TB/3043

A. RUSSELL BUCHANAN: The United States and World War II. † *Illus.* Vol. I TB/3044; Vol. II TB/3045

ABRAHAM CAHAN: The Rise of David Levinsky: *a documentary novel of social mobility in early twentieth century America. Intro. by John Higham* TB/1028

THOMAS C. COCHRAN: The American Business System: *A Historical Perspective, 1900-1955* TB/1080

FOSTER RHEA DULLES: America's Rise to World Power: 1898-1954. † *Illus.* TB/3021

JOHN D. HICKS: Republican Ascendancy: 1921-1933. † *Illus.* TB/3041

SIDNEY HOOK: Reason, Social Myths, and Democracy TB/1237

ROBERT HUNTER: Poverty: *Social Conscience in the Progressive Era. ‡ Edited by Peter d'A. Jones* TB/3065

WILLIAM L. LANGER & S. EVERETT GLEASON: The Challenge to Isolation: *The World Crisis of 1937-1940 and American Foreign Policy* Vol. I TB/3054; Vol. II TB/3055

WILLIAM E. LEUCHTENBURG: Franklin D. Roosevelt and the New Deal: 1932-1940. † *Illus.* TB/3025

ARTHUR S. LINK: Woodrow Wilson and the Progressive Era: 1910-1917. † *Illus.* TB/3023

GEORGE E. MOWRY: The Era of Theodore Roosevelt and the Birth of Modern America: 1900-1912. † *Illus.* TB/3022

RUSSEL B. NYE: Midwestern Progressive Politics: *A Historical Study of Its Origins and Development, 1870-1958* TB/1202

WILLIAM PRESTON, JR.: Aliens and Dissenters: *Federal Suppression of Radicals, 1903-1933* TB/1287

WALTER RAUSCHENBUSCH: Christianity and the Social Crisis. ‡ *Edited by Robert D. Cross* TB/3059

JACOB RIIS: The Making of an American. ‡ *Edited by Roy Lubove* TB/3070

PHILIP SELZNICK: TVA and the Grass Roots: *A Study in the Sociology of Formal Organization* TB/1230

IDA M. TARBELL: The History of the Standard Oil Company: *Briefer Version. ‡ Edited by David M. Chalmers* TB/3071

GEORGE B. TINDALL, Ed.: A Populist Reader ‡ TB/3069

TWELVE SOUTHERNERS: I'll Take My Stand: *The South and the Agrarian Tradition. Intro. by Louis D. Rubin, Jr., Biographical Essays by Virginia Rock* TB/1072

WALTER E. WEYL: The New Democracy: *An Essay on Certain Political Tendencies in the United States. ‡ Edited by Charles B. Forcey* TB/3042

Anthropology

JACQUES BARZUN: Race: *A Study in Superstition. Revised Edition* TB/1172

JOSEPH B. CASAGRANDE, Ed.: In the Company of Man: *Twenty Portraits of Anthropological Informants. Illus.* TB/3047

W. E. LE GROS CLARK: The Antecedents of Man: *Intro. to Evolution of the Primates.* ° △ *Illus.* TB/559

CORA DU BOIS: The People of Alor. *New Preface by the author. Illus.* Vol. I TB/1042; Vol. II TB/1043

RAYMOND FIRTH, Ed.: Man and Culture: *An Evaluation of the Work of Bronislaw Malinowski* ¶ ° △ TB/1133

DAVID LANDY: Tropical Childhood: *Cultural Transmission and Learning in a Puerto Rican Village* ¶ TB/1235

L. S. B. LEAKEY: Adam's Ancestors: *The Evolution of Man and His Culture.* △ *Illus.* TB/1019

ROBERT H. LOWIE: Primitive Society. *Introduction by Fred Eggan* TB/1056

EDWARD BURNETT TYLOR: The Origins of Culture. *Part I of "Primitive Culture." § Intro. by Paul Radin* TB/33

EDWARD BURNETT TYLOR: Religion in Primitive Culture. *Part II of "Primitive Culture." § Intro. by Paul Radin* TB/34

W. LLOYD WARNER: A Black Civilization: *A Study of an Australian Tribe.* ¶ *Illus.* TB/3056

Art and Art History

WALTER LOWRIE: Art in the Early Church. *Revised Edition. 452 illus.* TB/124

EMILE MÂLE: The Gothic Image: *Religious Art in France of the Thirteenth Century.* § △ *190 illus.* TB/44

MILLARD MEISS: Painting in Florence and Siena after the Black Death: *The Arts, Religion and Society in the Mid-Fourteenth Century. 169 illus.* TB/1148
ERICH NEUMANN: The Archetypal World of Henry Moore. △ *107 illus.* TB/2020
DORA & ERWIN PANOFSKY : Pandora's Box: *The Changing Aspects of a Mythical Symbol. Revised Edition. Illus.* TB/2021
ERWIN PANOFSKY: Studies in Iconology: *Humanistic Themes in the Art of the Renaissance.* △ *180 illustrations* TB/1077
ALEXANDRE PIANKOFF: The Shrines of Tut-Ankh-Amon. *Edited by N. Rambova. 117 illus.* TB/2011
JEAN SEZNEC: The Survival of the Pagan Gods: *The Mythological Tradition and Its Place in Renaissance Humanism and Art. 108 illustrations* TB/2004
OTTO VON SIMSON: The Gothic Cathedral: *Origins of Gothic Architecture and the Medieval Concept of Order.* △ *58 illus.* TB/2018
HEINRICH ZIMMER: Myth and Symbols in Indian Art and Civilization. *70 illustrations* TB/2005

Business, Economics & Economic History

REINHARD BENDIX: Work and Authority in Industry: *Ideologies of Management in the Course of Industrialization* TB/3035
GILBERT BURCK & EDITORS OF FORTUNE: The Computer Age: *And Its Potential for Management* TB/1179
THOMAS C. COCHRAN: The American Business System: *A Historical Perspective, 1900-1955* TB/1080
THOMAS C. COCHRAN: The Inner Revolution: *Essays on the Social Sciences in History* △ TB/1140
THOMAS C. COCHRAN & WILLIAM MILLER: The Age of Enterprise: *A Social History of Industrial America* TB/1054
ROBERT DAHL & CHARLES E. LINDBLOM: Politics, Economics, and Welfare: *Planning and Politico-Economic Systems Resolved into Basic Social Processes* TB/3037
PETER F. DRUCKER: The New Society: *The Anatomy of Industrial Order* △ TB/1082
EDITORS OF FORTUNE: America in the Sixties: *The Economy and the Society* TB/1015
ROBERT L. HEILBRONER: The Great Ascent: *The Struggle for Economic Development in Our Time* TB/3030
FRANK H. KNIGHT: The Economic Organization TB/1214
FRANK H. KNIGHT: Risk, Uncertainty and Profit TB/1215
ABBA P. LERNER: Everybody's Business: *Current Assumptions in Economics and Public Policy* TB/3051
ROBERT GREEN MC CLOSKEY: American Conservatism in the Age of Enterprise, 1865-1910 △ TB/1137
PAUL MANTOUX: The Industrial Revolution in the Eighteenth Century: *The Beginnings of the Modern Factory System in England* ° △ TB/1079
WILLIAM MILLER, Ed.: Men in Business: *Essays on the Historical Role of the Entrepreneur* TB/1081
RICHARD B. MORRIS: Government and Labor in Early America △ TB/1244
HERBERT SIMON: The Shape of Automation: *For Men and Management* TB/1245
PERRIN STRYKER: The Character of the Executive: *Eleven Studies in Managerial Qualities* TB/1041
PIERRE URI: Partnership for Progress: *A Program for Transatlantic Action* TB/3036

Contemporary Culture

JACQUES BARZUN: The House of Intellect △ TB/1051
CLARK KERR: The Uses of the University TB/1264
JOHN U. NEF: Cultural Foundations of Industrial Civilization △ TB/1024
NATHAN M. PUSEY: The Age of the Scholar: *Observations on Education in a Troubled Decade* TB/1157
PAUL VALÉRY: The Outlook for Intelligence △ TB/2016
RAYMOND WILLIAMS: Culture and Society, 1780-1950 ° △ TB/1252
RAYMOND WILLIAMS: The Long Revolution. ° △ *Revised Edition* TB/1253

Historiography & Philosophy of History

JACOB BURCKHARDT: On History and Historians. △ *Introduction by H. R. Trevor-Roper* TB/1216
WILHELM DILTHEY: Pattern and Meaning in History: *Thoughts on History and Society.* ° △ *Edited with an Introduction by H. P. Rickman* TB/1075
J. H. HEXTER: Reappraisals in History: *New Views on History & Society in Early Modern Europe* △ TB/1100
H. STUART HUGHES: History as Art and as Science: *Twin Vistas on the Past* TB/1207
RAYMOND KLIBANSKY & H. J. PATON, Eds.: Philosophy and History: *The Ernst Cassirer Festschrift. Illus.* TB/1115
ARNOLDO MOMIGLIANO: Studies in Historiography ° △ TB/1288
GEORGE H. NADEL, Ed.: Studies in the Philosophy of History: *Selected Essays from* History and Theory TB/1208
JOSE ORTEGA Y GASSET: The Modern Theme. *Introduction by Jose Ferrater Mora* TB/1038
KARL R. POPPER: The Open Society and Its Enemies △
Vol. I: The Spell of Plato TB/1101
Vol. II: The High Tide of Prophecy: Hegel, Marx and the Aftermath TB/1102
KARL R. POPPER: The Poverty of Historicism ° △ TB/1126
G. J. RENIER: History: Its Purpose and Method △ TB/1209
W. H. WALSH: Philosophy of History: *An Introduction* △ TB/1020

History: General

L. CARRINGTON GOODRICH: A Short History of the Chinese People. △ *Illus.* TB/3015
DAN N. JACOBS & HANS H. BAERWALD: Chinese Communism: *Selected Documents* TB/3031
BERNARD LEWIS: The Arabs in History △ TB/1029
BERNARD LEWIS: The Middle East and the West ° △ TB/1274

History: Ancient

A. ANDREWES: The Greek Tyrants △ TB/1103
ADOLF ERMAN, Ed. The Ancient Egyptians: *A Sourcebook of Their Writings. New material and Introduction by William Kelly Simpson* TB/1233
MICHAEL GRANT: Ancient History ° △ TB/1190
SAMUEL NOAH KRAMER: Sumerian Mythology TB/1055
NAPHTALI LEWIS & MEYER REINHOLD, Eds.: Roman Civilization. *Sourcebook I: The Republic* TB/1231
NAPHTALI LEWIS & MEYER REINHOLD, Eds.: Roman Civilization. *Sourcebook II: The Empire* TB/1232

History: Medieval

P. BOISSONNADE: Life and Work in Medieval Europe: *The Evolution of the Medieval Economy, the 5th to the 15th Century.* ° △ *Preface by Lynn White, Jr.* TB/1141
HELEN CAM: England before Elizabeth △ TB/1026
NORMAN COHN: The Pursuit of the Millennium: *Revolutionary Messianism in Medieval and Reformation Europe* △ TB/1037
G. G. COULTON: Medieval Village, Manor, and Monastery TB/1022
CHRISTOPHER DAWSON, Ed.: Mission to Asia: *Narratives and Letters of the Franciscan Missionaries in Mongolia and China in the 13th and 14 Centuries* △ TB/315
HEINRICH FICHTENAU: The Carolingian Empire: *The Age of Charlemagne* △ TB/1142
F. L. GANSHOF: Feudalism △ TB/1058
DENO GEANAKOPLOS: Byzantine East and Latin West: *Two Worlds of Christendom in the Middle Ages and Renaissance* TB/1265
EDWARD GIBBON: The Triumph of Christendom in the Roman Empire *(Chaps. XV-XX of "Decline and Fall," J. B. Bury edition).* § △ *Illus.* TB/46

W. O. HASSALL, Ed.: Medieval England: *As Viewed by Contemporaries* △ TB/1205

DENYS HAY: Europe: The Emergence of an Idea TB/1275

DENYS HAY: The Medieval Centuries ° △ TB/1192

J. M. HUSSEY: The Byzantine World △ TB/1057

ROBERT LATOUCHE: The Birth of Western Economy: *Economic Aspects of the Dark Ages.* ° △ *Intro. by Philip Grierson* TB/1290

FERDINAND LOT: The End of the Ancient World and the Beginnings of the Middle Ages. *Introduction by Glanville Downey* TB/1044

G. MOLLAT: The Popes at Avignon: 1305-1378 △ TB/308

CHARLES PETIT-DUTAILLIS: The Feudal Monarchy in France and England: *From the Tenth to the Thirteenth Century* ° △ TB/1165

HENRI PIRENNE: Early Democracies in the Low Countries: *Urban Society and Political Conflict in the Middle Ages and the Renaissance. Introduction by John H. Mundy* TB/1110

STEVEN RUNCIMAN: A History of the Crusades. △
Volume I: *The First Crusade and the Foundation of the Kingdom of Jerusalem. Illus.* TB/1143
Volume II: *The Kingdom of Jerusalem and the Frankish East, 1100-1187. Illus.* TB/1243

FERDINAND SCHEVILL: Siena: *The History of a Medieval Commune. Intro. by William M. Bowsky* TB/1164

SULPICIUS SEVERUS et al.: The Western Fathers: *Being the Lives of Martin of Tours, Ambrose, Augustine of Hippo, Honoratus of Arles and Germanus of Auxerre.* △ *Edited and trans. by F. O. Hoare* TB/309

HENRY OSBORN TAYLOR: The Classical Heritage of the Middle Ages. *Foreword and Biblio. by Kenneth M. Setton* TB/1117

F. VAN DER MEER: Augustine The Bishop: *Church and Society at the Dawn of the Middle Ages* △ TB/304

J. M. WALLACE-HADRILL: The Barbarian West: *The Early Middle Ages, A.D. 400-1000* △ TB/1061

History: Renaissance & Reformation

JACOB BURCKHARDT: The Civilization of the Renaissance in Italy. △ *Intro. by Benjamin Nelson & Charles Trinkaus. Illus.* Vol. I TB/40; Vol. II TB/41

JOHN CALVIN & JACOPO SADOLETO: A Reformation Debate. *Edited by John C. Olin* TB/1239

ERNST CASSIRER: The Individual and the Cosmos in Renaissance Philosophy. △ *Translated with an Introduction by Mario Domandi* TB/1097

FEDERICO CHABOD: Machiavelli and the Renaissance △ TB/1193

EDWARD P. CHEYNEY: The Dawn of a New Era, 1250-1453. * *Illus.* TB/3002

G. CONSTANT: The Reformation in England: *The English Schism, Henry VIII, 1509-1547* △ TB/314

R. TREVOR DAVIES: The Golden Century of Spain, 1501-1621 ° △ TB/1194

G. R. ELTON: Reformation Europe, 1517-1559 ° △ TB/1270

DESIDERIUS ERASMUS: Christian Humanism and the Reformation: *Selected Writings. Edited and translated by John C. Olin* TB/1166

WALLACE K. FERGUSON et al.: Facets of the Renaissance TB/1098

WALLACE K. FERGUSON et al.: The Renaissance: *Six Essays. Illus.* TB/1084

JOHN NEVILLE FIGGIS: The Divine Right of Kings. *Introduction by G. R. Elton* TB/1191

JOHN NEVILLE FIGGIS: Political Thought from Gerson to Grotius: 1414-1625: *Seven Studies. Introduction by Garrett Mattingly* TB/1032

MYRON P. GILMORE: The World of Humanism, 1453-1517. * *Illus.* TB/3003

FRANCESCO GUICCIARDINI: Maxims and Reflections of a Renaissance Statesman *(Ricordi). Trans. by Mario Domandi. Intro. by Nicolai Rubinstein* TB/1160

J. H. HEXTER: More's Utopia: *The Biography of an Idea, New Epilogue by the Author* TB/1195

HAJO HOLBORN: Ulrich von Hutten and the German Reformation TB/1238

JOHAN HUIZINGA: Erasmus and the Age of Reformation. △ *Illus.* TB/19

JOEL HURSTFIELD, Ed.: The Reformation Crisis △ TB/1267

ULRICH VON HUTTEN et al.: On the Eve of the Reformation: *"Letters of Obscure Men." Introduction by Hajo Holborn* TB/1124

PAUL O. KRISTELLER: Renaissance Thought: *The Classic, Scholastic, and Humanist Strains* TB/1048

PAUL O. KRISTELLER: Renaissance Thought II: *Papers on Humanism and the Arts* TB/1163

NICCOLÒ MACHIAVELLI: History of Florence and of the Affairs of Italy: *from the earliest times to the death of Lorenzo the Magnificent. Introduction by Felix Gilbert* △ TB/1027

ALFRED VON MARTIN: Sociology of the Renaissance. *Introduction by Wallace K. Ferguson* TB/1099

GARRETT MATTINGLY et al.: Renaissance Profiles. △ *Edited by J. H. Plumb* TB/1162

MILLARD MEISS: Painting in Florence and Siena after the Black Death: *The Arts, Religion and Society in the Mid-Fourteenth Century.* △ *169 illus.* TB/1148

J. E. NEALE: The Age of Catherine de Medici ° △ TB/1085

ERWIN PANOFSKY: Studies in Iconology: *Humanistic Themes in the Art of the Renaissance.* △ *180 illustrations* TB/1077

J. H. PARRY: The Establishment of the European Hegemony: 1415-1715: *Trade and Exploration in the Age of the Renaissance* △ TB/1045

J. H. PLUMB: The Italian Renaissance: *A Concise Survey of Its History and Culture* △ TB/1161

A. F. POLLARD: Henry VIII. ° △ *Introduction by A. G. Dickens* TB/1249

A. F. POLLARD: Wolsey. ° △ *Introduction by A. G. Dickens* TB/1248

CECIL ROTH: The Jews in the Renaissance. *Illus.* TB/834

A. L. ROWSE: The Expansion of Elizabethan England. ° △ *Illus.* TB/1220

GORDON RUPP: Luther's Progress to the Diet of Worms ° △ TB/120

FERDINAND SCHEVILL: The Medici. *Illus.* TB/1010

FERDINAND SCHEVILL: Medieval and Renaissance Florence. *Illus.* Volume I: *Medieval Florence* TB/1090
Volume II: *The Coming of Humanism and the Age of the Medici* TB/1091

G. M. TREVELYN: England in the Age of Wycliffe, 1368-1520 ° △ TB/1112

VESPASIANO: Renaissance Princes, Popes, and Prelates: *The Vespasiano Memoirs: Lives of Illustrious Men of the XVth Century. Intro. by Myron P. Gilmore* TB/1111

History: Modern European

FREDERICK B. ARTZ: Reaction and Revolution, 1815-1832. * *Illus.* TB/3034

MAX BELOFF: The Age of Absolutism, 1660-1815 △ TB/1062

ROBERT C. BINKLEY: Realism and Nationalism, 1852-1871. * *Illus.* TB/3038

ASA BRIGGS: The Making of Modern England, 1784-1867: *The Age of Improvement* ° △ TB/1203

CRANE BRINTON: A Decade of Revolution, 1789-1799. * *Illus.* TB/3018

D. W. BROGAN: The Development of Modern France. ° △
Volume I: *From the Fall of the Empire to the Dreyfus Affair* TB/1184
Volume II: *The Shadow of War, World War I, Between the Two Wars. New Introduction by the Author* TB/1185

J. BRONOWSKI & BRUCE MAZLISH: The Western Intellectual Tradition: *From Leonardo to Hegel* △ TB/3001

GEOFFREY BRUUN: Europe and the French Imperium, 1799-1814. * Illus. TB/3033

ALAN BULLOCK: Hitler, A Study in Tyranny. ° △ *Illus.* TB/1123

E. H. CARR: German-Soviet Relations Between the Two World Wars, 1919-1939 TB/1278

E. H. CARR: International Relations Between the Two World Wars, 1919-1939 ° △ TB/1279

E. H. CARR: The Twenty Years' Crisis, 1919-1939: *An Introduction to the Study of International Relations* ° △ TB/1122

GORDON A. CRAIG: From Bismarck to Adenauer: *Aspects of German Statecraft. Revised Edition* TB/1171

WALTER L. DORN: Competition for Empire, 1740-1763. * *Illus.* TB/3032

FRANKLIN L. FORD: Robe and Sword: *The Regrouping of the French Aristocracy after Louis XIV* TB/1217

CARL J. FRIEDRICH: The Age of the Baroque, 1610-1660. * *Illus.* TB/3004

RENÉ FUELOEP-MILLER: The Mind and Face of Bolshevism: *An Examination of Cultural Life in Soviet Russia. New Epilogue by the Author* TB/1188

M. DOROTHY GEORGE: London Life in the Eighteenth Century △ TB/1182

LEO GERSHOY: From Despotism to Revolution, 1763-1789. * *Illus.* TB/3017

C. C. GILLISPIE: Genesis and Geology: *The Decades before Darwin* § TB/51

ALBERT GOODWIN: The French Revolution △ TB/1064

ALBERT GUÉRARD: France in the Classical Age: *The Life and Death of an Ideal* △ TB/1183

CARLTON J. H. HAYES: A Generation of Materialism, 1871-1900. * *Illus.* TB/3039

J. H. HEXTER: Reappraisals in History: *New Views on History and Society in Early Modern Europe* △ TB/1100

STANLEY HOFFMANN et al.: In Search of France: *The Economy, Society and Political System in the Twentieth Century* TB/1219

A. R. HUMPHREYS: The Augustan World: *Society, Thought, & Letters in 18th Century England* ° △ TB/1105

DAN N. JACOBS, Ed.: The New Communist Manifesto and *Related Documents. Third edition, revised* TB/1078

HANS KOHN: The Mind of Germany: *The Education of a Nation* △ TB/1204

HANS KOHN, Ed.: The Mind of Modern Russia: *Historical and Political Thought of Russia's Great Age* TB/1065

WALTER LAQUEUR & GEORGE L. MOSSE, Eds.: International Fascism, 1920-1945. ° △ *Volume I of* Journal of Contemporary History TB/1276

WALTER LAQUEUR & GEORGE L. MOSSE, Eds.: The Left-Wing Intelligentsia between the Two World Wars. ° △ *Volume II of* Journal of Contemporary History TB/1286

FRANK E. MANUEL: The Prophets of Paris: *Turgot, Condorcet, Saint-Simon, Fourier, and Comte* TB/1218

KINGSLEY MARTIN: French Liberal Thought in the Eighteenth Century: *A Study of Political Ideas from Bayle to Condorcet* TB/1114

L. B. NAMIER: Facing East: *Essays on Germany, the Balkans, and Russia in the 20th Century* △ TB/1280

L. B. NAMIER: Personalities and Powers: *Selected Essays* △ TB/1186

L. B. NAMIER: Vanished Supremacies: *Essays on European History, 1812-1918* ° TB/1088

JOHN U. NEF: Western Civilization Since the Renaissance: *Peace, War, Industry, and the Arts* TB/1113

FRANZ NEUMANN: Behemoth: *The Structure and Practice of National Socialism, 1933-1944* TB/1289

FREDERICK L. NUSSBAUM: The Triumph of Science and Reason, 1660-1685. * *Illus.* TB/3009

DAVID OGG: Europe of the Ancien Régime, 1715-1783 ° △ TB/1271

JOHN PLAMENATZ: German Marxism and Russian Communism. ° △ *New Preface by the Author* TB/1189

RAYMOND W. POSTGATE, Ed.: Revolution from 1789 to 1906: *Selected Documents* TB/1063

PENFIELD ROBERTS: The Quest for Security, 1715-1740. * *Illus.* TB/3016

PRISCILLA ROBERTSON: Revolutions of 1848: *A Social History* TB/1025

GEORGE RUDÉ: Revolutionary Europe, 1783-1815 ° △ TB/1272

LOUIS, DUC DE SAINT-SIMON: Versailles, The Court, and Louis XIV. ° △ *Introductory Note by Peter Gay* TB/1250

ALBERT SOREL: Europe Under the Old Regime. *Translated by Francis H. Herrick* TB/1121

N. N. SUKHANOV: The Russian Revolution, 1917: *Eyewitness Account.* △ *Edited by Joel Carmichael* Vol. I TB/1066; Vol. II TB/1067

A. J. P. TAYLOR: From Napoleon to Lenin: *Historical Essays* ° △ TB/1268

A. J. P. TAYLOR: The Habsburg Monarchy, 1809-1918: *A History of the Austrian Empire and Austria-Hungary* ° △ TB/1187

G. M. TREVELYAN: British History in the Nineteenth Century and After: *1782-1919.* ° △ *Second Edition* TB/1251

H. R. TREVOR-ROPER: Historical Essays ° △ TB/1269

ELIZABETH WISKEMANN: Europe of the Dictators, 1919-1945 ° △ TB/1273

JOHN B. WOLF: The Emergence of the Great Powers, 1685-1715. * *Illus.* TB/3010

JOHN B. WOLF: France: 1814-1919: *The Rise of a Liberal-Democratic Society* TB/3019

Intellectual History & History of Ideas

HERSCHEL BAKER: The Image of Man: *A Study of the Idea of Human Dignity in Classical Antiquity, the Middle Ages, and the Renaissance* TB/1047

R. R. BOLGAR: The Classical Heritage and Its Beneficiaries: *From the Carolingian Age to the End of the Renaissance* △ TB/1125

RANDOLPH S. BOURNE: War and the Intellectuals: *Collected Essays, 1915-1919.* △ ‡ *Edited by Carl Resek* TB/3043

J. BRONOWSKI & BRUCE MAZLISH: The Western Intellectual Tradition: *From Leonardo to Hegel* △ TB/3001

ERNST CASSIRER: The Individual and the Cosmos in Renaissance Philosophy. △ *Translated with an Introduction by Mario Domandi* TB/1097

NORMAN COHN: The Pursuit of the Millennium: *Revolutionary Messianism in Medieval and Reformation Europe* △ TB/1037

C. C. GILLISPIE: Genesis and Geology: *The Decades before Darwin* § TB/51

G. RACHEL LEVY: Religious Conceptions of the Stone Age *and Their Influence upon European Thought.* △ *Illus. Introduction by Henri Frankfort* TB/106

ARTHUR O. LOVEJOY: The Great Chain of Being: *A Study of the History of an Idea* TB/1009

FRANK E. MANUEL: The Prophets of Paris: *Turgot, Condorcet, Saint-Simon, Fourier, and Comte* △ TB/1218

PERRY MILLER & T. H. JOHNSON, Editors: The Puritans: *A Sourcebook of Their Writings* Vol. I TB/1093; Vol. II TB/1094

MILTON C. NAHM: Genius and Creativity: *An Essay in the History of Ideas* TB/1196

ROBERT PAYNE: Hubris: *A Study of Pride. Foreword by Sir Herbert Read* TB/1031

RALPH BARTON PERRY: The Thought and Character of William James: *Briefer Version* TB/1156

GEORG SIMMEL et al.: Essays on Sociology, Philosophy, and Aesthetics. ¶ *Edited by Kurt H. Wolff* TB/1234

BRUNO SNELL: The Discovery of the Mind: *The Greek Origins of European Thought* △ TB/1018

PAGET TOYNBEE: Dante Alighieri: *His Life and Works. Edited with Intro. by Charles S. Singleton* △ TB/1206

ERNEST LEE TUVESON: Millennium and Utopia: *A Study in the Background of the Idea of Progress.* ¶ *New Preface by the Author* TB/1134

PAUL VALÉRY: The Outlook for Intelligence △ TB/2016

PHILIP P. WIENER: Evolution and the Founders of Pragmatism. △ *Foreword by John Dewey* TB/1212

BASIL WILLEY: Nineteenth Century Studies: *Coleridge to Matthew Arnold* ° △ TB/1261

BASIL WILLEY: More Nineteenth Century Studies: *A Group of Honest Doubters* ° △ TB/1262

Literature, Poetry, The Novel & Criticism

JAMES BAIRD: Ishmael: *The Art of Melville in the Contexts of International Primitivism* TB/1023

JACQUES BARZUN: The House of Intellect △ TB/1051

W. J. BATE: From Classic to Romantic: *Premises of Taste in Eighteenth Century England* TB/1036

RACHEL BESPALOFF: On the Iliad TB/2006

R. P. BLACKMUR et al.: Lectures in Criticism. *Introduction by Huntington Cairns* TB/2003

JAMES BOSWELL: The Life of Dr. Johnson & The Journal of a Tour to the Hebrides with Samuel Johnson LL.D.: *Selections.* ° △ *Edited by F. V. Morley. Illus. by Ernest Shepard* TB/1254

ABRAHAM CAHAN: The Rise of David Levinsky: *a documentary novel of social mobility in early twentieth century America. Intro. by John Higham* TB/1028

ERNST R. CURTIUS: European Literature and the Latin Middle Ages △ TB/2015

GEORGE ELIOT: Daniel Deronda: *a novel. Introduction by F. R. Leavis* TB/1039

ADOLF ERMAN, Ed.: The Ancient Egyptians: *A Sourcebook of Their Writings. New Material and Introduction by William Kelly Simpson* TB/1233

ÉTIENNE GILSON: Dante and Philosophy TB/1089

ALFRED HARBAGE: As They Liked It: *A Study of Shakespeare's Moral Artistry* TB/1035

STANLEY R. HOPPER, Ed: Spiritual Problems in Contemporary Literature § TB/21

A. R. HUMPHREYS: The Augustan World: *Society, Thought and Letters in 18th Century England* ° △ TB/1105

ALDOUS HUXLEY: Antic Hay & The Giaconda Smile. ° △ *Introduction by Martin Green* TB/3503

ALDOUS HUXLEY: Brave New World & Brave New World Revisited. ° △ *Introduction by Martin Green* TB/3501

HENRY JAMES: The Tragic Muse: *a novel. Introduction by Leon Edel* TB/1017

ARNOLD KETTLE: An Introduction to the English Novel. △
Volume I: *Defoe to George Eliot* TB/1011
Volume II: *Henry James to the Present* TB/1012

RICHMOND LATTIMORE: The Poetry of Greek Tragedy △ TB/1257

J. B. LEISHMAN: The Monarch of Wit: *An Analytical and Comparative Study of the Poetry of John Donne* ° △ TB/1258

J. B. LEISHMAN: Themes and Variations in Shakespeare's Sonnets ° △ TB/1259

ROGER SHERMAN LOOMIS: The Development of Arthurian Romance △ TB/1167

JOHN STUART MILL: On Bentham and Coleridge. △ *Introduction by F. R. Leavis* TB/1070

KENNETH B. MURDOCK: Literature and Theology in Colonial New England TB/99

SAMUEL PEPYS: The Diary of Samuel Pepys. ° *Edited by O. F. Morshead. Illus. by Ernest Shepard* TB/1007

ST.-JOHN PERSE: Seamarks TB/2002

V. DE S. PINTO: Crisis in English Poetry, 1880-1940 ° TB/1260

GEORGE SANTAYANA: Interpretations of Poetry and Religion § TB/9

C. K. STEAD: The New Poetic: *Yeats to Eliot* △ TB/1263

HEINRICH STRAUMANN: American Literature in the Twentieth Century. △ *Third Edition, Revised* TB/1168

PAGET TOYNBEE: Dante Alighieri: *His Life and Works. Edited with Intro. by Charles S. Singleton* TB/1206

DOROTHY VAN GHENT: The English Novel: *Form and Function* TB/1050

E. B. WHITE: One Man's Meat. *Introduction by Walter Blair* TB/3505

BASIL WILLEY: Nineteenth Century Studies: *Coleridge to Matthew Arnold* △ TB/1261

BASIL WILLEY: More Nineteenth Century Studies: *A Group of Honest Doubters* ° △ TB/1262

RAYMOND WILLIAMS: Culture and Society, 1780-1950 ° △ TB/1252

RAYMOND WILLIAMS: The Long Revolution. ° △ *Revised Edition* TB/1253

MORTON DAUWEN ZABEL, Editor: Literary Opinion in America Vol. I TB/3013; Vol. II TB/3014

Myth, Symbol & Folklore

JOSEPH CAMPBELL, Editor: Pagan and Christian Mysteries *Illus.* TB/2013

MIRCEA ELIADE: Cosmos and History: *The Myth of the Eternal Return* § △ TB/2050

MIRCEA ELIADE: Rites and Symbols of Initiation: *The Mysteries of Birth and Rebirth* § △ TB/1236

THEODOR H. GASTER: Thespis: *Ritual, Myth and Drama in the Ancient Near East* △ TB/1281

C. G. JUNG & C. KERÉNYI: Essays on a Science of Mythology: *The Myths of the Divine Child and the Divine Maiden* TB/2014

DORA & ERWIN PANOFSKY: Pandora's Box: *The Changing Aspects of a Mythical Symbol.* △ *Revised edition. Illus.* TB/2021

ERWIN PANOFSKY: Studies in Iconology: *Humanistic Themes in the Art of the Renaissance.* △ *180 illustrations* TB/1077

JEAN SEZNEC: The Survival of the Pagan Gods: *The Mythological Tradition and its Place in Renaissance Humanism and Art.* △ *108 illustrations* TB/2004

HELLMUT WILHELM: Change: *Eight Lectures on the I Ching* △ TB/2019

HEINRICH ZIMMER: Myths and Symbols in Indian Art and Civilization. △ *70 illustrations* TB/2005

Philosophy

G. E. M. ANSCOMBE: An Introduction to Wittgenstein's Tractatus. ° △ *Second Edition, Revised* TB/1210

HENRI BERGSON: Time and Free Will: *An Essay on the Immediate Data of Consciousness* ° △ TB/1021

H. J. BLACKHAM: Six Existentialist Thinkers: *Kierkegaard, Nietzsche, Jaspers, Marcel, Heidegger, Sartre* ° △ TB/1002

CRANE BRINTON: Nietzsche. *New Preface, Bibliography and Epilogue by the Author* TB/1197

MARTIN BUBER: The Knowledge of Man. △ *Ed. with an Intro. by Maurice Friedman. Trans. by Maurice Friedman and Ronald Gregor Smith* TB/135

ERNST CASSIRER: The Individual and the Cosmos in Renaissance Philosophy. △ *Translated with an Introduction by Mario Domandi* TB/1097

ERNST CASSIRER: Rousseau, Kant and Goethe. *Introduction by Peter Gay* TB/1092

FREDERICK COPLESTON: Medieval Philosophy ° △ TB/376

F. M. CORNFORD: Principium Sapientiae: *A Study of the Origins of Greek Philosophical Thought. Edited by W. K. C. Guthrie* TB/1213

F. M. CORNFORD: From Religion to Philosophy: *A Study in the Origins of Western Speculation* § TB/20

WILFRID DESAN: The Tragic Finale: *An Essay on the Philosophy of Jean-Paul Sartre* TB/1030

A. P. D'ENTRÈVES: Natural Law: *An Historical Survey* △ TB/1223

MARVIN FARBER: The Aims of Phenomenology: *The Motives, Methods, and Impact of Husserl's Thought* TB/1291

HERBERT FINGARETTE: The Self in Transformation: *Psychoanalysis, Philosophy and the Life of the Spirit* ¶ TB/1177

PAUL FRIEDLÄNDER: Plato: *An Introduction* △ TB/2017

ÉTIENNE GILSON: Dante and Philosophy TB/1089

WILLIAM CHASE GREENE: Moira: *Fate, Good, and Evil in Greek Thought* TB/1104

W. K. C. GUTHRIE: The Greek Philosophers: *From Thales to Aristotle* ° △ TB/1008
F. H. HEINEMANN: Existentialism and the Modern Predicament △ TB/28
ISAAC HUSIK: A History of Medieval Jewish Philosophy JP/3
EDMUND HUSSERL: Phenomenology and the Crisis of Philosophy. *Translated with an Introduction by Quentin Lauer* TB/1170
IMMANUEL KANT: The Doctrine of Virtue, *being Part II of the* Metaphysic of Morals. *Trans. with Notes & Intro. by Mary J. Gregor. Foreword by H. J. Paton* TB/110
IMMANUEL KANT: Groundwork of the Metaphysic of Morals. *Trans. & analyzed by H. J. Paton* TB/1159
IMMANUEL KANT: Lectures on Ethics. § △ *Introduction by Lewis W. Beck* TB/105
IMMANUEL KANT: Religion Within the Limits of Reason Alone. § *Intro. by T. M. Greene & J. Silber* TB/67
QUENTIN LAUER: Phenomenology: *Its Genesis and Prospect* TB/1169
GABRIEL MARCEL: Being and Having: *An Existential Diary.* △ *Intro. by James Collins* TB/310
GEORGE A. MORGAN: What Nietzsche Means TB/1198
PHILO, SAADYA GAON, & JEHUDA HALEVI: Three Jewish Philosophers. *Ed. by Hans Lewy, Alexander Altmann, &Isaak Heinemann* TB/813
MICHAEL POLANYI: Personal Knowledge: *Towards a Post-Critical Philosophy* △ TB/1158
WILLARD VAN ORMAN QUINE: Elementary Logic: *Revised Edition* TB/577
WILLARD VAN ORMAN QUINE: From a Logical Point of View: *Logico-Philosophical Essays* TB/566
BERTRAND RUSSELL et al.: The Philosophy of Bertrand Russell. *Edited by Paul Arthur Schilpp*
Vol. I TB/1095; Vol. II TB/1096
L. S. STEBBING: A Modern Introduction to Logic △ TB/538
ALFRED NORTH WHITEHEAD: Process and Reality: *An Essay in Cosmology* △ TB/1033
PHILIP P. WIENER: Evolution and the Founders of Pragmatism. *Foreword by John Dewey* TB/1212
WILHELM WINDELBAND: A History of Philosophy
Vol. I: *Greek, Roman, Medieval* TB/38
Vol. II: *Renaissance, Enlightenment, Modern* TB/39
LUDWIG WITTGENSTEIN: The Blue and Brown Books ° TB/1211

Political Science & Government

JEREMY BENTHAM: The Handbook of Political Fallacies: *Introduction by Crane Brinton* TB/1069
KENNETH E. BOULDING: Conflict and Defense: *A General Theory* TB/3024
CRANE BRINTON: English Political Thought in the Nineteenth Century TB/1071
EDWARD S. CORWIN: American Constitutional History: *Essays edited by Alpheus T. Mason and Gerald Garvey* TB/1136
ROBERT DAHL & CHARLES E. LINDBLOM: Politics, Economics, and Welfare: *Planning and Politico-Economic Systems Resolved into Basic Social Processes* TB/3037
JOHN NEVILLE FIGGIS: The Divine Right of Kings. *Introduction by G. R. Elton* TB/1191
JOHN NEVILLE FIGGIS: Political Thought from Gerson to Grotius: 1414-1625: *Seven Studies. Introduction by Garrett Mattingly* TB/1032
F. L. GANSHOF: Feudalism △ TB/1058
G. P. GOOCH: English Democratic Ideas in the Seventeenth Century TB/1006
J. H. HEXTER: More's Utopia: *The Biography of an Idea. New Epilogue by the Author* TB/1195
SIDNEY HOOK: Reason, Social Myths and Democracy △ TB/1237
ROBERT H. JACKSON: The Supreme Court in the American System of Government △ TB/1106
DAN N. JACOBS, Ed.: The New Communist Manifesto *and Related Documents. Third Edition, Revised* TB/1078
DAN N. JACOBS & HANS BAERWALD, Eds.: Chinese Communism: *Selected Documents* TB/3031
HANS KOHN: Political Ideologies of the 20th Century TB/1277
ROBERT GREEN MC CLOSKEY: American Conservatism in the Age of Enterprise, 1865-1910 TB/1137
KINGSLEY MARTIN: French Liberal Thought in the Eighteenth Century: *Political Ideas from Bayle to Condorcet* △ TB/1114
ROBERTO MICHELS: First Lectures in Political Sociology. *Edited by Alfred de Grazia* ¶ ° TB/1224
JOHN STUART MILL: On Bentham and Coleridge. △ *Introduction by F. R. Leavis* TB/1070
BARRINGTON MOORE, JR.: Political Power and Social Theory: *Seven Studies* ¶ TB/1221
BARRINGTON MOORE, JR.: Soviet Politics—The Dilemma of Power: *The Role of Ideas in Social Change* ¶ TB/1222
BARRINGTON MOORE, JR.: Terror and Progress—USSR: *Some Sources of Change and Stability in the Soviet Dictatorship* ¶ TB/1266
JOHN B. MORRALL: Political Thought in Medieval Times △ TB/1076
JOHN PLAMENATZ: German Marxism and Russian Communism. ° △ *New Preface by the Author* TB/1189
KARL R. POPPER: The Open Society and Its Enemies △
Vol. I: *The Spell of Plato* TB/1101
Vol. II: *The High Tide of Prophecy: Hegel, Marx and the Aftermath* TB/1102
HENRI DE SAINT-SIMON: Social Organization, The Science of Man, and Other Writings. *Edited and Translated by Felix Markham* TB/1152
JOSEPH A. SCHUMPETER: Capitalism, Socialism and Democracy △ TB/3008
CHARLES H. SHINN: Mining Camps: *A Study in American Frontier Government.* ‡ *Edited by Rodman W. Paul* TB/3062
PETER WOLL, Ed.: Public Administration and Policy: *Selected Essays* TB/1284

Psychology

ALFRED ADLER: The Individual Psychology of Alfred Adler. △ *Edited by Heinz L. and Rowena R. Ansbacher* TB/1154
ALFRED ADLER: Problems of Neurosis. *Introduction by Heinz L. Ansbacher* TB/1145
ANTON T. BOISEN: The Exploration of the Inner World: *A Study of Mental Disorder and Religious Experience* TB/87
ARTHUR BURTON & ROBERT E. HARRIS, Eds.: Clinical Studies of Personality
Vol. I TB/3075; Vol. II TB/3076
HADLEY CANTRIL: The Invasion from Mars: *A Study in the Psychology of Panic* ¶ TB/1282
HERBERT FINGARETTE: The Self in Transformation: *Psychoanalysis, Philosophy and the Life of the Spirit* ¶ TB/1177
SIGMUND FREUD: On Creativity and the Unconscious: *Papers on the Psychology of Art, Literature, Love, Religion.* § △ *Intro. by Benjamin Nelson* TB/45
C. JUDSON HERRICK: The Evolution of Human Nature TB/545
WILLIAM JAMES: Psychology: *The Briefer Course. Edited with an Intro. by Gordon Allport* TB/1034
C. G. JUNG: Psychological Reflections △ TB/2001
C. G. JUNG: Symbols of Transformation: *An Analysis of the Prelude to a Case of Schizophrenia.* △ *Illus.*
Vol. I TB/2009; Vol. II TB/2010
C. G. JUNG & C. KERÉNYI: Essays on a Science of Mythology: *The Myths of the Divine Child and the Divine Maiden* TB/2014
JOHN T. MC NEILL: A History of the Cure of Souls TB/126
KARL MENNINGER: Theory of Psychoanalytic Technique TB/1144

ERICH NEUMANN: Amor and Psyche: *The Psychic Development of the Feminine* △ TB/2012

ERICH NEUMANN: The Archetypal World of Henry Moore. △ *107 illus.* TB/2020

ERICH NEUMANN: The Origins and History of Consciousness △ Vol. I *Illus.* TB/2007; Vol. II TB/2008

C. P. OBERNDORF: A History of Psychoanalysis in America TB/1147

RALPH BARTON PERRY: The Thought and Character of William James: *Briefer Version* TB/1156

JEAN PIAGET, BÄRBEL INHELDER, & ALINA SZEMINSKA: The Child's Conception of Geometry ° △ TB/1146

JOHN H. SCHAAR: Escape from Authority: *The Perspectives of Erich Fromm* TB/1155

MUZAFER SHERIF: The Psychology of Social Norms TB/3072

Sociology

JACQUES BARZUN: Race: *A Study in Superstition. Revised Edition* TB/1172

BERNARD BERELSON, Ed.: The Behavioral Sciences Today TB/1127

ABRAHAM CAHAN: The Rise of David Levinsky: *A documentary novel of social mobility in early twentieth century America. Intro. by John Higham* TB/1028

THOMAS C. COCHRAN: The Inner Revolution: *Essays on the Social Sciences in History* TB/1140

ALLISON DAVIS & JOHN DOLLARD: Children of Bondage: *The Personality Development of Negro Youth in the Urban South* ¶ TB/3049

ST. CLAIR DRAKE & HORACE R. CAYTON: Black Metropolis: *A Study of Negro Life in a Northern City.* △ *Revised and Enlarged. Intro. by Everett C. Hughes* Vol. I TB/1086; Vol. II TB/1087

EMILE DURKHEIM et al.: Essays on Sociology and Philosophy: *With Analyses of Durkheim's Life and Work.* ¶ *Edited by Kurt H. Wolff* TB/1151

LEON FESTINGER, HENRY W. RIECKEN & STANLEY SCHACHTER: When Prophecy Fails: *A Social and Psychological Account of a Modern Group that Predicted the Destruction of the World* ¶ TB/1132

ALVIN W. GOULDNER: Wildcat Strike: *A Study in Worker-Management Relationships* ¶ TB/1176

FRANCIS J. GRUND: Aristocracy in America: *Social Class in the Formative Years of the New Nation* △ TB/1001

KURT LEWIN: Field Theory in Social Science: *Selected Theoretical Papers.* ¶ △ *Edited with a Foreword by Dorwin Cartwright* TB/1135

R. M. MAC IVER: Social Causation TB/1153

ROBERT K. MERTON, LEONARD BROOM, LEONARD S. COTTRELL, JR., Editors: Sociology Today: *Problems and Prospects* ¶ Vol. I TB/1173; Vol. II TB/1174

ROBERTO MICHELS: First Lectures in Political Sociology. *Edited by Alfred de Grazia* ¶ ° TB/1224

BARRINGTON MOORE, JR.: Political Power and Social Theory: *Seven Studies* ¶ TB/1221

BARRINGTON MOORE, JR.: Soviet Politics—The Dilemma of Power: *The Role of Ideas in Social Change* ¶ TB/1222

TALCOTT PARSONS & EDWARD A. SHILS, Editors: Toward a General Theory of Action: *Theoretical Foundations for the Social Sciences* TB/1083

JOHN H. ROHRER & MUNRO S. EDMONDSON, Eds.: The Eighth Generation Grows Up: *Cultures and Personalities of New Orleans Negroes* ¶ TB/3050

ARNOLD ROSE: The Negro in America: *The Condensed Version of Gunnar Myrdal's* An American Dilemma TB/3048

KURT SAMUELSSON: Religion and Economic Action: *A Critique of Max Weber's* The Protestant Ethic and the Spirit of Capitalism. ¶ ° *Trans. by E. G. French. Ed. with Intro. by D. C. Coleman* TB/1131

PHILIP SELZNICK: TVA and the Grass Roots: *A Study in the Sociology of Formal Organization* TB/1230

GEORG SIMMEL et al.: Essays on Sociology, Philosophy, and Aesthetics. ¶ *Edited by Kurt H. Wolff* TB/1234

HERBERT SIMON: The Shape of Automation: *For Men and Management* △ TB/1245

PITIRIM A. SOROKIN: Contemporary Sociological Theories. *Through the First Quarter of the 20th Century* TB/3046

MAURICE R. STEIN: The Eclipse of Community: *An Interpretation of American Studies* TB/1128

FERDINAND TÖNNIES: Community and Society: *Gemeinschaft und Gesellschaft. Translated and edited by Charles P. Loomis* TB/1116

W. LLOYD WARNER & Associates: Democracy in Jonesville: *A Study in Quality and Inequality* TB/1129

W. LLOYD WARNER: Social Class in America: *The Evaluation of Status* TB/1013

RELIGION

Ancient & Classical

J. H. BREASTED: Development of Religion and Thought in Ancient Egypt. *Intro. by John A. Wilson* TB/57

HENRI FRANKFORT: Ancient Egyptian Religion: *An Interpretation* TB/77

G. RACHEL LEVY: Religious Conceptions of the Stone Age *and their Influence upon European Thought.* △ *Illus. Introduction by Henri Frankfort* TB/106

MARTIN P. NILSSON: Greek Folk Religion. *Foreword by Arthur Darby Nock* TB/78

ALEXANDRE PIANKOFF: The Shrines of Tut-Ankh-Amon. △ *Edited by N. Rambova. 117 illus.* TB/2011

ERWIN ROHDE: Psyche: *The Cult of Souls and Belief in Immortality Among the Greeks.* △ *Intro. by W. K. C. Guthrie* Vol. I TB/140; Vol. II TB/141

H. J. ROSE: Religion in Greece and Rome △ TB/55

Biblical Thought & Literature

W. F. ALBRIGHT: The Biblical Period from Abraham to Ezra TB/102

C. K. BARRETT, Ed.: The New Testament Background: *Selected Documents* △ TB/86

C. H. DODD: The Authority of the Bible △ TB/43

M. S. ENSLIN: Christian Beginnings △ TB/5

M. S. ENSLIN: The Literature of the Christian Movement △ TB/6

JOHN GRAY: Archaeology and the Old Testament World. △ *Illus.* TB/127

JAMES MUILENBURG: The Way of Israel: *Biblical Faith and Ethics* △ TB/133

H. H. ROWLEY: The Growth of the Old Testament △ TB/107

GEORGE ADAM SMITH: The Historical Geography of the Holy Land. ° △ *Revised and reset* TB/138

D. WINTON THOMAS, Ed.: Documents from Old Testament Times △ TB/85

The Judaic Tradition

LEO BAECK: Judaism and Christianity. *Trans. with Intro. by Walter Kaufmann* JP/23

SALO W. BARON: Modern Nationalism and Religion JP/18

MARTIN BUBER: Eclipse of God: *Studies in the Relation Between Religion and Philosophy* △ TB/12

MARTIN BUBER: For the Sake of Heaven TB/801

MARTIN BUBER: Hasidism and Modern Man. △ *Ed. and Trans. by Maurice Friedman* TB/839

MARTIN BUBER: The Knowledge of Man. △ *Edited with an Introduction by Maurice Friedman. Translated by Maurice Friedman and Ronald Gregor Smith* TB/135

MARTIN BUBER: Moses: *The Revelation and the Covenant* △ TB/837

MARTIN BUBER: The Origin and Meaning of Hasidism △ TB/835

MARTIN BUBER: Pointing the Way. △ *Introduction by Maurice S. Friedman* TB/103

MARTIN BUBER: The Prophetic Faith TB/73

MARTIN BUBER: Two Types of Faith: *the interpenetration of Judaism and Christianity* ° △ TB/75

ERNST LUDWIG EHRLICH: A Concise History of Israel: *From the Earliest Times to the Destruction of the Temple in A.D. 70* ° △ TB/128

MAURICE S. FRIEDMAN: Martin Buber: *The Life of Dialogue* △ TB/64

GENESIS: *The NJV Translation* TB/836

SOLOMON GRAYZEL: A History of the Contemporary Jews TB/816

WILL HERBERG: Judaism and Modern Man TB/810

ARTHUR HERTZBERG: The Zionist Idea TB/817

ABRAHAM J. HESCHEL: God in Search of Man: *A Philosophy of Judaism* JP/7

ISAAC HUSIK: A History of Medieval Jewish Philosophy JP/3

FLAVIUS JOSEPHUS: The Great Roman-Jewish War, *with* The Life of Josephus. *Introduction by William R. Farmer* TB/74

JACOB R. MARCUS: The Jew in the Medieval World TB/814

MAX L. MARGOLIS & ALEXANDER MARX: A History of the Jewish People TB/806

T. J. MEEK: Hebrew Origins TB/69

C. G. MONTEFIORE & H. LOEWE, Eds.: A Rabbinic Anthology. JP/32

JAMES PARKES: The Conflict of the Church and the Synagogue: *The Jews and Early Christianity* JP/21

PHILO, SAADYA GAON, & JEHUDA HALEVI: Three Jewish Philosophers. *Ed. by Hans Lewey, Alexander Altmann, & Isaak Heinemann* TB/813

CECIL ROTH: A History of the Marranos TB/812

CECIL ROTH: The Jews in the Renaissance. *Illus.* TB/834

HERMAN L. STRACK: Introduction to the Talmud and Midrash TB/808

JOSHUA TRACHTENBERG: The Devil and the Jews: *The Medieval Conception of the Jew and its Relation to Modern Anti-Semitism* JP/22

Christianity: General

ROLAND H. BAINTON: Christendom: *A Short History of Christianity and its Impact on Western Civilization.* △ *Illus.* Vol. I TB/131; Vol. II TB/132

Christianity: Origins & Early Development

AUGUSTINE: An Augustine Synthesis. △ *Edited by Erich Przywara* TB/335

ADOLF DEISSMANN: Paul: *A Study in Social and Religious History* TB/15

EDWARD GIBBON: The Triumph of Christendom in the Roman Empire *(Chaps. XV-XX of "Decline and Fall," J. B. Bury edition).* § △ *Illus.* TB/46

MAURICE GOGUEL: Jesus and the Origins of Christianity. ° △ *Introduction by C. Leslie Mitton*
Volume I: *Prolegomena to the Life of Jesus* TB/65
Volume II: *The Life of Jesus* TB/66

EDGAR J. GOODSPEED: A Life of Jesus TB/1

ROBERT M. GRANT: Gnosticism and Early Christianity. △ *Revised Edition* TB/136

ADOLF HARNACK: The Mission and Expansion of Christianity in the First Three Centuries. *Introduction by Jaroslav Pelikan* TB/92

R. K. HARRISON: The Dead Sea Scrolls : *An Introduction* ° △ TB/84

EDWIN HATCH: The Influence of Greek Ideas on Christianity. § △ *Introduction and Bibliography by Frederick C. Grant* TB/18

ARTHUR DARBY NOCK: Early Gentile Christianity and Its Hellenistic Background TB/111

ARTHUR DARBY NOCK: St. Paul ° △ TB/104

ORIGEN: On First Principles. △ *Edited by G. W. Butterworth. Introduction by Henri de Lubac* TB/311

JAMES PARKES: The Conflict of the Church and the Synagogue: *The Jews and Early Christianity* JP/21

SULPICIUS SEVERUS et al.: The Western Fathers: *Being the Lives of Martin of Tours, Ambrose, Augustine of Hippo, Honoratus of Arles and Germanus of Auxerre.* △ *Edited and translated by F. R. Hoare* TB/309

F. VAN DER MEER: Augustine the Bishop: *Church and Society at the Dawn of the Middle Ages* △ TB/304

JOHANNES WEISS: Earliest Christianity: *A History of the Period A.D. 30-150. Introduction and Bibliography by Frederick C. Grant* Volume I TB/53
Volume II TB/54

Christianity: The Middle Ages and The Reformation

JOHN CALVIN & JACOPO SADOLETO: A Reformation Debate. *Edited by John C. Olin* TB/1239

G. CONSTANT: The Reformation in England: *The English Schism, Henry VIII, 1509-1547* △ TB/314

CHRISTOPHER DAWSON, Ed.: Mission to Asia: *Narratives and Letters of the Franciscan Missionaries in Mongolia and China in the 13th and 14th Centuries* △ TB/315

JOHANNES ECKHART: Meister Eckhart: *A Modern Translation by R. B. Blakney* TB/8

DESIDERIUS ERASMUS: Christian Humanism and the Reformation: *Selected Writings. Edited and translated by John C. Olin* TB/1166

ÉTIENNE GILSON: Dante and Philosophy △ TB/1089

WILLIAM HALLER: The Rise of Puritanism △ TB/22

HAJO HOLBORN: Ulrich von Hutten and the German Reformation TB/1238

JOHAN HUIZINGA: Erasmus and the Age of Reformation. △ *Illus.* TB/19

A. C. MC GIFFERT: Protestant Thought Before Kant △ *Preface by Jaroslav Pelikan* TB/93

JOHN T. MC NEILL: Makers of the Christian Tradition: *From Alfred the Great to Schleiermacher* △ TB/121

G. MOLLAT: The Popes at Avignon, 1305-1378 △ TB/308

GORDON RUPP: Luther's Progress to the Diet of Worms ° △ TB/120

Christianity: The Protestant Tradition

KARL BARTH: Church Dogmatics: *A Selection* △ TB/95

KARL BARTH: Dogmatics in Outline △ TB/56

KARL BARTH: The Word of God and the Word of Man TB/13

RUDOLF BULTMANN et al: Translating Theology into the Modern Age: *Historical, Systematic and Pastoral Reflections on Theology and the Church in the Contemporary Situation. Volume 2 of* Journal for Theology and the Church, *edited by Robert W. Funk in association with Gerhard Ebeling* TB/252

WHITNEY R. CROSS: The Burned-Over District: *The Social and Intellectual History of Enthusiastic Religion in Western New York, 1800-1850* △ TB/1242

WINTHROP HUDSON: The Great Tradition of the American Churches TB/98

SOREN KIERKEGAARD: On Authority and Revelation: *The Book on Adler. Translated by Walter Lowrie. Intro. by Frederick Sontag* TB/139

SOREN KIERKEGAARD: Edifying Discourses. *Edited with an Introduction by Paul Holmer* TB/32

SOREN KIERKEGAARD: The Journals of Kierkegaard. ° △ *Ed. with Intro. by Alexander Dru* TB/52

SOREN KIERKEGAARD : The Point of View for My Work as an Author: *A Report to History.* § *Preface by Benjamin Nelson* TB/88

SOREN KIERKEGAARD: The Present Age. § △ *Translated and edited by Alexander Dru. Introduction by Walter Kaufmann* TB/94

SOREN KIERKEGAARD: Purity of Heart △ TB/4

SOREN KIERKEGAARD: Repetition: *An Essay in Experimental Psychology.* △ *Translated with Introduction & Notes by Walter Lowrie* TB/117

SOREN KIERKEGAARD: Works of Love: *Some Christian Reflections in the Form of Discourses* △ TB/122

WALTER LOWRIE: Kierkegaard: *A Life* Vol. I TB/89
Vol. II TB/90

JOHN MACQUARRIE: The Scope of Demythologizing: *Bultmann and his Critics* △ TB/134

PERRY MILLER & T. H. JOHNSON, Editors: The Puritans: *A Sourcebook of Their Writings* Vol. I TB/1093
Vol. II TB/1094

JAMES M. ROBINSON et al.: The Bultmann School of Biblical Interpretation: New Directions? *Volume 1 of* Journal for Theology and the Church, *edited by Robert W. Funk in association with Gerhard Ebeling* TB/251

F. SCHLEIERMACHER: The Christian Faith. △ *Introduction by Richard R. Niebuhr* Vol. I TB/108
Vol. II TB/109

F. SCHLEIERMACHER: On Religion: *Speeches to Its Cultured Despisers. Intro. by Rudolf Otto* TB/36

TIMOTHY L. SMITH: Revivalism and Social Reform: *American Protestantism on the Eve of the Civil War* TB/1229

PAUL TILLICH: Dynamics of Faith △ TB/42

PAUL TILLICH: Morality and Beyond TB/142

EVELYN UNDERHILL: Worship △ TB/10

G. VAN DER LEEUW: Religion in Essence and Manifestation: *A Study in Phenomenology.* △ *Appendices by Hans H. Penner* Vol. I TB/100; Vol. II TB/101

Christianity: The Roman and Eastern Traditions

DOM CUTHBERT BUTLER: Western Mysticism: *The Teaching of Augustine, Gregory and Bernard on Contemplation and the Contemplative Life* § ° △ TB/312

A. ROBERT CAPONIGRI, Ed.: Modern Catholic Thinkers I: *God and Man* △ TB/306

A. ROBERT CAPONIGRI, Ed.: Modern Catholic Thinkers II: *The Church and the Political Order*△ TB/307

THOMAS CORBISHLEY, S.J.: Roman Catholicism △ TB/112

CHRISTOPHER DAWSON: The Historic Reality of Christian Culture TB/305

G. P. FEDOTOV: The Russian Religious Mind: *Kievan Christianity, the 10th to the 13th centuries* TB/370

G. P. FEDOTOV, Ed.: A Treasury of Russian Spirituality TB/303

ÉTIENNE GILSON: The Spirit of Thomism TB/313

DAVID KNOWLES: The English Mystical Tradition △ TB/302

GABRIEL MARCEL: Being and Having: *An Existential Diary.* △ *Introduction by James Collins* TB/310

GABRIEL MARCEL: Homo Viator: *Introduction to a Metaphysic of Hope* TB/397

FRANCIS DE SALES: Introduction to the Devout Life. *Trans. by John K. Ryan* TB/316

GUSTAVE WEIGEL, S. J.: Catholic Theology in Dialogue TB/301

Oriental Religions: Far Eastern, Near Eastern

TOR ANDRAE: Mohammed: *The Man and His Faith* △ TB/62

EDWARD CONZE: Buddhism: *Its Essence and Development.* ° △ *Foreword by Arthur Waley* TB/58

EDWARD CONZE et al., Editors: Buddhist Texts Through the Ages △ TB/113

ANANDA COOMARASWAMY: Buddha and the Gospel of Buddhism. △ *Illus.* TB/119

H. G. CREEL: Confucius and the Chinese Way TB/63

FRANKLIN EDGERTON, Trans. & Ed.: The Bhagavad Gita TB/115

SWAMI NIKHILANANDA, Trans. & Ed.: The Upanishads: *A One-Volume Abridgment* △ TB/114

HELLMUT WILHELM: Change: *Eight Lectures on the I Ching* △ TB/2019

Philosophy of Religion

NICOLAS BERDYAEV: The Beginning and the End § △ TB/14

NICOLAS BERDYAEV: Christian Existentialism: *A Berdyaev Synthesis.* △ *Ed. by Donald A. Lowrie* TB/130

NICOLAS BERDYAEV: The Destiny of Man △ TB/61

RUDOLF BULTMANN: History and Eschatology: *The Presence of Eternity* ° TB/91

RUDOLF BULTMANN AND FIVE CRITICS: Kerygma and Myth: *A Theological Debate* △ TB/80

RUDOLF BULTMANN and KARL KUNDSIN: Form Criticism: *Two Essays on New Testament Research.* △ *Translated by Frederick C. Grant* TB/96

MIRCEA ELIADE: The Sacred and the Profane TB/81

LUDWIG FEUERBACH: The Essence of Christianity. § *Introduction by Karl Barth. Foreword by H. Richard Niebuhr* TB/11

ÉTIENNE GILSON: The Spirit of Thomism TB/313

ADOLF HARNACK: What is Christianity? § △ *Introduction by Rudolf Bultmann* TB/17

FRIEDRICH HEGEL: On Christianity: *Early Theological Writings. Ed. by R. Kroner and T. M. Knox* TB/79

KARL HEIM: Christian Faith and Natural Science △ TB/16

IMMANUEL KANT: Religion Within the Limits of Reason Alone. § *Intro. by T. M. Greene & J. Silber* TB/67

K. E. KIRK: The Vision of God: *The Christian Doctrine of the Summum Bonum* § △ TB/137

JOHN MACQUARRIE: An Existentialist Theology: *A Comparison of Heidegger and Bultmann.* ° △ *Preface by Rudolf Bultmann* TB/125

PAUL RAMSEY, Ed.: Faith and Ethics: *The Theology of H. Richard Niebuhr* TB/129

PIERRE TEILHARD DE CHARDIN: The Divine Milieu ° △ TB/384

PIERRE TEILHARD DE CHARDIN: The Phenomenon of Man ° △ TB/383

Religion, Culture & Society

JOSEPH L. BLAU, Ed.: Cornerstones of Religious Freedom in America: *Selected Basic Documents, Court Decisions and Public Statements. Revised and Enlarged Edition* TB/118

C. C. GILLISPIE: Genesis and Geology: *The Decades before Darwin* § TB/51

KYLE HASELDEN: The Racial Problem in Christian Perspective TB/116

WALTER KAUFMANN, Ed.: Religion from Tolstoy to Camus: *Basic Writings on Religious Truth and Morals. Enlarged Edition* TB/123

JOHN T. MC NEILL: A History of the Cure of Souls TB/126

KENNETH B. MURDOCK: Literature and Theology in Colonial New England TB/99

H. RICHARD NIEBUHR: Christ and Culture △ TB/3

H. RICHARD NIEBUHR: The Kingdom of God in America TB/49

R. B. PERRY: Puritanism and Democracy TB/1138

PAUL PFUETZE: Self, Society, Existence: *Human Nature and Dialogue in the Thought of George Herbert Mead and Martin Buber* TB/1059

WALTER RAUSCHENBUSCH: Christianity and the Social Crisis. ‡ *Edited by Robert D. Cross* TB/3059

KURT SAMUELSSON: Religion and Economic Action: *A Critique of Max Weber's* The Protestant Ethic and the Spirit of Capitalism ¶ ° △ *Trans. by E. G. French. Ed. with Intro. by D. C. Coleman* TB/1131

TIMOTHY L. SMITH: Revivalism and Social Reform: *American Protestantism on the Eve of the Civil War* △ TB/1229

ERNST TROELTSCH: The Social Teaching of the Christian Churches ° △ Vol. I TB/71; Vol. II TB/72

NATURAL SCIENCES AND MATHEMATICS

Biological Sciences

CHARLOTTE AUERBACH: The Science of Genetics Σ △ TB/568

MARSTON BATES: The Natural History of Mosquitoes. *Illus.* TB/578

A. BELLAIRS: Reptiles: *Life History, Evolution, and Structure.* △ *Illus.* TB/520

LUDWIG VON BERTALANFFY: Modern Theories of Development: *An Introduction to Theoretical Biology* TB/554

LUDWIG VON BERTALANFFY: Problems of Life: *An Evaluation of Modern Biological and Scientific Thought* △ TB/521

HAROLD F. BLUM: Time's Arrow and Evolution TB/555

JOHN TYLER BONNER: The Ideas of Biology. Σ △ *Illus.* TB/570

A. J. CAIN: Animal Species and their Evolution. △ *Illus.* TB/519

WALTER B. CANNON: Bodily Changes in Pain, Hunger, Fear and Rage. *Illus.* TB/562

W. E. LE GROS CLARK: The Antecedents of Man: *An Introduction to Evolution of the Primates.* ° △ *Illus.* TB/559

W. H. DOWDESWELL: Animal Ecology. △ *Illus.* TB/543

W. H. DOWDESWELL: The Mechanism of Evolution. △ *Illus.* TB/527

R. W. GERARD: Unresting Cells. *Illus.* TB/541

DAVID LACK: Darwin's Finches. △ *Illus.* TB/544

ADOLF PORTMANN: Animals as Social Beings. ° △ *Illus.* TB/572

O. W. RICHARDS: The Social Insects. △ *Illus.* TB/542

P. M. SHEPPARD: Natural Selection and Heredity. △ *Illus.* TB/528

EDMUND W. SINNOTT: Cell and Psyche: *The Biology of Purpose* TB/546

C. H. WADDINGTON: How Animals Develop. △ *Illus.* TB/553

C. H. WADDINGTON: The Nature of Life: *The Main Problems and Trends in Modern Biology* △ TB/580

Chemistry

J. R. PARTINGTON: A Short History of Chemistry. △ *Illus.* TB/522

Communication Theory

J. R. PIERCE: Symbols, Signals and Noise: *The Nature and Process of Communication* △ TB/574

Geography

R. E. COKER: This Great and Wide Sea: *An Introduction to Oceanography and Marine Biology. Illus.* TB/551

F. K. HARE: The Restless Atmosphere △ TB/560

History of Science

MARIE BOAS: The Scientific Renaissance, 1450-1630 ° △ TB/583

W. DAMPIER, Ed.: Readings in the Literature of Science. *Illus.* TB/512

A. HUNTER DUPREE: Science in the Federal Government: *A History of Policies and Activities to 1940* △ TB/573

ALEXANDRE KOYRÉ: From the Closed World to the Infinite Universe: *Copernicus, Kepler, Galileo, Newton, etc.* △ TB/31

A. G. VAN MELSEN: From Atomos to Atom: *A History of the Concept* Atom TB/517

O. NEUGEBAUER: The Exact Sciences in Antiquity TB/552

HANS THIRRING: Energy for Man: *From Windmills to Nuclear Power* △ TB/556

STEPHEN TOULMIN & JUNE GOODFIELD: The Architecture of Matter: *Physics, Chemistry & Physiology of Matter, Both Animate & Inanimate, As it Evolved Since the Beginning of Science* ° △ TB/584

STEPHEN TOULMIN & JUNE GOODFIELD: The Discovery of Time ° △ TB/585

LANCELOT LAW WHYTE: Essay on Atomism: *From Democritus to 1960* △ TB/565

Mathematics

E. W. BETH: The Foundations of Mathematics: *A Study in the Philosophy of Science* △ TB/581

H. DAVENPORT: The Higher Arithmetic: *An Introduction to the Theory of Numbers* △ TB/526

H. G. FORDER: Geometry: *An Introduction* △ TB/548

S. KÖRNER: The Philosophy of Mathematics: *An Introduction* △ TB/547

D. E. LITTLEWOOD: Skeleton Key of Mathematics: *A Simple Account of Complex Algebraic Problems* △ TB/525

GEORGE E. OWEN: Fundamentals of Scientific Mathematics TB/569

WILLARD VAN ORMAN QUINE: Mathematical Logic TB/558

O. G. SUTTON: Mathematics in Action. ° △ *Foreword by James R. Newman. Illus.* TB/518

FREDERICK WAISMANN: Introduction to Mathematical Thinking. *Foreword by Karl Menger* TB/511

Philosophy of Science

R. B. BRAITHWAITE: Scientific Explanation TB/515

J. BRONOWSKI: Science and Human Values. △ *Revised and Enlarged Edition* TB/505

ALBERT EINSTEIN et al.: Albert Einstein: Philosopher-Scientist. *Edited by Paul A. Schilpp* Vol. I TB/502
Vol. II TB/503

WERNER HEISENBERG: Physics and Philosophy: *The Revolution in Modern Science* △ TB/549

JOHN MAYNARD KEYNES: A Treatise on Probability. ° △ *Introduction by N. R. Hanson* TB/557

KARL R. POPPER: Logic of Scientific Discovery △ TB/576

STEPHEN TOULMIN: Foresight and Understanding: *An Enquiry into the Aims of Science.* △ *Foreword by Jacques Barzun* TB/564

STEPHEN TOULMIN: The Philosophy of Science: *An Introduction* △ TB/513

G. J. WHITROW: The Natural Philosophy of Time ° △ TB/563

Physics and Cosmology

JOHN E. ALLEN: Aerodynamics: *A Space Age Survey* △ TB/582

STEPHEN TOULMIN & JUNE GOODFIELD: The Fabric of the Heavens: *The Development of Astronomy and Dynamics.* △ *Illus.* TB/579

DAVID BOHM: Causality and Chance in Modern Physics. △ *Foreword by Louis de Broglie* TB/536

P. W. BRIDGMAN: Nature of Thermodynamics TB/537

P. W. BRIDGMAN: A Sophisticate's Primer of Relativity △ TB/575

A. C. CROMBIE, Ed.: Turning Point in Physics TB/535

C. V. DURELL: Readable Relativity. △ *Foreword by Freeman J. Dyson* TB/530

ARTHUR EDDINGTON: Space, Time and Gravitation: *An Outline of the General Relativity Theory* TB/510

GEORGE GAMOW: Biography of Physics Σ △ TB/567

MAX JAMMER: Concepts of Force: *A Study in the Foundation of Dynamics* TB/550

MAX JAMMER: Concepts of Mass *in Classical and Modern Physics* TB/571

MAX JAMMER: Concepts of Space : *The History of Theories of Space in Physics. Foreword by Albert Einstein* TB/533

G. J. WHITROW: The Structure and Evolution of the Universe: *An Introduction to Cosmology.* △ *Illus.* TB/504